A Field Guide in Colour to GARDEN PLANTS

A Field Guide in Colour to

GARDEN PLANTS

by Jan Tykač
and Vlastimil Vaněk

Picture acknowledgements:
448 colour photographs; by M. Blažek (4), D. Dršata (7), Z. Humpál (6), J. Marco (6),
F. Přeučil (7), Č. Raab (8), V. J. Staněk (9), A. Tykačová (118), V. Vaněk (282), V. Vrblík (1),
1 black-and-white photograph by E. Hase.
Line drawings by I. Kincl.

Frontispiece by Pat Brindley

Translated by Olga Kuthanová
Graphic design Antonín Chmel
English version first published 1978 by
Octopus Books Limited
59 Grosvenor Street, London W 1
Reprinted 1980, 1983, 1985
© 1978 Artia, Prague
ISBN 0 7064 1037 8

Printed in Czechoslovakia
3/07/07/51-04

Contents

Flowers in the Garden

It is impossible to imagine a garden without flowers. Even if the greatest expanse is taken up by a well-tended lawn with trees and shrubs forming an enclosure and dominant features, it is flowers that give it the bright colourful touch no garden can be without.

In general, flowers are all plants that bear blossoms and are coloured. Flowers are divided according to their characteristics into three groups: annuals, perennials and woody plants. Annuals are plants that normally complete their life cycle within one growing season. Biennials, which are included among annuals, live for two years. Perennials live for more than two years and the top parts of the plants are soft—herbaceous. Woody plants also live for a number of years but their top parts are woody. These divisions, however, are not always clear-cut: some flowers that are classed as annuals may live longer than one year in a congenial climate, and many species that are classed as perennials are in reality woody plants, because their top parts turn woody. There is no precise demarcation between the groups; the divisions are not botanical but rather a convenience in general use.

Annuals, as stated above, are flowers that in temperate regions usually live for only one growing season. They are generally raised from seed, and they flower, produce seeds and die within the four seasons of the year. The range of annuals is wide; their flowers come in glowing colours, are abundant and often borne over a long period, which is why they are so popular in the garden.

Most annuals are easily propagated, and seed establishments offer a wide choice of seeds. The full beauty of their blossoms may be enjoyed sometimes as early as late May, but mostly they flower in summer. Most species require a sunny position; a few tolerate shade or partial shade. Annuals are thus planted in open parts of the garden where large patches of colour are required throughout the summer.

Biennials are usually grouped together with annuals and are treated as such, though their life cycle lasts two years. They are sown one year, to produce flowers and die the following year. This group includes some species that flower in early spring, such as pansies, forget-me-nots, etc., which go well together with annuals. Some biennials are also very popular for cutting, for example carnations and pinks, and bellflowers.

Perennials are another important group of garden flowers. They live more than two— on average four to six—years, though some species last as long as ten, or even up to fifty years. Perennials make up the largest group of flowers, numbering several thousand species and varieties. Because they have markedly different characteristics they are divided into several further groups.

Low, prostrate perennials are called **rock plants.** These are planted mainly in rock gardens, though many can also be used in a dry wall, as carpeting plants to cover flat areas in place of turf, as edging plants, and elsewhere. Most are alpine plants, but the group also includes others. Likewise many, but not all, are xerophilous (able to thrive in dry conditions); many are lowland plants, and many more lovely species and varieties have been produced by breeders. Generally spoken, in this group are classed all perennials that grow no taller than 20 to 30 cm.

Perennials proper are species more than 40 cm high. Some even grow to a height of two to three metres.

Most perennials have decorative flowers; many, however, also have decorative foliage or an attractive habit of growth. Some are grown chiefly for their foliage, which is often beautifully coloured or of an interesting shape, e.g. *Hosta, Artemisia, Stachys olympica,* etc.

Some perennials have top parts that die down for the winter and grow in again in spring. In others they remain green throughout the winter. Some species die back after flowering in the same way as bulbs, e.g. *Papaver orientale, Adonis amurensis, Dicentra spectabilis,* etc.

Perennials with special characteristics or ones that live in special conditions are classed in separate independent groups. These are mainly ornamental grasses, aquatic plants and ferns. All have their special place in the garden.

Grasses, with their light, airy habit and often attractively coloured foliage, have become inseparable companions of floral décor in modern gardens, particularly in natural settings. Aquatic plants, of which the best known are water lilies, are ornamental features of pools and boggy parts of the garden. **Ferns,** with their beautiful foliage, are invaluable for shady or partially shaded areas. All these locations are unsuitable for both annuals and bulbs.

Bulbs and tubers, like perennials, live more than two years, but they differ both because of the existence of a fleshy storage organ—a bulb, corm or tuber—and in their manner of growth.

Most plants in this group are of steppe origin, and are thus adapted to conditions where the moist period of spring is followed by a long hot, dry period poorly tolerated by other plants. Steppe plants have a brief vegetative period in spring, marked by rapid growth and flowering. Shortly after, all the reserve food materials are stored in the bulb or tuber, and the plant enters a dormant period that lasts through the summer until autumn. In this state plants are able to survive even the most severe heat and drought. With the arrival of cold weather they resume activity in order to ensure that the top parts grow and flower as soon as spring comes.

These plants have their dormant period at different times of the year and also exhibit varying degrees of hardiness to low temperatures, depending on their original habitat. Some are hardy and will withstand even severe frosts—for example, tulips, narcissi, hyacinths, crocuses, lilies and many more. Others, however, will not withstand frost and must be lifted in the autumn and stored in frost-free premises for the winter, after which they are planted out again in spring. These include gladioli, dahlias, tuberous begonias, Indian Shot (Cannas), and tiger flowers. In areas where the temperature remains above freezing point in winter they may, however, be left outdoors in the ground.

Woody plants are likewise invaluable in the garden. Trees serve as structural elements in the garden and also provide shade. Shrubs are used to separate various parts of the garden, and when in flower add extra colour.

The two main groups — broad-leaved and coniferous trees and shrubs — are equally important. Broad-leaved species may be deciduous, shedding their leaves in winter, or evergreen, retaining their leaves in winter. Besides having decorative flowers some species also have distinctive foliage or fruits. Climbing plants form a special group of their own.

Conifers, with few exceptions, are evergreen. Some grow into fairly large trees in time, so care should be taken when selecting them for the garden, particularly if it is a small one. Of greater interest are shrub-like and dwarf conifers, which range in shape from pyramidal and columnar to ones of shrubby and prostrate habit, and have many different uses in the garden.

All the above groups are important in the garden; selected and combined with forethought and taste, they will together provide a lovely, harmonious and pleasant setting.

Use of Flowers and Woody Plants in the Modern Garden

Even a brief glance at the catalogues of establishments which grow and supply plants for gardens will show how vast is the selection offered for sale in the various groups. Truly good use of plants in the garden requires taste, an eye for shape and colour, and also knowledge of the plants' needs. The most important thing is to choose the best and most suitable species for any particular garden setting, and then to care for them properly. There are as many possibilities as there are sites and types of gardens; it is impossible to follow any set pattern.

Flower Beds and Borders

These are usually of regular outline and are a traditional and still widely used method of planting flowers in the garden. They date from a period when gardens were usually landscaped along formal lines. Nowadays, with the trend towards more natural, informal schemes, beds and borders are giving way to natural gardens, even though they are far from being a thing of the past.

Borders vary in width, depending on the situation; the most usual size is between 100 and 150 cm across. As a rule, they are viewed from only one side, generally being located either beside a path, next to a house, a wall, in front of a hedge or pergola. They often form an important part of the scheme, and it is best if they are set against a suitable backdrop, such as a green hedge or the wall of a house.

In borders designed to be seen from one side the tallest plants should be put in the rear, with the others graduating downwards towards the front. Mixed borders are most popular, composed of several species of flowers and providing a brightly coloured display. With a careful choice of plants it is possible to have colour throughout the year.

It is not easy to create a truly attractive border, for it requires a fairly broad knowledge of flowers. In the first place one must choose species suitable for the site, and it is necessary to know the final height of the various plants in order to group and place them. Very important, also, is the arrangement of colours to achieve harmonious contrasts in the border. Species planted together should have complementary colours, and should naturally flower at the same time. For example, red contrasts well with white or yellow, yellow with blue, violet or pink, etc.

To make an effective display the various species should be planted out in groups of three to five plants. The richest display of blossoms is provided by borders containing plants that flower during the same specific period, either spring, summer or autumn. It is also possible to obtain continual flowering throughout the growing season by planting species that bloom at different times, but then one must be prepared for the fact that the border will contain patches empty of colour at certain times. Even though some species are noted for their long period of flowering, none bears blossoms continuously for months on end.

Flowers that may be used in the border include annuals, perennials, bulbs and some woody plants.

Annuals are very rewarding bedding plants because of their profusely produced flowers and bright colours, and because some species also bear flowers for a long time. Their chief drawback, however, is their short life-span, which means that they must be planted out anew every year, and also the fact that they do not bear flowers in spring but mainly in summer. The flowering period of annuals can be prolonged by purchasing grown-on seedlings, often ones already in bloom, but even then flowering will not begin before mid-May. Spring colour can be obtained by using bulbs as fill-ups, particularly tulips, which flower from as early as April. One drawback, however, is that if good healthy bulbs are wanted for future years they must be left to mature after flowering before being lifted, and new plants being put out in their stead. This means that there will be empty spaces in the borders for a period of about one month. If the bulbs are not to be preserved they can be lifted immediately after flowering; this arrangement does, of course, necessitate the purchase of new bulbs every year.

The most important flowers for the border are the perennials. Their great advantage is their longevity, and thus also the fact that they require far less work on the part of the gardener. A well laid-out perennial border will provide an effective display for several years before replacements are needed — all it requires is normal care.

The rules for laying out a perennial border are the same as for annuals. Here, too, the individual species should be graduated according to height and placed according to colour and period of flowering so as to provide an effective display. Compared with annuals, perennials have the added advantage of including species that flower either from early spring into late autumn, when annuals have long since been killed by the first frosts. The drawback of perennials compared with certain annuals is their shorter flowering period, which averages about four weeks, though they do include some species that flower for longer, even as long as two to three months, e.g. *Heliopsis, Oenothera missouriensis, Gaillardia aristata, Viola cornuta, Rudbeckia* hybrid 'Gloriosa Daisy', and others. A suitable choice of plants can provide a display of colour from early spring until late autumn. Many species have decorative foliage and habit of growth and are an ornamental feature even when not in flower.

The perennial border can also include bulbs and annuals. Several suitable spots should be left free for this purpose when putting out perennials. If bulbs are used which are to be left in the ground a number of years (narcissi, certain botanical tulips, hyacinths, etc.), the later-flowering perennials should be placed so that they mask the dying-down parts of the bulbs. Empty spaces left by dying-down perennials such as *Dicentra, Papaver orientale,* etc. should be masked in the same manner. Putting bulbs in a perennial border will provide colour in early spring, and even though the summer months bring a profusion of flowering perennials, the addition of some long-flowering annuals will heighten the effect.

In modern gardens the structured border is increasingly being replaced by freer, more informal arrangements. Plants are not arranged in such rigid graduating lines, and in some places taller plants are put as solitary specimens or perhaps in small groups among lower-growing species. Such specimens must have an attractive habit of growth and foliage in order to be an ornamental feature even when not in flower. A number of ornamental grasses are also good for this purpose. This type of border creates a lighter, more diversified effect and is a sort of intermediate stage between a formal border and a natural perennial garden.

A third type is the so-called low border, which has a somewhat different purpose and a different location in the garden. Whereas the normal border is usually designed to be viewed from one side and is placed against a suitable background, low borders or beds may be sited so they can be viewed from both sides. They may be located near a bench or other resting place, between house and pathway, etc. Low-growing perennials, no more than 40 to 50 cm high and mostly carpeting or cushion-forming plants, are suited to this type of border. They are planted in sections of irregular outline separated by perennials of medium height, or grasses such as *Avena, Deschampsia, Pennisetum, Festuca*, etc. Good fill-ins for such beds or borders are several small bulbs that provide colour in spring and are hidden from view by the carpeting perennials after they have died down. Also good in such a border are certain low woody plants, in particular *Erica carnea, Calluna vulgaris*, certain low species of *Cotoneaster*, of *Potentilla*, and of dwarf conifers such as *Pinus mugo*, etc.

Of the woody plants, floribunda roses are best suited for borders. These may be combined with perennials or used by themselves. Some varieties flower profusely for a long period and come in beautiful colours, but borders consisting entirely of roses do have the disadvantage of not coming into flower before the end of June, and the requirements of their proper care and maintenance do not allow for the planting of any other flowers in their midst.

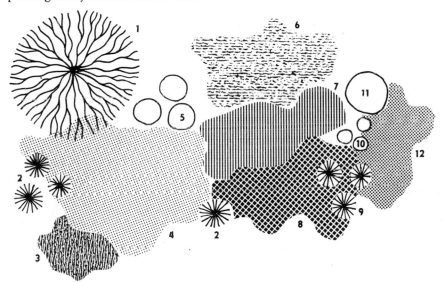

A spring garden:
1. *Daphne mezereum* 2. *Avena sempervirens* 3. *Crocus neapolitanus* 'Dutch Yellow' 4. *Erica carnea* 'Winter Beauty' 5. *Helleborus niger* 6. *Doronicum columnae* 7. *Primula elatior* hybrid, red 8. *Tulipa fosteriana* hybrid 'Princeps' 9. *Brunnera macrophylla* 10. *Primula denticulata* 'Alba' 11. *Dicentra spectabilis* 12. *Crocus chrysanthus* in a mixture of colours

Free-style, Natural Groupings

Unlike beds and borders, these flower groupings are irregular in outline, can be any shape, and may contain a wide variety of flowers selected for their pleasing combined appearance. They are composed mainly of low-growing perennials that form a 'carpet' in which are set groups of medium-high and taller species. Also used in these schemes are grasses and both broad-leaved and coniferous woody plants of dwarf habit. Well-designed sections of this type should look as natural as possible, even though cultivated species of flowers have been used for the purpose — simplicity and a loose, open effect are best. For this reason it is best to use only a few species, selecting them with care. The inclusion of grasses adds an airy touch; of the bulbs, the ones best suited for the purpose are those which, like perennials, may be left in the ground for a number of years.

Their character makes such free-style, natural groupings the best form of colour decoration in the modern, informal garden. They should be sited where they make an attractive display, perhaps near a bench, or in the background but within direct view of bench or patio; they should also be kept in mind when planning areas of garden that are seen from indoors. The effect of free-style flower groupings is heightened if they are set in an expanse of green lawn or are backed by darker shrubs.

The Heath Garden

This is a type of natural garden containing heathers *(Calluna vulgaris)* and heaths *(Erica carnea)* of various colours, interspersed with various woody plants such as *Juniperus communis* 'Stricta', *Pinus mugo, Cytisus praecox, Berberis thunbergii* and the like as vertical elements. The heaths and heathers, planted out in smaller or larger patches of irregular contours, may be accompanied by various prostrate

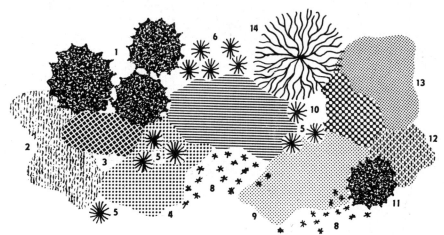

A heath garden:
1. *Pinus mugo* 2. *Calluna vulgaris* 'Alportii' 3. *Lavandula angustifolia* 4. *Erica carnea* 'Rubra' 5. *Avena sempervirens* 6. *Deschampsia cespitosa* 7. *Erica carnea* 'Snow Queen' 8. *Festuca glauca* 9. *Thymus serpyllum* 10. *Aster linosyris* 11. *Juniperus communis* 'Hibernica' 12. *Calluna vulgaris* 'J. H. Hamilton' 13. *Aster dumosus* hybrid 'Prof. Kippenberg' 14. *Cytisus praecox*

plants, such as *Thymus serpyllum, Antennaria dioica, Dianthus deltoides,* etc. Clumps of grasses are also good, e.g. *Avena sempervirens, Deschampsia cespitosa, Festuca scoparia,* etc. A group of pines, with perhaps a birch tree or two, serves as an effective backdrop. The heath garden should be sited in a sunny position, and the soil mixed with sand and peat; heath mould can also be added.

Paths, which in the modern garden are usually paved with natural stone, may lead through the heath garden so that its beauty can be admired close at hand. As with the free-style perennial groupings, a heath garden should ideally be fronted by a green expanse of lawn.

The Steppe Garden

This type of garden is laid out along the same lines as the heath garden but contains a different selection of plants. The flat, horizontal element is formed by prostrate plants such as *Thymus serpyllum, Antennaria dioica* and *Dianthus deltoides.* Among these larger or smaller groups of grasses are planted: of the low-growing forms chiefly various species of *Festuca* and *Koeleria glauca,* and of those of medium height *Avena sempervirens, Deschampsia cespitosa, Pennisetum alopecuroides* and *Stipa barbata.* The annual ornamental grass *Hordeum jubatum* is also very beautiful and effective, and as it seeds itself freely it needs only to be kept in check.

Other features in this garden are perennials of steppe character, for instance *Iris pumila, Adonis vernalis, Pulsatilla vulgaris, Pulsatilla halleri, Lavandula angustifolia, Dictamnus albus* and the like, which are planted in small or larger groups; and, of course, certain bulbous and tuberous plants such as botanical tulips, *Allium karataviense, A. christophii, A. moly,* various species of *Crocus, Muscari armeniacum, Scilla sibirica,* etc. Small or larger patches of these, depending on the character of the species, may be scattered at random throughout the section. The steppe garden should also contain certain species of *Eremurus,* particularly *E. stenophyllus* 'Bungei'.

All the above plants like, or at least tolerate, sun and dry conditions, and the steppe garden should be sited accordingly; well-drained soil is also important. The steppe garden is lovely throughout the spring, and continues to be attractive in later months even though it is not as colourful.

Section Containing Xerophilous Plants

This is a special, unique part of the garden. Even though it has its attractive features it is not a common decorative element. The selection of plants links up in part with the steppe garden, but is limited solely to xerophilous species that tolerate extreme drought. The ground for such a section is prepared in a slightly different way. It is sited either on sloping ground with a southern exposure or else on level ground that is contoured so it has a slightly undulating surface. Well-drained soil is a must. Large stones or groups of stones should be embedded firmly here and there to create the impression of rocks and the ground should be covered with stone rubble and smaller stones of the same sort. The plants should cover no more than two-thirds of the area, leaving at least one-third bare. It is also possible to use certain woody plants in limited numbers, depending on the size of this

A garden with ornamental grasses:
1. *Hippophae rhamnoides* 2. *Spartina pectinata* 3. *Avena sempervirens* 4. *Festuca glauca* 5. *Festuca scoparia* 6. *Sedum telephium* 7. *Thymus serpyllum* 8. *Allium christophii* 9. *Dictamnus albus* 10. *Calamagrostis epigejos* 11. *Deschampsia cespitosa* 12. *Geranium platypetalum* 13. *Dianthus deltoides* 14. *Avena sempervirens* 15. *Miscanthus sinensis* 'Gracillimus' 16. *Festuca scoparia* 17. *Pennisetum alopecuroides* 18. *Berberis thunbergii* 'Atropurpurea'

section. Of the conifers only certain prostrate or shrubby forms of *Juniperus communis,* of the broad-leaved species for instance *Caragana jubata, Hippophae rhamnoides, Perovskia atriplicifolia* etc., and of the larger species *Yucca filamentosa, Eryngium giganteum* and *Lavandula angustifolia.* Further plants that are suitable include *Carlina acaulis, Thymus serpyllum,* all hardy species of *Opuntia, Euphorbia myrsinites, Antennaria dioica* and *Marrubium velutinum.* These, however, should not be planted in large masses as in the steppe garden, but in relatively small groups interspersed with stones.

Such xerophilous sections require a minimum of care and maintenance: as a rule they do not need to be watered; they should, however, be provided with a light protective cover of evergreen twigs for the winter.

Flat Flower Schemes

Flat flower schemes are extremely effective in some parts of the garden, for instance beside a bench or patio, or near the entrance to the house. These areas, of varying dimensions and regular or irregular shape, are intended to provide a bright display for a long period. Smaller spaces should be of one colour, while larger ones may contain a mixture of colours although the effect should remain harmonious.

If such a space is to provide a display of colour throughout the growing season, plants must be put out twice a year. Bulbs are best for a spring display, chiefly varieties of low double tulips and certain botanical tulips of the *Tulipa fosteriana, T. kaufmanniana and T. greigii* groups. These should be spaced 12 to 15 cm apart so as to form a continuous sheet of colour. Tulips come mainly in red, yellow, white and pink; if blue is desired in the scheme, then use should be made of *Muscari armeniacum* or *Scilla sibirica*. When the bulbs have finished flowering they are replaced by annuals or other plants that flower the whole summer long, are of low height, and come in striking colours. Of the annuals particularly good for this purpose because of their long flowering period are *Ageratum houstonianum, Petunia hybrida, Salvia splendens, Tagetes patula* and *Verbena* hybrids, of the other plants chiefly *Begonia tuberhybrida* and *Pelargonium zonale*.

Low perennials are less suitable for such large plantings because none can rival the annuals in brilliance of colour and length of flowering. They can, however, be used to create a patchwork effect. Various carpeting species are planted out to cover spaces of different shapes and sizes. If, besides flowering, they also have decorative foliage the colour effect is permanent. Species with strikingly decorative foliage include *Achillea tomentosa, Ajuga reptans* and *Stachys olympica,* and of the grasses chiefly *Festuca glauca, F. scoparia* and *Koeleria glauca*. Of the flowering, but evergreen perennials suitable for the purpose are *Androsace sarmentosa, Saxifraga arendsii* hybrid, *Thymus serpyllum* and *Viola cornuta*. Flat plantings of perennials may be brightened also by groups of low bulbs such as *Crocus* hybrid, *Muscari armeniacum, Leucojum vernum* and *Eranthis hyemalis*.

Turf Substitutes

Where conditions prevent the successful growth of green lawn, perhaps because of too much sun or the shade of trees and shrubs, or places so small that it is difficult to keep turf in good condition, prostrate perennials serve as good substitutes. These not only grow well in such places but also require hardly any care, and in time form dense clumps which cover the ground like a carpet.

For dry, sunny situations *Achillea tomentosa, Hieracium aurantiacum, Phlox subulata, Thymus serpyllum* and various species of *Sedum* are all good. For partial and full shade *Ajuga reptans, Lysimachia nummularia* and *Vinca minor* are best.

Rock Gardens and Dry Walls

The problem of differences in level between various parts of a garden situated on sloping ground may be solved in several ways: by grass-covered terraces, a series of dry walls or by a rock garden. Of the three possibilities the rock garden is the prettiest, but it does require a great deal more work than any of the other garden sections already considered.

The proper construction of a rock garden, as well as a selection of suitable plants, are most important. The principal construction material is stone, and the rocks should be large—the smallest should weigh at least 50 kg, and most should be larger than this. They may be of various kinds; best of all are pale-coloured rocks with a weathered surface—stone that has recently been cut is unsuitable for this purpose.

The slope on which the rock garden is to be located should first of all be roughly shaped to the contours required. Then the rocks are laid in place—either individually or in groups—and firmly embedded in the ground. They should be arranged to give a natural effect and to create spaces of various sizes to receive the various plants. If the rock garden is a large one it may contain paths and steps made of flat stones. Even before planting, the rock garden should be attractive.

All rock gardens require well-drained soil. If the soil is not naturally permeable it should be mixed with sand and peat, and if necessary provided with drainage. The hollows where the plants are to go should be filled with some porous material (gravel, coarse sand, etc.) topped by a layer of permeable soil. Some rock plants have special soil requirements, and the soil should be suitably prepared for them before planting begins.

Proper setting out of plants is as important as the construction of the rock garden. Rock plants are best considered according to height, which also determines their location in the rockery. Species of prostrate habit or which form cushions are put in the spaces between the stones. These include *Achillea tomentosa, Alyssum montanum, Campanula cochleariifolia, Dianthus deltoides, Saxifraga × arendsii, Sedum acre, Thymus serpyllum* and *Veronica prostrata.* A number of the same species planted together in a group are most effective, and this method of planting is recommended. Species that hang down over the stones, forming colourful cascades, are also attractive.

Species that form clumps or small shrublets should be planted individually or in small groups. There should not be too many of these in the rockery, which should contain mostly ground-hugging plants. *Aster alpinus, Adonis vernalis, Primula denticulata, Pulsatilla vulgaris* and *Santolina chamaecyparissus* are all examples of plants in this category.

Some species are excellent for filling cracks and crevices—some even thrive better thus than when they are planted in open spaces. Plants for this purpose include *Campanula tridentata, Dianthus alpinus, Saxifraga longifolia,* all species of *Sempervivum* and *Sedum spinosus.*

Grasses also have their place in the rock garden as a supplementary element to give it a natural look. All low species of *Festuca, Carex* and *Koeleria coerulea* are good for the purpose, of the medium-high grasses chiefly *Avena sempervirens* and *Pennisetum alopecuroides.*

As for bulbs, spaces between the rocks may be filled with groups of botanical as well as hybrid crocuses, certain low species of botanical tulips—in particular *Tulipa tarda, T. fosteriana* and *T. kaufmanniana*—and most small bulbs such as *Eranthis hyemalis, Scilla sibirica, Puschkinia scilloides, Chionodoxa luciliae* and *Colchicum bornmuelleri.*

The rock garden should also include woody plants, chiefly of dwarf or prostrate habit. Of the junipers, for instance, *Juniperus chinensis* 'Globosa Cinerea', *J. communis* 'Depressa' and *J. sabina* 'Tamariscifolia'; of the pines chiefly the dwarf form of *Pinus mugo;* and of the spruces *Picea abies* 'Nidiformis', *Picea glauca* 'Echiniformis' and *P. glauca* 'Liliput'. Broad-leaved species suited for the purpose include *Cotoneaster horizontalis, Euonymus fortunei, Erica carnea, Berberis thunbergii* 'Kobold' and *Cytisus decumbens.*

Dry walls provide another solution to the problem of landscaping a garden situated on a slope. The stones are joined not by cement but by filling the gaps between them with carefully sieved soil in which the rock plants are put; the construction is further strengthened by their root system. These walls are constructed of layers of stones, each successively some three to four centimetres closer towards the slope. The finished wall should be inclined backwards, not only to hold up the bank but also to direct the rain into the soil, where it is retained for the plants, which usually thrive better in such a wall than in open ground.

The species used in crevices in the rock garden, and those which form hanging cushions are also the best to plant in walls. The top of the wall may either give directly on to the lawn, or a border of low perennials may be placed there.

The Water Garden

Water creates a pleasant, soothing effect in gardens, and may be used in various ways. If water is available from a natural source, it is quite easy to have lovely streams, cascades, natural pools and marshy places in the garden. If, however, the only source of water is the public mains then pools of concrete or plastic are generally the rule.

Pools are usually located in the part of the garden set for family living, perhaps near a patio. The attractiveness of pools is heightened if they contain aquatic

An aquatic garden:
Water lilies and other aquatic
plants planted in pools

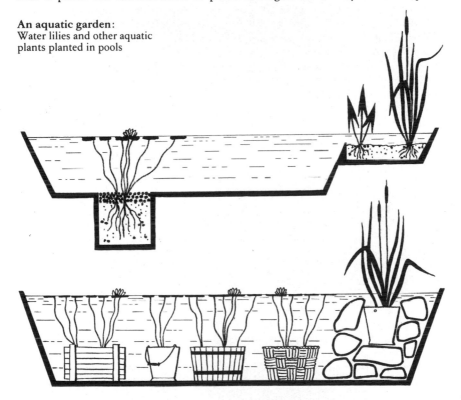

plants, the most popular being water lilies. Nowadays these are available in many species, varieties and colours, ranging from white, pink and red to yellow, orange and bronze. The various species have different depth requirements. Leaving aside the natural species, which generally require a depth of more than 80 cm, most species and varieties do well at a depth of 40 to 50 cm, although miniature varieties will be content with a depth of 15 to 20 cm. These have smaller leaves and flowers and are suitable for even quite small pools. In all instances the leaves should not cover too great an expanse of water; at least one-third of the water's surface should remain exposed, particularly in small pools.

Water lilies are not, of course, the only plants grown in pools. There are many other decorative plants which can be used for the purpose. The narrow, grass-like leaves of *Acorus calamus,* which also has a variegated form, *Juncus effusus, Scirpus lacustris, S. tabernaemontani* and its yellow-ribbed form, *Typha angustifolia* and the smaller *Typha minima* are all very decorative. Many other plants with decorative foliage and flowers are also lovely, such as *Alisma plantago-aquatica, Butomus umbellatus, Hippuris vulgaris, Hottonia palustris, Menyanthes trifoliata, Orontium aquaticum* and *Sagittaria sagittifolia.* Most of these do best at a depth of 10 to 20 cm. Pools are generally deeper than this, so a pocket at a shallower depth near the edge of the pool needs to be made to receive the plants. Some aquatic species float on the surface of the water and become submerged only towards the end of the growing season. The best known of these are *Stratiotes aloides, Utricularia vulgaris, Hydrocharis morsus-ranae* and *Trapa natans.*

Marshy places can be created in the garden with the aid of concrete bowls about 25 to 30 cm deep. The bowl should be placed in the ground so the edge is just below the level of the surface and does not show, then filled with soil and soaked with water. Water should be added as required so the soil does not dry out. Not only bog plants but also certain moisture-loving species which make unusual and interesting plants, will grow well in these conditions. The loveliest of these is without a doubt the Clematis Iris — *Iris kaempferi* — with flowers which sometimes look more like orchids than irises. For the edge of such a marshy spot, whether it is situated by itself or beside a pool, low species such as *Calla palustris, Myosotis palustris* and *Primula rosea* are a good choice.

The immediate vicinity of pools should contain perennials which resemble bog plants even though they grow in dry conditions. Best suited for this purpose are *Hemerocallis* hybrid, *Trollius* hybrids, *Bergenia cordifolia, Iris sibirica, Brunnera macrophylla, Filipendula ulmaria, Kniphofia* hybrids, *Ligularia dentata* and *Tradescantia andersoniana* hybrid.

Shaded and Partly Shaded Sections of the Garden

Every garden has some areas which are partly or fully shaded, usually under trees and on the northern side of house or wall. They, too, can be made attractive by a suitable choice of plants. With only a few exceptions, annuals do not tolerate such situations: only *Ageratum houstonianum* 'Nicotiana' and *Impatiens walleriana* will grow successfully; all other species must have sun. Nor is there a wide choice among bulbs and tubers, although they may, of course, be planted under deciduous trees that do not come into full leaf until the end of April. The early-flo-

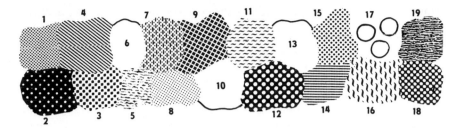

**Arrangement of flowers for cutting
(annuals, perennials and bulbs):**
1. *Chrysanthemum indicum* hybrid 2. *Narcissus* 3. *Heliopsis helianthoides* 4. *Callistephus chinensis* 5. *Tagetes erecta* 6. *Doronicum plantagineum* 7. *Campanula persicifolia* 8. *Venidium fastuosum* 9. *Chrysanthemum maximum* 10. *Zinnia elegans* 11. *Liatris spicata* 12. *Matthiola incana* 13. *Scabiosa caucasica* 14. *Cosmos bipinnatus* 15. *Chrysanthemum coccineum* 16. *Calendula officinalis* 17. *Paeonia lactiflora* hybrid 18. *Tulipa* (Darwin and Lily-flowered) 19. *Gypsophila paniculata*

wering species will grow and flower before the trees are in full leaf, by which time they are beginning to die back and shade no longer matters. Species of small bulbs such as *Eranthis hyemalis, Erythronium dens-canis, Iris reticulata, Leucojum vernum, Muscari armeniacum* and *Scilla sibirica* are the most suitable. Some spread freely and form dense masses even in shade and partial shade — e.g. *Galanthus nivalis, Eranthis hyemalis.* These can be planted not only under deciduous trees but also under shrubs. Even they, however, do not thrive under trees that have a shallow, aggressive root system, such as the birch. Under tall deciduous trees it is also possible to plant more demanding bulbs, such as early tulips, hyacinths and narcissi. These can be used to form beautiful colour combinations.
Woody plants and perennials offer a wider choice for partly and fully shaded locations. Of the conifers, those that tolerate permanent shade are all species of *Taxus,* of the junipers chiefly *Juniperus chinensis* 'Pfitzeriana' and most species of *Chamaecyparis.* Deciduous, broad-leaved woody plants that can be put in shade include *Lonicera xylosteum, Symphoricarpus albus,* and the Mollis hybrids and Ghent hybrids of the azalea *(Azalea pontica)* group. Evergreen broad-leaved species which tolerate partial shade include *Cotoneaster salicifolius, Pyracantha coccinea* and most species and varieties of *Rhododendron.* The rhododendrons are most attractive in partially shaded spots and when in flower are true gems. They must, of course, be provided with properly prepared soil and plenty of moisture. These are requirements shared by certain perennials which make very good companions to groups of rhododendrons, e.g. *Astilbe arendsii* hybrids, *Cypripedium calceolus, Aruncus dioicus, Trillium sessile* and all species of *Rodgersia.* Most ferns, with their graceful fronds, likewise make good companion plants.

Flowers for Cutting

Cut flowers are a common decorative element in modern homes, and they too may be grown in one's own garden. Usually, however, one is loathe to cut flowers in borders or groupings which form a decorative feature in the garden; the solution to the problem is to lay out special beds in which to grow them. These should be located in an inconspicuous place, where the sight of areas left bare by cutting will not offend the eye.

The choice of flowers good for cutting, not only for the beauty of their blossoms but also for their longevity in the vase, is quite large, and includes species that bloom throughout the growing season. Another, equally important problem is how to keep flowers fresh and lovely for as long as possible. This depends partly on what stage of flowering they have reached when they are cut (for instance, flowers of the family Compositae should be cut when they are as we wish to have them in the vase), and also on the conditions indoors—greater atmospheric moisture is beneficial, higher temperatures are detrimental to the flowers. It is also possible to purchase a variety of chemical agents which, when added to the water in the vase, prolong the life of cut flowers. The simplest method, however, is to have a constant and adequate supply from one's own garden from spring until autumn.

Terraces, Pergolas, Balconies

A terrace is a raised, paved area immediately adjacent to the house and connected with the living quarters. It usually overlooks a lawn or garden, to which it is linked by steps. The method of anchoring the terrace depends on the difference in height between the paved area and the surrounding terrain. If it is fairly great then the terrace usually has a stone or concrete foundation, whereas if it is less than 60 to 70 cm the solution may be a dry wall planted with flowers, or a contoured slope with a rock garden.

A pool adjoining the terrace looks very attractive, either below or on the same level as the paved area. The size of the pool depends on the size of the terrace. It should naturally be sited slightly to one side so as not to be in the way, and its shape, which may be either regular or asymmetrical, should be in harmony with that of the terrace. It should naturally also contain aquatic plants.

Another method of brightening the terrace is to leave several spaces of varying dimensions unpaved and fill them with plants. Such spaces are usually sited at the edge of the terrace or by the wall of the house. If the terrace is laid directly on soil then plants will thrive without any trouble. If, however, it is laid on a foundation layer of other material it will be necessary to dig pockets to a depth of at least 40 cm, depending on the plants to be put there, and count on the need for regular watering. Plants used for the purpose are mainly dwarf pines, junipers, certain species of *Cotoneaster, Potentilla fruticosa,* etc. Some of the grasses are also lovely: *Avena sempervirens, Pennisetum alopecuroides,* of the taller ones *Spartina pectinata* and various forms of *Miscanthus sinensis.*

If the pockets are large, they may contain a combination of different plants, for instance a dwarf pine and grasses *(Avena sempervirens, Festuca glauca* or *F. scoparia),* plus a prostrate perennial *(Thymus serpyllum, Phlox subulata* and *Iberis sempervirens).* It is also possible to put only flowering plants in these spaces, e.g. tulips for colour in spring, followed in summer by *Petunia* hybrids, *Pelargonium zonale, Salvia splendens, Tagetes patula,* etc.

Even if there are no such unpaved spaces in the terrace it can still be brightened with portable greenery—containers of various shapes and sizes, made of earthenware or other material, containing plants that do well in limited space. These consist primarily of certain flowering annuals, but it is also possible to use certain woody plants, grasses and perennials referred to in preceding paragraphs, of which the best are *Pinus mugo, Cotoneaster praecox, Cytisus decumbens, Avena sempervirens* and all species of *Festuca*.

The edges of balconies are generally brightened by troughs filled with flowers, mostly annuals. Besides those that are suitable for growing in unpaved spaces and containers on the terrace, pendent species are also attractive and good for this purpose, in particular *Pelargonium peltatum, Petunia* hybrids, *Tropaeolum* hybrids and *Begonia tuberhybrida* "Pendula" (if the site is not too exposed to sun).

Pergolas are used to separate two different parts of the garden or to link the house or entranceway with the garden. There are many kinds of pergolas; in general they

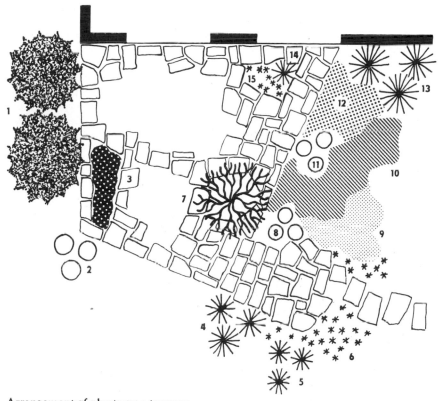

Arrangement of plants on a terrace:
1. *Juniperus virginiana* 'Tripartita' 2. *Helianthus salicifolius* 3. *Tulipa fosteriana* hybrid 'Princeps' 4. *Spartina pectinata* 5. *Avena sempervirens* 6. *Thymus serpyllum* 7. *Cotoneaster praecox* 8. *Sedum telephium* 9. *Veronica prostrata* 10. *Phlox subulata* 'Rosea' 11. *Lavandula angustifolia* 12. *Doronicum columnae* 13. *Miscanthus sinensis* 'Giganteus' 14. *Avena sempervirens* 15. *Thymus serpyllum* and *Festuca glauca*

consist of upright poles or lengths of wood linked together with a number of horizontal sections to form an attractive pattern or design. The wood may either be just treated, or painted white—the most suitable colour. The pergola may also be used to shade a bench, in which case it is usually constructed as a lattice of scantlings suspended above the bench. Various climbing plants are trained over the pergola to create a green or flowering screen, which besides being a lovely decorative feature also provides more shade.

The best woody plants for the purpose are climbing roses, *Clematis* hybrids, *Wistaria sinensis, Aristolochia macrophylla, Lonicera* × *tellmanniana* and *Polygonum aubertii*. Of the perennials, *Lathyrus latifolius* and *Asparagus verticillatus* are particularly good, and of the annuals *Lathyrus odoratus* and *Phaseolus coccineus*.

Hedges

The various sections of the garden as a rule either end with or are separated from each other by hedges. These may consist of freely-growing shrubs, or they may be clipped. Both evergreen and deciduous shrubs may be used for this purpose. For symmetrical, clipped hedges the best conifers are *Thuja plicata,* which grows fairly rapidly, *Taxus baccata,* which grows rather slowly, and certain taller, upright species of *Chamaecyparis*. Broad-leaved shrubs good for making thick hedges include *Acer campestre, Carpinus betulus, Crataegus monogyna, Ligustrum vulgare, L. ovalifolium* and *Ribes alpinum*. Species recommended for free-growing, untrimmed hedges are *Deutzia* × *magnifica, Forsythia* × *intermedia, Lonicera caerulea, Syringa vulgaris* and *Weigela* hybrids, which also flower, thus adding a further decorative element to the garden.

Hedge planting—isolation of roots and clipping

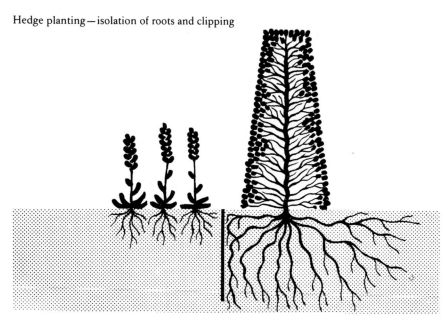

Cultivation and Care of Flowers in the Garden

Annuals and biennials generally like a warm and sunny situation. They do best in good, permeable garden soil with plenty of moisture and nutrients. They do not tolerate soggy soil. Over-feeding is likely to lead to lush growth and fewer flowers. The soil should be forked over to aerate it and then levelled before planting. If it is too dry it should be watered.

The time to plant depends on both the species and the geographical location. Hardier species are usually put out in April, while species sensitive to the late frosts which usually occur up to mid-May in central Europe are planted in the second half of May. Most species should be spaced 25 to 35 cm apart, but those that develop into large plants should be given more space. In recent years nurseries have been supplying seedlings grown-on in pots. This has many advantages, the foremost being the possibility of putting out larger, properly developed plants, often already in flower, which root well and grow rapidly because they have firm balls of soil round the roots.

When the bed is ready, measure out and mark the places where the plants are to be put, make holes with a dibber, and after putting the plants in press the soil in well round the roots and water thoroughly. Watering should be repeated at frequent intervals until the plants become established. After that it is only necessary to water them in dry weather.

Species with tap roots or poorly branched roots that do not tolerate disturbance are generally sown directly in the place where they are to grow. Seeds are sown either in drills or in pinches in a marked-out bed, and the seedlings thinned to give enough growing space to the healthiest among them. The time for sowing varies depending on the species; however, most species suited to this method of growing are sown from March to April.

Care of annuals during the growing season is fairly simple, consisting of watering as needed, occasional hoeing and weeding. When the plants have become established they may be given an application of compound fertilizer, best of all in liquid form when watering. This may be repeated two or three times more at about three-week intervals.

Biennials, which are usually planted in the late summer and autumn, should be provided with a light cover of evergreen twigs for the winter, particularly where there is danger of dry frosts.

All annuals and biennials are propagated from seed. Some species are sown directly into the ground where the plants are to grow; others must first be raised under glass and then planted out as seedlings. The best method for most of the latter type is in a cold or semi-warm frame. Most species are sown in March, although those sensitive to frost and which grow rapidly are sown in April. Slow-growing species are sown in February into boxes in the greenhouse or by the window, e.g. *Ageratum houstonianum, Begonia semperflorens, Lobelia erinus, Petunia* hybrids and *Portulaca grandiflora*.

When they have germinated, seedlings are pricked out about 5 cm apart into another frame, where they continue to grow under glass being provided with greater ventilation and if necessary with shade on warm, sunny days. About a week before being put in their permanent site the seedlings are hardened off by removing the glass. They should be watered before being moved.

Perennials, unlike annuals, do not all have the same soil and site requirements. The various genera have their origin in widely differing conditions, which must be provided for them in the garden if they are to thrive. There are, nevertheless, many species tolerant enough to adapt themselves to conditions different from those of their native habitat.

Most perennials do well in good, slightly permeable garden soil that is reasonably moist. Some species require a certain type of soil, e.g. acidic soil containing humus (*Astilbe arendsii* hybrids, *Anemone japonica* hybrids). If the soil in a garden does not have the requiered characteristics, it must be replaced to a depth of at least 30 cm in those places where the plants are to be put. Proper preparation of the topsoil is important, particularly in the case of certain rock plants, grasses and ferns. Before planting, the soil should be well aerated by digging over to a depth of 30 cm, and all weeds should be removed. It is the persistent, rhizomatous weeds that pose the greatest danger. Annual weeds are easier to eliminate by hoeing. Prior to planting only old, well-rotted compost should be added to the soil as fertilizer. Artificial fertilizers should never be applied until after the plants have become established. Heavy soil can be improved by adding sand and peat.

Perennials are planted out mainly in spring (usually in April and early May) and autumn (from the end of August until the beginning of October). Planting at a later date can be risky for some species. The plants must have time to become well rooted before winter, as they may otherwise suffer serious damage from dry frosts, particularly if these come early. If the gardener has no choice and they must be planted out later in the autumn, then they should be covered with evergreen twigs after being put in the ground.

If the plants have firm soil balls round the roots, as they will if they are container-grown, they may be put out at any time during the growing season, though it is better to avoid planting during a hot summer, as the dry conditions will necessitate far more frequent watering. Most species can be planted with success either in spring or autumn. The general rule of thumb, however, is that spring-flowering species should be planted in autumn and vice versa.

Plants should be put in holes of adequate size made with a hoe, spade, trowel or dibber. The soil must be firmly pressed in round the roots of the plants, then lightly raked over and watered thoroughly. At first the plants should be watered at frequent intervals, later only according to need. Occasional shallow hoeing will destroy germinating weeds and keep the soil moist. Routine care in following years is minimal. It includes spring hoeing to suppress weeds, and watering during lengthy dry, hot spells. Prompt removal of faded flowers will prevent the formation of seed and in some species (e.g. *Lupinus polyphyllus* hybrids, *Delphinium* hybrids, etc.) will promote continued flowering. In autumn the top parts of the plants are cut back and the soil between them loosened with a hoe. A protective cover of evergreen twigs should be provided for species likely to be damaged by frost.

Perennials are propagated from seed as well as by offshoots, cuttings, division, etc. Most botanical species can be multiplied by seed, as can certain cultivated perennials, but only if top-quality seed is obtained from a breeder (e.g. *Primula vulgaris, P. elatior, Lupinus polyphyllus* hybrids, *Aquilegia* hybrids and *Gaillardia aristata*). Sowing and raising seedlings under glass is carried out in the same way as for annuals. March and April are the best time for sowing. Some plants, such as *Trollius* hybrids, all species of *Eryngium,* etc., will not germinate unless exposed to frost and should therefore be sown in autumn. Other species germinate best if the seed is sown as soon as it is harvested, e.g. *Helleborus niger, Dictamnus albus,* etc.

Vegetative propagation is used in the case of all species with a large number of varieties in order to ensure the preservation of the characteristics of the parent plants. The easiest method is by division of clumps, which does not require any special tools. Larger numbers of young plants may be obtained by cuttings. This method requires a frame or greenhouse: the cuttings are taken from the tips of young shoots and inserted in clean sand, to which peat may be added. They must be kept under glass until they take root, during which time they should be shaded and misted frequently. When they have rooted the cuttings should be provided with increasing ventilation until they are left uncovered altogether. There are several other methods, but these are used only by nurseries, for example propagation by root cuttings in the case of *Papaver orientale, Anemone hupehensis, Brunnera macrophylla, Primula denticulata, Phlox paniculata,* etc. Grafting is used mostly for double varieties of *Gypsophila paniculata.*

Rock garden plants generally require a rather light, permeable soil and do not tolerate wet conditions. If the soil is not permeable then good drainage must be provided when constructing the rockery. Most species are happy in ordinary garden soil to which sand and peat have been added. In the case of lime-loving (calcicole) plants limestone rubble should be added. Preparation of the soil is especially important in the case of lime-hating plants (calcifuge). These do best in a mixture of well-rotted leaf mould, sand, peat and garden soil.

Rock garden plants are planted chiefly in April so that they become well established by winter. Plants that have been grown in pots and have soil balls round the roots may be put out also in May and June. Autumn planting is risky. After being put in place they, like all other plants, must be watered. Care during the course of the year consists of regular weeding, and watering as required; misting equipment is very good for this purpose. In regions with a harsh climate and the danger of dry frost, rock plants should be provided with a protective cover of evergreen twigs for the winter.

Ornamental perennial grasses may be divided according to their requirements into two groups: undemanding species, which do best in fairly poor, permeable soil, e.g. *Avena sempervirens,* all species of *Festuca, Pennisetum alopecuroides, Deschampsia cespitosa* and *Calamagrostis epigejos;* and demanding species, e.g. all species of *Miscanthus, Cortaderia selloana* and *Spartina michauxiana,* which should be provided with deep, nourishing and well-drained soil. In spring they require abundant moisture and nutrients, but in the autumn rather dry conditions. They do not tolerate waterlogged soil, particularly in winter.

Most grasses are planted in spring; only some species may be planted in the autumn, e.g. *Avena sempervirens, Deschampsia cespitosa* and all species of *Festuca.* Planting and care are the same as for all other perennials, although grasses should always be cut back in spring. The chief method of propagation is by division, also in spring.

Aquatic and bog plants are a special group of perennials. The soil in which they are put should be rather heavy, free of lime and fertilized with bonemeal. The plants are put out in spring (April to May), which is also the time to propagate by division. The most important aquatic plants — water-lilies — were formerly put in wicker or wire baskets or other containers, lifted out for the winter and stored in a cellar until spring when they were again put back into the pool. A better and easier method is to put water-lilies in hollows made for this purpose in the bottom of the pool. These should be at least 30 cm across and 40 cm deep. Water-lilies may be left there for the winter if the pool is drained and the bottom covered with a layer of leaves at least 50 cm thick. Larger pools, particularly ones in which the sides slope at a sufficient angle, need not be drained for the winter; water-lilies do not mind if the water freezes over. Every three years, however, they must be lifted, divided, the soil replaced and young plants put out again.

Ferns have specific needs. Most species require shade or partial shade and rich soil that contains no lime and is sufficiently moist. In most cases the soil must be prepared beforehand. The areas where ferns are to be put should contain a mixture of peat, forest litter and leaf mould.

Ferns should be planted only in spring when they begin to put out leaves. The majority are propagated by division, some by means of rooting offshoots (e.g. *Matteucia struthiopteris*). They may also be propagated by using the spores, but this requires special equipment.

Bulbs and tubers generally require good, well-drained soil which should be forked over to aerate it before planting; well-rotted compost may also be added.

Most species are planted in autumn, best of all in September, and should be thoroughly watered-in so that they will root quickly. Frost-sensitive species are planted in spring; these include *Dahlia, Gladiolus, Tigridia pavonia, Acidanthera bicolor, Begonia tuberhybrida* and *Canna indica.* Begonia tubers are put by a window or in the greenhouse about mid-April before they have started growth; after this has started they are put outdoors, at about the end of May. Watering and aftercare is the same as for other flowers. Tubers of species sensitive to frost must be lifted in the autumn—from late September till mid-October—, put in dry, frost-free premises for the winter, and put out again in spring.

Hardy species may remain in the same spot for a number of years, like other perennials. Only tulips, apart from a few botanical species, should be lifted every year after they have died back. The bulbs should be kept in a dry, well-aired place during the summer and put out in the autumn. If tulips are left in the ground undisturbed for a number of years, the bulbs become increasingly smaller as they multiply, and in two or three years' time the plants begin to cease flowering.

Propagation depends on the species. Most produce bulblets which are then grown to normal size. Some are propagated from seed as, for instance, all species of *Allium, Scilla, Chionodoxa, Puschkinia, Anemone, Eranthis, Eremurus, Leucojum, Galanthus* and *Tigridia*. Most species begin to bear flowers two to three years after sowing. Hardy species are sown in autumn.

Broad-leaved trees and shrubs generally all do well in any good garden soil. Some do have special requirements: *Acer palmatum, Magnolia × soulangeana, M. stellata* and all species of *Rhododendron* need humus-rich, sufficiently moist and non-alkaline soil; *Erica carnea* and *Calluna vulgaris* must have well-drained soil with a mixture of sand and peat added; *Calluna vulgaris* is also intolerant of lime. The application of good, well-rotted compost when planting is always beneficial, as is the addition of peat.

Except for the evergreen species, which are supplied by nurseries with a root ball, plants are delivered with bare roots and must be trimmed before being put out in the ground. It is necessary to cut off the root tips and cut back the branches to between a third and a half of their original length. The hole in which they are to be put should be somewhat larger than the root system. The bottom of the hole is covered with a layer of good, friable soil on which the plant is placed, and the hole filled with soil, which should be settled between the roots by giving the plant a slight shake. The soil should be tamped down firmly, the surface levelled and then thoroughly soaked with water.

Woody plants may be put out in spring, best of all in March to April before they begin growth, as well as in autumn from October to November. The increasing practice of growing woody plants in containers in the nursery means all year round planting.

Pruning of roses

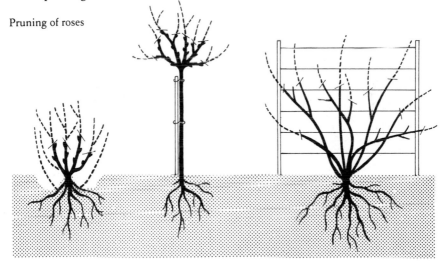

Most woody plants must be pruned the first two or three years so that they branch well and develop into dense bushes (the same applies to the crowns of trees). Branches are cut back by about a third in spring; as a rule this is no longer necessary in later years.

Roses, however, need regular pruning, in particular hybrid tea and floribunda roses. In the autumn they should be cut back to about half their length, which also makes it easier to mound the soil as protection against damage by frost. In spring, before growth starts, the soil should be raked level and the shoots cut back to the second or third bud from the base. In the case of climbing roses long, unbranched shoots are cut back by about a third, and side shoots by between a third and a half. Shrub roses are pruned in the same way as other ornamental shrubs.

Trimmed hedges should be clipped every year. Pruning is important in the first few years to encourage dense growth at the base. Then they should be allowed to

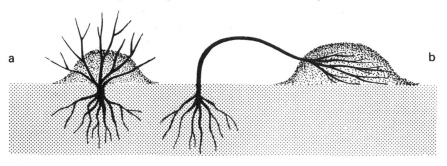

a   b

Winter care for a) shrub roses b) tree roses c) climbing roses

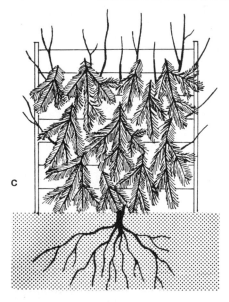

Winter care for rhododendrons

c

28

grow to the required height and clipped with electric or hand shears to the required shape. The first clipping should be done in spring before growth begins, the second in late spring while the shoots are still soft. In summer they will put out further young shoots, thus making the hedge thicker.

Some species of woody plants are propagated from seed, but all varieties and forms are propagated by vegetative means, either by cuttings, grafting or budding. These require skill and expertise and are usually not a task for the amateur gardener. It is best to purchase the plants one wants from a nursery.

Coniferous trees and shrubs are supplied to shops with root balls and in containers. The method of planting is the same as for evergreen broad-leaved species;

Planting of conifers

it is again always advisable to add peat when planting in order to promote root growth. The best time for planting is in spring, from March to April, and in autumn from August to November. It is important to water the plants thoroughly as soon as they are put in the ground, and several times more after that; once established, conifers require only routine care. In most cases they are not trimmed, except for certain shrub species such as *Taxus baccata* and certain species of *Juniperus,* which may be made more attractive by cutting off unduly long, unbranched twigs.

All evergreens, both broad-leaved and coniferous, require ample moisture in winter and should thus be watered thoroughly before the arrival of long-term frosts.

The propagation of conifers is a difficult task which usually requires a greenhouse. Some species are multiplied by seed, others by cuttings or grafting. They grow fairly slowly and are only supplied for sale when they are three to five years old. They are not propagated by the amateur gardener.

In the foregoing we have discussed the many different problems that confront the gardener, indicated how they can be solved, and suggested suitable species for the various sections of the garden. We have purposely dealt chiefly with the uses of plants and the layout of the various sections of the garden, and not with routine care and maintenance, which is discussed in detail in many handbooks. The illustrated section provides a survey of the various species and varieties grown in the garden, though it is of course far from comprehensive. More detailed information on the many available plants may be found in garden catalogues. The assortment of available species, of course, depends in great measure on the current demand, and it may happen that some of those described in the book are not to be found. However, a related species or variety of the same genus is sure to be available. The principal rules of cultivation, propagation and use remain valid not only for the illustrated species but for all related plants as well. Information on chemical agents, machines, equipment, tools and the like may be obtained from special establishments. The list of special literature at the end of the book includes a number of recent publications which may serve as a suitable supplement to this book.

Plates

The heading to each species described gives the following items of information:

The height of the plant in centimetres (cm)
The time of flowering, months of the year being indicated in roman numerals.
Light requirements —
    ○ sun   ◑ semi-shade   ● shade
Watering requirements —
    ○ no need for regular watering, except in periods of prolonged drought
    ◪ occasional watering recommended
    ■ regular watering

The plants illustrated are divided into the following sections:

      Annuals and biennials
      Perennials
      Ornamental grasses
      Aquatic plants
      Ferns
      Rock garden plants
      Bulbs and tubers
    Broad-leaved trees and shrubs
    Coniferous trees and shrubs

Annuals

Floss Flower   *Ageratum houstonianum* MILL. *(A. mexicanum* SIMS*)*

Compositae   10—50 cm   V—X   ○ ☑

Origin: Mexico. *Description:* Thickly branched stem. Leaves heart-shaped, softly hairy, margins serrate. Inflorescence: clusters of small blue-violet flower-heads; some varieties are white or pink. *Requirements:* Humus-rich soil. *Cultivation:* Plant out in second half of May. *Propagation:* Sow in February in boxes. Germination within 8 to 10 days at a temperature of 12 to 15°C. Prick out as soon as possible and pinch to promote branching. May also be multiplied by cuttings. *Uses:* As a carpeting and edging plant, in boxes and earthenware urns; taller varieties also for cutting. *Varieties:* 'Blue Mink'—blue-violet, and others.

Hollyhock   *Althaea rosea* CAV.

Malvaceae   150—250 cm   VII—IX   ○ ☑

Origin: Orient. *Description:* Ground rosette of leaves from which rises a tall stem with heart-shaped, felted leaves. Long spike of single or double flowers. *Requirements:* Deep, nourishing soil; sunny and sheltered situation. *Propagation:* Sow in May directly in the ground. *Uses:* Beside a fence or wall or in front of tall ornamental shrubs; also to conceal unsightly spots. *Varieties:* Usually available as seedling strains in single or double flowered selections of many colours.

Love Lies Bleeding   *Amaranthus caudatus* L.

Amaranthaceae   40—80 cm   VII—X   ○ ☑

Origin: Tropical Africa and Asia. *Description:* Reddish stems with longish ovate leaves. Long, thick, drooping clusters of small flowers. *Requirements:* Rather light, nourishing soil; ample sun and warmth. *Cultivation:* Water liberally during the growing period. *Propagation:* Sow outdoors in flowering position in early May. *Uses:* In larger or smaller groups; cut flowers last about a week in water. *Varieties:* The variety 'Atropurpureus' is dark purple; also dark red and white strains.

Snapdragon   *Antirrhinum majus* L.

Scrophulariaceae   15—100 cm   VI—IX   ○ ☑

Origin: Southern Europe. *Description:* Thickly branched plant with longish lanceolate leaves. Lipped flowers arranged in long spikes. *Requirements:* Well-drained, humus-rich soil. In a sheltered site it may even overwinter. *Cultivation:* Plant grown-on seedlings outdoors in April. *Propagation:* Sow seeds thinly under glass in March. Prick out shortly after and pinch to promote branching. *Uses:* In annual beds, shorter varieties in boxes and bowls; cut flowers last 6 to 10 days in water. *Varieties:* The "Grandiflorum" (majus) group includes large-flowered varieties, 60 to 100 cm high, good for cutting, the "Nanum" group varieties 40 to 60 cm high, for bedding and cutting, the "Pumilum" group varieties of thickly branched habit, 15 to 25 cm high. Available as separate varieties or mixtures.

Top left: *Ageratum houstonianum.* Top right: *Althaea rosea.* Bottom left: *Amaranthus caudatus.* Bottom right: *Antirrhinum majus.*

Annuals

Begonia semperflorens hybrids

Begoniaceae   15—35 cm   V—IX   ○ ▨

Origin: Brazil. *Description:* Compact habit. Leaves leathery, pale green to dark brown. Masses of white, pink, carmine or scarlet-red flowers. *Requirements:* Nourishing, slightly acid soil. *Cultivation:* Plant out after the last spring frosts. *Propagation:* Sow in boxes in January and February. Prick out as soon as possible to a spacing of 2 × 2 cm and again in April into a frame. *Uses:* As a carpeting and edging plant, in boxes and bowls. *Varieties:* Attractive varieties include 'Carmen'—pink with bronze foliage; 'Lucifer'—scarlet with brown foliage; 'Schneeteppich'—white with green foliage, etc.

Common Daisy   *Bellis perennis* L.

Compositae   12—15 cm   III—VI   ○ ◐ ▨

Origin: Europe, America, Australia. *Description:* Ground rosette of longish ovate leaves. White, pink or red flower heads; usually grown is the double form. *Requirements:* Any good garden soil. *Cultivation:* Put out in beds in September, provide a light cover of evergreen twigs as protection against frost. *Propagation:* By division after flowering. Also by seeds sown in July under glass or directly in their outdoor position. *Uses:* For spring decoration in beds together with bulbs, as edging plants, on graves in a cemetery, in boxes and bowls, and also for cutting. *Varieties:* Those of the "Monstrosa" group have tongue-shaped flowers; those of the "Fistulosa" group are tube-shaped.

Swan River Daisy   *Brachycome iberidifolia* BENTH.

Compositae   25—30 cm   VII—IX   ○ ▨

Origin: Australia. *Description:* Thickly branched stem with narrow leaves. Flower-heads about 25 mm across, pleasantly scented. *Requirements:* Well-drained, nourishing soil. *Cultivation:* Put out in beds in second half of May. *Propagation:* Sow in March under glass or in late April directly in the bed. Prick out or thin shortly after germination. *Uses:* In mixed beds, in rock gardens after bulbs have finished, in boxes and bowls. *Varieties:* Mainly grown as violet-blue, pink and white mixtures.

Pot or Garden Marigold   *Calendula officinalis* L.

Compositae   30—60 cm   VI—X   ○ ◐ ▨

Origin: Mediterranean region. *Description:* Branching plants with longish ovate, sessile leaves. Flower-heads double, semi-double or single. *Requirements:* Any garden soil. *Cultivation:* When flowers have faded the plants may be cut back to about 15 cm—they will then put out new shoots and flower anew. *Propagation:* Sow in permanent site in early April; for earlier flowering sow in autumn. *Uses:* In mixed beds; cut flowers last 5 to 8 days in water. *Varieties:* Mixtures and also separate varieties, e.g. 'Orange King'—orange with brown centre; 'Lemon Queen'—lemon yellow, and many others.

Top left: *Begonia semperflorens* hybrid. Top right: *Bellis perennis* "Monstrosa". Bottom left: *Brachycome iberidifolia.* Bottom right: *Calendula officinalis.*

Annuals

China Aster   *Callistephus chinensis* NEES *(Aster chinensis* L.)

Compositae   15 — 100 cm   VII — X   ○ ◪

Origin: China. *Description:* Erect, branching stem covered with light down. Leaves longish ovate, long-stalked. Flower-heads of varying shapes and colours. *Requirements:* Loamy-sandy soil with ample nutrients and lime; susceptible to various fungus diseases, especially wilt, and should therefore be planted in a different place each year. *Cultivation:* Plant grown-on seedlings in beds in May with spacing of 30 × 30 cm. *Propagation:* Seeds are usually sown under glass in March, but may also be sown outdoors in flowering position and thinned as soon as possible to 15 to 20 cm apart. *Uses:* In annual beds; low-growing varieties also in boxes, bowls or pots; taller varieties also for cutting — will last 8 to 14 days in water. *Varieties:* Because these asters are so popular, breeders are constantly producing new varieties. To aid selection they have been divided according to their characteristics into the following groups: "Dwarf" — flower-heads about 4 cm across, produced in abundance. Plants of semi-spherical habit, 15 to 30 cm high. Good also for flower pots. Flower in August. Most widely cultivated varieties include scarlet, carmine-pink, white, and blue colours.
"Low Comet" — flower-heads loose with narrow, slightly wavy petals. Generally only 25 cm high. Flower in late August and September. Available in a mixture of colours — blue-violet, scarlet and white — and also as separate varieties.
"Single" — flower-heads semi-double, 9 to 10 cm across. Plants 60 to 70 cm high. Flower in August to September. Available in the following colours: white, pink, carmine, dark red and blue-violet *(Sinensis* mixed).
"Quilled, semi-quilled" — delicate ray florets. Flower-heads 10 to 12 cm across. Plants 70 to 100 cm tall. Flower in August and September. Available in a mixture of colours.
"Bouquet" — flower-heads 8 to 10 cm across, central disc of tube-shaped flowers surrounded by tongue-shaped flowers. Plants 60 to 90 cm tall. Flower in August. Available in separate colours — white, pink, carmine, scarlet, blue — as well as in a mixture of colours.
"Princess" — flower-heads 8 to 11 cm across, central disc of tube-shaped flowers, ray petals tongue-shaped. Plants 60 to 90 cm tall. Flower in August to September. Most widely grown are the varieties 'Bellablanca' — yellow-white; 'Carmen' — dark red; 'Roter Edelstein' — scarlet; 'Veronica' — violet-blue.
"Ostrich Feather" — flower-heads 10 to 12 cm across, petals narrow and slightly wavy. Plants 70 to 90 cm tall. Flower from July to August. Available in separate colours — white, pink, red, blue — as well as in mixtures.
Besides these seedsmen's catalogues offer many other types of China asters listed under the following names: "American Beauty", "Market Queen", "Chrysanthemum-flowered", "Pompon", "Ball-type", "Florist", "Unicum", "Madeleine Single", "Powder Puffs", "Totem Pole" etc.

Top left: *Callistephus chinensis* "Comet". Top right: *Callistephus chinensis* "Single". Bottom left: *Callistephus chinensis* "Quilled". Bottom right: *Callistephus chinensis* "Princess".

Annuals

Canterbury Bell *Campanula medium* L.

Campanulaceae   50—90 cm   VI—VII   ○ ◪

Origin: Southern Europe. *Description:* Biennial with ground rosette of felted leaves. Pyramidal panicles of bell-like flowers. *Requirements:* Loamy-sandy soil, rich in nutrients. *Cultivation:* Plant in beds in August. Provide with a light cover of evergreen twigs as protection against severe frosts. *Propagation:* Sow thinly under glass in June. *Uses:* In smaller groups in beds. Cut flowers remain attractive in water for about 10 days. *Varieties:* "Single" and "Double" strains, in white, pink and blue.

Cockscomb *Celosia argentea* L.

Amaranthaceae   15—80 cm   VII—IX   ○ ◪

Origin: Eastern India. *Description:* Ground rosette of leaves from which rises a flattened stem with flower-head of pyramidal or comb-like shape. *Requirements:* Well-drained, nourishing soil; a warm situation. *Cultivation:* Plant out in spring after all danger of frost is past. *Propagation:* Sow in boxes in February or in a frame in March. Prick out seedlings early. *Uses:* In annual beds, on graves, in flower boxes and bowls. Plants may be dried and used for winter decoration. *Varieties:* "Cristata" resembles a cockscomb; "Plumosa" has erect, feathery flower-heads of narrow pyramidal shape. Varieties: yellow, orange, red, pink and violet.

Sweet Sultan *Centaurea moschata* L.

Compositae   60—90 cm   VII—VIII   ○ ◪

Origin: Asia Minor. *Description:* Densely branched stem with lanceolate leaves. Flower-heads about 6 cm across, pleasantly scented. *Requirements:* No special needs. *Cultivation:* Seedlings may be moved only when very young. *Propagation:* Sow outdoors in flowering position in April, thinning as soon as seed germinates. *Uses:* In annual beds. Cut flowers last about 8 days in water. *Varieties:* Available as mixtures as well as in separate colours, e.g. 'Alba'—yellow-white; Graciosa'—pink; 'Purpurea'—purple.

Common Wallflower *Cheiranthus cheiri* L.

Cruciferae   25—70 cm   IV—VI   ○ ◪

Origin: Europe. *Description:* Biennial with narrow, entire leaves. Racemes of single or double flowers, pleasantly scented. *Requirements:* Fairly heavy, well-fertilized soil with plenty of lime. *Cultivation:* Put grown-on seedlings out in beds in autumn, and cover with evergreen twigs as protection against dry frost. *Propagation:* Sow under glass in May and June. *Uses:* For spring decoration in beds with biennials and bulbs; also for forcing in the greenhouse. *Varieties:* Cultivated varieties are divided into the following groups: "Tall Double", "Dwarf Double", "Tall Single" and "Dwarf Single", coloured golden-yellow, canary yellow, bronze and violet; 'Tom Thumb' is a very dwarf strain.

Top left: *Campanula medium.* Top right: *Celosia argentea* 'Plumosa'. Bottom left: *Centaurea moschata* 'Alba'. Bottom right: *Cheiranthus cheiri.*

Annuals

Painted Lady   *Chrysanthemum carinatum* SHOUSB. *(C. tricolor* ANDR.*)*

Compositae   40—80 cm   VII—IX   ○ ▨

Origin: Morocco. *Description:* Erect, branching stems with deeply incised leaves. Flower-heads about 7 cm across, borne on long, firm stalks. *Requirements:* Practically any garden soil. *Cultivation:* Plant outdoors in mid-May. *Propagation:* May also be sown directly in the bed in late April, and the seedlings thinned. *Uses:* In mixed beds. Cut flowers last about 10 days in water. *Varieties:* Popular varieties include 'Kokarde' — white with a yellow or red ring round the central disc, 'Atrococcineum' — dark red with yellow ring; 'Pole Star' — white with dark centre; 'Dunetti aureum' — yellow, double, and many other colours.

Corn Marigold   *Chrysanthemum segetum* L.

Compositae   30—60 cm   VII—X   ○ ▨

Origin: Mediterranean region. *Description:* Broadly branching habit, leaves toothed, flower-heads about 8 cm across, on long, thick stalks. *Requirements:* No special needs. *Cultivation, propagation* and *uses:* As for the preceding species. *Varieties:* Pure varieties include 'Eldora-do' — pale yellow with brown centre; 'Eastern Star' — pale yellow with dark centre and yellow ring; 'Helios' — golden-yellow with pale centre.

Clarkia unguiculata LINDL.   *(C. elegans* DOUGL. non POIR.*)*

Onagraceae   40—60 cm   VII—VIII   ○ ▨

Origin: California. *Description:* Fairly fragile stems with heart-shaped, elongate, hoary leaves. Flowers, about 4 cm across, borne in leaf axils. *Requirements:* A warm and sheltered situation. *Cultivation:* Pinch plants to promote branching, but then they flower later. *Propagation:* Sow seed outdoors in permanent site in April, then thin. *Uses:* In mixed annual beds. Cut flowers last 8 to 10 days in water. *Varieties:* Available in mixture as well as separate varieties as single or double-flowered pink, white, violet and red.

Spider Plant   *Cleome spinosa* JACQ.

Capparidaceae   80—150 cm   VI—X   ○ ▨

Origin: Central America. *Description:* Erect stems with palmate, hairy leaves. Attractive flow-ers arranged in clusters. *Requirements:* Rather light, humus-rich soil. *Cultivation:* Plant out in beds after all danger of frost is past. *Propagation:* Sow under glass in March, and prick out as soon as possible into small pots. *Uses:* As a solitary specimen or in small groups in front of ornamental shrubs. Cut flowers are very decorative and last up to 2 weeks in water. *Varieties:* The following are generally cultivated: 'Helen Campbell' — white; 'Pink Queen' — pink; and other colours.

Top left: *Chrysanthemum carinatum.* Top right: *Chrysanthemum segetum.* Bottom left: *Clarkia unguiculata.* Bottom right: *Cleome spinosa.*

Annuals

Coleus blumei hybrids   (*C. blumei* BENTH.)

Labiatae   25 — 40 cm   ○ ◑ ▣

Origin: Java. *Description:* Erect stem with opposite, heart-shaped, beautifully variegated leaves. Flowers composed of small, pale violet florets. *Requirements:* A warm and sheltered situation; likes sun but tolerates partial shade. *Cultivation:* Should not be put outdoors before mid-May. Overwinter in a warm and light greenhouse. *Propagation:* Sow seeds in February in boxes in a warm greenhouse, and in winter also by cuttings, which will root in 5 to 7 days at a temperature of 22 to 25°C. *Uses:* Chiefly as carpeting plants in parks, or in bowls together with annuals. Also a popular house plant. *Varieties:* Though generally grown only in mixtures it is also possible to obtain certain varieties such as 'Blutrot' — blood-red with narrow, yellow-green margin; 'Firnelicht' — coppery-red; 'Gold' — green with yellow markings.

Convolvulus tricolor L.

Convolvulaceae   25 — 50 cm   VII — IX   ○ ▣

Origin: Southern Europe/North Africa. *Description:* Branched, bushy plants with ovate leaves. Funnel-shaped flowers about 5 cm across, open only in the morning. *Requirements:* A warm and sheltered situation; in soil that is too rich it bears few flowers. *Cultivation:* Does not tolerate transplanting. *Propagation:* Sow in April outdoors where it is to flower, and thin to a spacing of 15 cm. *Uses:* In flower boxes and bowls. Also for early bedding. *Varieties:* Generally the varieties of 'Minor', 'Royal Ensign' (bright blue) and 'Blue Flash' are grown; also available in a mixture of blue, violet, red and pink.

Tickseed   *Coreopsis tinctoria* NUTT (*Calliopsis bicolor* RCHB.)

Compositae   15 — 100 cm   VII — VIII   ○ ▣

Origin: North America. *Description:* Erect, branching stems with deeply divided leaves. Flowerheads up to 8 cm across. *Requirements:* Good, well-drained garden soil in a sunny location. *Cultivation:* Plant out grown-on seedlings in beds in May, spaced 20 × 20 cm. If plants are cut back after flowering they will put out new shoots and flower again in autumn. *Propagation:* Sow under glass in March; seeds will germinate in 8 to 10 days. Pricked-out seedlings should be hardened off before being put outdoors. *Uses:* Shorter species and varieties for bedding in parks and gardens. Taller plants are also good for cutting; they will last about 9 days in water. *Varieties:* The flowers come in various shades of yellow, red and brown: the variety 'Flaming Ray' is 35 cm high with reddish-brown flowers; 'Nana radiata tigrina' has about 4-cm-wide flowers coloured reddish-brown with yellow spots. Double forms are also cultivated; 'Grandiflora' strains make good cut flowers.

Top left: *Coleus blumei* hybrid. Top right: *Convolvulus tricolor*. Bottom left: *Coreopsis tinctoria* 'Flaming Ray'. Bottom right: *Coreopsis tinctoria* 'Nana radiata tigrina'.

Annuals

Cosmea   *Cosmos bipinnatus* CAV.

Compositae   80—120 cm   VII—X   ○ ▨

Origin: Mexico. *Description:* Richly branching plant with delicately cut leaves. Single flowers up to 10 cm across. *Requirements:* Any light, loamy-sandy soil. *Cultivation:* Must be watered regularly. *Propagation:* Sow outdoors in late April in flowering position; thin seedlings. *Uses:* Singly or in groups in beds. Cut flowers soon wilt. *Varieties:* Most widely grown are 'Blender' — dark red; 'Gloria' — carmine-pink with central boss; 'Pinkie' — pink; 'Radiance' — dark pink with central boss; 'Sensation' — single mixed for cutting.

Cosmea   *Cosmos sulphureus* CAV.

Compositae   60—90 cm   VIII—IX   ○ ▨

Origin: Brazil and Mexico. *Description:* Flowers only 6 cm across. *Requirements, cultivation, propagation* and *uses:* As for the preceding species. *Varieties:* Only the varieties 'Goldcrest' — yellow, and 'Orangeflamme' — orange, are grown.

Gourd   *Cucurbita pepo* L.

Cucurbitaceae   150—250 cm   VII—IX (fruits)   ○ ▨

Origin: America. *Description:* Climbing plant with large, rough leaves. The yellow flowers are followed by variously shaped ornamental fruits. *Requirements:* Fertilized, well-drained soil, liberal watering. *Cultivation:* Plant grown-on seedlings with two leaves outdoors after danger of spring frosts is past. *Propagation:* Sow seeds in pinches of three into pots, plunge in the ground in a frame until time for planting out. In warmer regions sow outdoors in permanent site in the first half of May. *Uses:* To cover walls, pergolas and other constructions; also in larger containers on the terrace or balcony. The inedible fruits are attractive as winter decoration in the home. *Varieties:* Seeds are usually available in mixtures.

Larkspur   *Delphinium ajacis* L. *(Consolida ajacis* SCHUR*)*

Ranunculaceae   40—130 cm   VI—VIII   ○ □ ▨

Origin: Mediterranean region. *Description:* Erect, thinly-branched stems with dark green, needle-like leaves. Long spike of fairly large flowers. *Requirements:* Nourishing, well-drained soil, in a sheltered situation. *Cultivation:* Space 25 × 25 cm. *Propagation:* Sow outdoors in permanent site in April, and thin newly-germinated seedlings. *Uses:* In mixed annual beds. Cut flowers last up to 8 days in water. *Varieties:* The many varieties are divided into several groups according to common characteristics: **"Low-growing hyacinth-flowered"** — 50 to 60 cm high, with thick spikes of fairly large flowers; **"Giant hyacinth-flowered"** — 100 to 130 cm high, likewise thick spikes of large flowers; **"Tall double"** — 110 to 130 cm high, looser spikes of smaller, double flowers; **"Exquisite"** — 100 to 120 cm high, richly branched with long, thick spikes of large flowers. Varieties in each group are available in a mixture of colours as well as separately — white, salmon, pink, carmine, pale blue and dark blue.

Top left: *Cosmos bipinnatus* 'Blender'. Top right: *Cosmos sulphureus* 'Orangeflamme'. Bottom left: *Cucurbita pepo.* Bottom right: *Delphinium ajacis.*

Annuals

Sweet William *Dianthus barbatus* L.

Caryophyllaceae   25—60 cm   VI—VII   ○ ▰

Origin: Southern Europe. *Description:* Leaves dark green, lanceolate. Flowers fairly small, single or double, on short stalks, borne in umbels about 10 cm across. *Requirements:* Nourishing, loamy-sandy soil rich in lime. *Cultivation:* Plant out in beds in late August. *Propagation:* Sow outdoors in well-prepared seed bed in late May, and prick out seedlings as soon as possible to a spacing of 2 × 3 cm. *Uses:* Popular flowers for cutting, lasting about 9 days in water. Also for bedding, on graves, in flower boxes and bowls. *Varieties:* Grown in a mixture of colours as well as in separate colours.

Carnation *Dianthus caryophyllus* L.

Caryophyllaceae   25—90 cm   VI—VII   ○ ▰

Origin: Southern Europe. *Description:* Noded stems with sessile, narrow, blue-green leaves. Flowers fairly large, single or double, with entire or toothed margins, pleasantly scented. *Requirements:* Well-fertilized soil. *Cultivation:* Plant out after all danger of frost is past. Pinch to promote branching. *Propagation:* Sow seed in boxes in the greenhouse in February. *Uses:* For bedding and cutting. *Varieties:* The type species is no longer cultivated, but there are many attractive varieties which are divided into several groups: **"Chabaud"** carnations have large blossoms borne continuously until the first frosts; **"Enfant de Nice"**—carnations are only 50 to 60 cm high with somewhat smaller, wavy petals; **"Dwarf Fragrance"** are scented, double, 25 to 30 cm, in many colours.

Chinese or Indian Pink *Dianthus chinensis* L.

Caryophyllaceae   25—40 cm   VII—IX   ○ ▰

Origin: China. *Description:* Richly branched plants with grey-green leaves. Unscented flowers about 8 cm across, petals usually with toothed margins; generally multicoloured with characteristic black line on each petal, dark centre and white edge, sometimes differently coloured on the underside. *Requirements:* Nourishing, loamy-sandy soil. Should not be put outdoors before mid-May. *Cultivation:* As soon as plants have rooted pinch the growing points to promote branching. *Propagation:* Sow seed under glass in March, then prick out. *Uses:* Same as for preceding species. *Varieties:* Chinese pinks are generally grown in a mixture of colours, but are also available in separate colours, e.g. 'Baby Doll'—red with white edge; 'Bravo'—scarlet; 'Lucifer'—orange-red; 'Schneeball'—white; 'Trauermantel'—blackish-purple. Besides single varieties breeders have also developed varieties with double blooms in various colours.

Top left: *Dianthus barbatus.* Top right: *Dianthus caryophyllus.* Bottom left: *Dianthus chinensis* 'Baby Doll'. Bottom right: *Dianthus chinensis* 'Flore Pleno'.

Annuals

Star of the Veldt   *Dimorphotheca sinuata* DC.
                               (D. aurantiaca HORT. non DC.*)*

Compositae   15 — 40 cm   VI — IX   ○ □

Origin: South Africa. *Description:* Branching plant with longish, lanceolate leaves. Flower-heads about 5 cm across. *Requirements:* Warm situation and well-drained soil. *Cultivation:* Remove faded flowers promptly. *Propagation:* Does not transplant well: sow directly where it is to flower at the end of April. *Uses:* In annual beds, on a dry slope, in the rock garden after spring bulbs have finished. *Varieties:* Generally grown in a mixture of colours with orange, yellow or white predominating. Some varieties available are 'Giant Orange' — orange; 'Goliath' — dark orange with brown centre; 'Glistening White'.

Livingstone Daisy   *Dorotheanthus bellidiformis* N. E. BR.
                               (Mesembryanthemum criniflorum SCHWANT.*)*

Aizoaceae   3 — 10 cm   VI — VIII   ○ □

Origin: South Africa. *Description:* Prostrate, reddish stems with blue-green fleshy leaves. Flowers about 5 cm across. *Requirements:* Rather dry soil and a warm situation. *Cultivation:* Plant grown-on seedlings outdoors after mid-May. In very rich soil they bear few flowers. *Propagation:* Sow under glass in late March, later prick out into small pots. *Uses:* As a carpeting plant, as edging for beds, on dry slopes, in the rock garden after spring bulbs have finished. *Varieties:* Available only in a mixture of white, yellow, pink, salmon, carmine and violet colours.

Viper's Bugloss   *Echium lycopsis* L. *(E. plantagineum* L.*)*

Boraginaceae   35 — 100 cm   VI — VIII   ○ □

Origin: Southern Europe. *Description:* Leaves broadly lanceolate, hairy. Spikes of bell-like, outward-facing flowers. *Requirements:* Does best in full sun and dry soil. *Cultivation:* Larger plants do not transplant well. *Propagation:* Sow outdoors in permanent site in March. *Uses:* In annual beds. *Varieties:* Generally available in a multicoloured mixture of varieties such as "Dwarf Hybrids" (height 35 cm). Best-known varieties are 'Blue Bedder' — flowers reddish at first, later azure blue, and 'White Bedder' — white.

Californian Poppy   *Eschscholtzia californica* CHAM.

Papaveraceae   30 — 50 cm   VI — X   ○ □ ◪

Origin: California. *Description:* Broadly branching plant with grey-green, finely-cut foliage. Cup-shaped flowers, about 8 cm across, open only in sunny weather. *Requirements:* Does not tolerate soggy soil. *Cultivation:* Cannot be transplanted. *Propagation:* Sow outdoors in permanent site in spring or autumn. *Uses:* In annual beds, on dry slopes, in the rock garden, or at the top of a dry wall. *Varieties:* Available in a mixture of colours, single or double forms.

Top left: *Dimorphotheca sinuata* 'Giant Orange'. Top right: *Dorotheanthus bellidiformis.* Bottom left: *Echium lycopsis* "Dwarf Hybrids". Bottom right: *Eschscholtzia californica* 'Orange King'.

Annuals

Blanket Flower *Gaillardia pulchella* FOUG. *(G. bicolor* LAM.*)*

Compositae   25—70 cm   VII—X   ○ □ — ☑

Origin: North America. *Description:* Broadly branching plant with rough, elongate leaves. Flower heads about 6 cm across. *Requirements:* Well-drained, nourishing soil and a warm, sheltered situation. *Cultivation:* Put outdoors in beds in May. *Propagation.* Sow under glass in March. *Uses:* In mixed beds. Rewarding as cut flowers, lasting 5 to 8 days in water. *Varieties:* Seedsmen offer mixtures of double or single forms, only occasionally separate varieties such as 'Lorenziana'—double, brownish-yellow, and 'Goblin'—dwarf, carmine-red flowers with yellow bands.

Treasure Flower *Gazania* hybrids

Compositae   15—30 cm   VI—X   ○ □ ☑

Origin: South Africa. *Description:* Ground rosette of dark green leaves silvery-felted on the underside. Flowers about 8 cm across, on long stems. *Requirements:* Well-drained, warm soil; in even partial shade the flowers will not open. *Cultivation:* Plant out in mid-May. Remove faded flowers promptly. *Propagation:* Sow under glass in March. Prick out in threes into small pots. *Uses:* In annual beds, in boxes and bowls. *Varieties:* Cultivated varieties are usually available only in a mixture of yellow, orange, red and coppery-brown.

Godetia grandiflora LINDL.

Onagraceae   20—40 cm   VII—VIII   ○ ☑

Origin: California. *Description:* Thinly branched plant with longish, lanceolate leaves, from the axils of which grow flowers about 8 cm across. *Requirements:* Does not tolerate soggy soil. *Cultivation:* Plant grown-on seedlings outdoors in May. *Propagation:* Sow under glass in late March and prick out soon afterward. *Uses:* In annual beds, and low-growing varieties also in the rock garden. *Varieties:* Of the single varieties, "Dwarf Selected Mixed"—in pastel colours; 'Blitzstrahl'—dark red; 'Pelargonium'—spotted pale pink; 'Scarlet Emblem'—large, single, red; 'Sybil Sherwood'—salmon pink; 'Azalea-flowered' mixtures.

Helipterum roseum BENTH.   *(Acroclinium roseum* HOOK.*)*

Compositae   30—55 cm   VI—IX   ○ □ ☑

Origin: Australia. *Description:* Branching plants with narrow, sessile leaves. Flower-heads about 5 cm across with dry bracts curved round the central yellow disc. *Requirements:* Well-drained, humus-rich soil. Intolerant of lime. A warm and sheltered situation. *Cultivation:* Plant grown-on seedlings outdoors after mid-May. *Propagation:* Sow under glass in late March. *Uses:* Chiefly as cut flowers, and dried for 'everlasting' winter decoration. *Varieties:* Usually offered only in a mixture of various shades of pink, white and red.

Top left: *Gaillardia pulchella* 'Lorenziana'. Top right: *Gazania* hybrid. Bottom left: *Godetia grandiflora* "Dwarf Selected Mixed". Bottom right: *Helipterum roseum*.

Annuals

Squirrel-tail Grass   *Hordeum jubatum* L.

Gramineae   40—60 cm   VI—VIII   ○ ◪

Origin: North America. *Description:* Grass forming tufts of upright stems with soft leaves. Spikes 5 to 12 cm long, generally curving to the side. *Requirements:* None; very adaptable species. *Cultivation:* Space plants about 15 cm apart. *Propagation:* Sow outdoors in permanent site in late April. May be grown on in pots plunged in the ground in a frame. *Uses:* In smaller or larger groups in bedding schemes. Also in floral arrangements as freshly cut or dried flowers. *Varieties:* Only the type species is cultivated, no known varieties to date.

Rocket Candytuft   *Iberis amara* L. *(I. coronaria* HORT.*)*

Cruciferae   20—30 cm   V—VIII   ○ ◪

Origin: Southern Europe. *Description:* Richly branched stems, leaves stiff, finely toothed, lanceolate with blunt tip. Flower clusters almost flat, later lengthening into spikes. Very fragrant. *Requirements:* Well-drained, rather moist garden soil. *Cultivation:* Plant out spaced 25 × 25 cm. *Propagation:* Sow directly in flowering position in April. *Uses:* In mixed annual beds, boxes and bowls. Attractive also as underplanting between dahlias, gladioli and similar plants. Cut flowers last about one week in water. *Varieties:* 'Fairy Mixed'—dwarf, brilliant colour range; 'Red Flash'—vivid carmine-red.

Globe Candytuft   *Iberis umbellata* L.

Cruciferae   25—35 cm   VI—VIII   ○ ◪

Origin: Southern Europe. *Description:* Leaves lanceolate with pointed tip. Umbrella-shaped flower clusters do not lengthen into spikes. *Requirements, cultivation, propagation* and *uses:* As for the preceding species. *Varieties:* The type form has pinkish-violet flowers about 1 cm across. Other varieties include 'Alba'—pure white; 'Dunettii'—purplish-violet; 'Rose Cardinal'—pure pink; 'Vulkan'—carmine-red.

Balsam, Touch-me-not   *Impatiens walleriana* HOOK. *(I. holstii* ENGL. et WARB.*)*

Balsaminaceae   15—60 cm   VI—X   ○ ◑ ◪

Origin: Tropical Africa. *Description:* Richly branched, thick, fleshy stems, leaves elliptic lanceolate. Flowers about 4 cm across, borne in leaf axils. *Requirements:* Well-drained, rather moist soil. Tolerant of partial shade. *Cultivation:* Plant out after all danger of frost is past. *Propagation:* Sow thinly under glass in mid-March, and prick out into small pots. *Uses:* In beds under tall trees, also in flower boxes and bowls. *Varieties:* Offered in colour mixtures as well as separate colours; also 'Camellia-flowered' mixtures and dwarf 'Tom Thumb' mixed.

Top left: *Hordeum jubatum.* Top right: *Iberis amara.* Bottom left: *Iberis umbellata.* Bottom right: *Impatiens walleriana.*

Annuals

Morning Glory *Ipomoea purpurea* ROTH *(Convolvulus purpureus* L.*)*

Convolvulaceae   200—400 cm   VI—X   ○ ◩

Origin: Tropical America. *Description:* Twining plant with branching stem and heart-shaped leaves. Large, trumpet-shaped flowers that open early in the morning and close before noon. *Requirements:* A warm and sheltered situation. In excessively rich soil it does not bear flowers. *Cultivation:* Requires support, such as a wooden framework, wire netting, etc. *Propagation:* Sow in flowering position in early April. *Uses:* To cover pergolas and fences. Also in boxes on balconies and terraces. *Varieties:* Offered in mixed colours as well as in separate varieties such as 'Heavenly Blue' ('Rubrocoerulea') and 'Scarlet O'Hara' with scarlet trumpets.

Summer Cypress, Fire Bush *Kochia scoparia* SCHRAD.

Chenopodiaceae   60—100 cm   VIII—IX   ○ ◩

Origin: Southern Europe and Middle East. *Description:* Erect, richly branched plants with linear leaves. Small, insignificant, yellow-green flowers. *Requirements:* Will grow in almost any garden soil. *Cultivation:* Put out in beds in the second half of May. *Propagation:* Sow seeds in pots under glass in early April or later directly in the ground where they are to flower. *Uses:* Singly in gardens, parks or cemetery. Also as a temporary hedge, as it can be easily trimmed into various shapes. *Varieties:* 'Trichophylla'—foliage turns wine-red in autumn; 'Childsii' is an improved form.

Hare's Tail Grass *Lagurus ovatus* L.

Gramineae   30—40 cm   VI—VIII   ○ □ ◩

Origin: Mediterranean region. *Description:* Ornamental grass with narrow leaves forming thick clumps. Stems terminated by oval white spikes with long awns. *Requirements:* Well-drained soil and a warm situation. *Cultivation:* Put grown-on seedlings outdoors in early May. *Propagation:* Sow under glass in late March, preferably in pots plunged in the ground. *Uses:* In annual beds and for edging. Rewarding as a cut flower, particularly in the winter months. *Varieties:* Only the species is cultivated.

Sweet Pea *Lathyrus odoratus* L.

Leguminosae   100—200 cm   VI—IX   ○ ◩

Origin: Southern Italy. *Description:* Climbing plant. Stem with paired leaves terminates in tendrils which hold it to the support. Fragrant flowers in loose racemes on long stalks. *Requirements:* Rich soil and a warm situation. *Cultivation:* Requires a support on which to climb. *Propagation:* Sow in pinches of three in small hollows in permanent site in April. *Uses:* To cover fences, pergolas and railings. Also in boxes on a balcony or as cut flowers in a small vase. *Varieties:* Many in pastel hues, divided into groups such as "Praecox", "Spencer", "Grandiflora", "Semi-dwarf Multiflora" and "Dwarf Bijou". The "Grandiflora" strains are usually very sweet scented.

Top left: *Ipomoea purpurea.* Top right: *Kochia scoparia.* Bottom left: *Lagurus ovatus.* Bottom right: *Lathyrus odoratus.*

Annuals

Annual Mallow   *Lavatera trimestris* L.

Malvaceae   60—100 cm   VI—IX   ○ □ ▨

Origin: Mediterranean region. *Description:* Richly branching plant with heart-shaped kidney-like leaves covered with light down. Flowers funnel-shaped, about 6 cm across, on long stalks. *Requirements:* Rather light, dry, poor soil. *Cultivation:* In excessively rich soil it makes lush growth and bears few flowers. *Propagation:* Sow in permanent site in April. *Uses:* In beds; cut flowers last only briefly in water. *Varieties:* Besides the type species with pink flowers, available varieties are 'Albiflora'—white; 'Splendens'—carmine; 'Loveliness'—dark pink; 'Sunset'—lilac-pink with darker stripes; 'Tanagra'—pink.

Statice   *Limonium sinuatum* MILL.

Plumbaginaceae   60—80 cm   VII—IX   ○ □ ▨

Origin: Mediterranean region. *Description:* Ground rosette of longish, lobed leaves covered with fine hairs from which rises a richly branching stem with numerous small flowers. *Requirements:* A light, well-drained, nourishing soil. *Cultivation:* Put out in beds at the end of April. *Propagation:* Sow under glass in March, prick out seedlings. *Uses:* In annual beds. Invaluable as a dried everlasting for winter decoration. *Varieties:* The type species has a blue calyx and yellow petals. More widely cultivated nowadays are the varieties 'Candidissimum'—white; 'Roseum Superbum'—carmine-pink; and those with blue and lavender colours.

Sea Lavender, Statice   *Limonium suworowii* O. KUNTZE

Plumbaginaceae   40—70 cm   VII—IX   ○ □ ▨

Origin: Turkestan. *Description:* Ground rosette of entire leaves. Long, dense spikes of small rose-pink flowers pressed tightly to the stem. *Requirements, cultivation, propagation* and *uses:* As for the preceding species. *Varieties:* Only the type species is grown.

Sweet Alyssum   *Lobularia maritima* DESV. *(Alyssum maritimum* LAM.*)*

Cruciferae   8—40 cm   VI—IX   ○ □ ▨

Origin: Mediterranean region. *Description:* Richly branched plant with creeping, ascending stems, small, longish lanceolate leaves, and profusion of small, white, fragrant flowers arranged in racemes. *Requirements:* Does well in almost any garden soil. *Cultivation:* Plant outdoors in early May. If cut back after flowering it will produce new flowers later the same year. *Uses:* As a carpeting plant in beds of annuals, under taller plants such as *Dahlia, Ricinus,* etc., in flower boxes and bowls. *Varieties:* Most widely cultivated are the varieties 'Little Dorrit'—white; 'Snow Carpet'—white; 'Rosie O'Day'—rose-pink.

Top left: *Lavatera trimestris.* Top right: *Limonium sinuatum* —blue-coloured variety. Bottom left: *Limonium suworowii.* Bottom right: *Lobularia maritima* 'Rosie O'Day'.

Annuals

African Daisy *Lonas annua* VINES et DRUCE *(L. inodora* GAERTN.*)*

Compositae   30—40 cm   VII—X   ○ ◪

Origin: Algeria. *Description:* Erect plant of broadly branching habit with longish lobed leaves and clusters of small tubular flowers. *Requirements:* Ordinary garden soil and a warm situation. *Cultivation:* Put grown-on plants outdoors in beds in May. *Propagation:* Sow in boxes in the greenhouse in early March. Prick out as soon as possible and grow on in a frame. *Uses:* In mixed beds, and dried for winter decoration. *Varieties:* Only the type species with yellow flowers is cultivated.

Matricaria inodora L.   *(Chrysanthemum maritimum* PERS.*)*

Compositae   25—40 cm   VI—VII   ○ ◪

Origin: Mediterranean region. *Description:* Richly branched stem with finely cut leaves. Flowers about 4 cm across with a ray of white petals and yellow central disc. *Requirements:* An adaptable species with no special needs. *Cultivation:* Put grown-on plants outdoors in May. *Propagation:* Sow under glass in late May. Harden off pricked-out seedlings before planting outside. *Uses:* In mixed annual beds. Cut flowers last 12 to 14 days in water. *Varieties:* The double varieties are popular: 'Brautkleid'—with large white flowers; 'Bridal Robe'—white; 'Schneeball'—cream yellow.

Stock *Matthiola incana* R. BR.

Cruciferae   25—70 cm   VI—VII   ○ ◪

Origin: Mediterranean region. *Description:* Stems with long leaves felted on the underside, pleasantly scented flowers about 4 cm across. *Requirements:* Nourishing, loamy-sandy soil. *Cultivation:* Put hardened-off plants outside in the second half of April. *Propagation:* Sow in boxes in February or in a frame in March; prick out into small pots. *Uses:* For bedding and cutting. *Varieties:* Cultivated varieties come in white, yellow, pink, red, carmine and blue, as well as in a mixture of colours. They are divided according to height, flowering period and flower shape into 'Ten Week'—summer flowering; 'Brompton'—winter flowering; 'Night-Scented' *(Matthiola bicomis)*; and many bedding varieties.

Monkey Flower *Mimulus* hybrids

Scrophulariaceae   20—30 cm   VI—VIII   ○ ◪

Origin: Latin America. *Description:* Branching stems with oval, heart-shaped leaves. Flowers about 6 cm across, borne in clusters. *Requirements:* Fresh soil and partial shade. *Cultivation:* Put outside in beds in mid-May. *Propagation:* Sow in boxes or in a frame in the second half of March; prick out into small pots. Pinching promotes branching. *Uses:* In annual beds, window-boxes and bowls on the terrace. *Varieties:* Available mostly in mixed colours. The best-known varieties are 'Bonfire'—orange-red with rusty throat; 'Rubens'—white with red patches.

Top left: *Lonas annua.* Top right: *Matricaria inodora* 'Bridal Robe'. Bottom left: *Matthiola incana.* Bottom right: *Mimulus* hybrid.

Annuals

Marvel of Peru *Mirabilis jalapa* L.

Nyctaginaceae   60—80 cm   VI—X   ○ ▨

Origin: Mexico. *Description:* Tuberous root, richly branching stem with heart-shaped leaves. Trumpet-shaped, pleasantly scented flowers open at night and close again in the morning. *Requirements:* Deep, nourishing and warm soil. *Cultivation:* Put outdoors at the end of May as it does not tolerate even a slight frost. *Propagation:* Sow under glass in early April. Tubers can be stored for the winter in the same way as with dahlias. *Uses:* Singly or in small groups in bedding schemes; also in large bowls on terrace or balcony. *Varieties:* Cultivated in a mixture of glowing colours—yellow, pink, red and white.

Forget-me-not *Myosotis* hybrids

Boraginaceae   10—35 cm   II—VI   ○ ◕ ▨

Origin: Alps. *Description:* Biennial with numerous stems branching from the ground and long, hoary leaves. *Requirements:* Well-prepared, nourishing soil. *Cultivation:* Best planted out in spring; provide a light cover of evergreen twigs for the winter. *Propagation:* Sow sparsely in the first half of July. *Uses:* In spring bedding schemes, particularly combined with tulips and narcissi; also in boxes and bowls, as well as for cutting. *Varieties:* Most widely cultivated nowadays are the hybrids obtained by interbreeding several species. There are many attractive varieties with blue, pink or white flowers.

Nemesia hybrids

Scrophulariaceae   20—45 cm   VI—IX   ○ ▨

Origin: South Africa. *Description:* Narrow leaves and profusion of flowers, about 25 cm across, borne in racemes. *Requirements:* Well-drained, nourishing soil. *Cultivation:* Put out in May when all danger of frost is past. *Propagation:* Sow sparsely under glass in late March. *Uses:* In annual beds, boxes and bowls, and for cutting. *Varieties:* Usually cultivated in a mixture of pastel colours.

Tobacco Plant *Nicotiana* × *sanderae* HORT.

Solanaceae   60—100 cm   VII—IX   ○ ▨

Origin: Latin America. *Description:* Large, elliptical, finely hairy leaves. Funnel-shaped flowers with five-pointed corolla that open only in the evening. *Requirements:* Loamy, humus-rich soil, liberal watering, a warm, sheltered situation. *Cultivation:* Put out grown-on plants at the end of May. *Propagation:* Sow under glass in April. Seedlings must be hardened off gradually. *Uses:* In small or larger groups to conceal unattractive spots in the garden. *Varieties:* Originally only varieties with bright red flowers were cultivated, but in recent years breeders have produced varieties in other hues such as 'Crimson Rock'—deep red, 'Lime Green' and 'White Idol'.

Top left: *Mirabilis jalapa.* Top right: *Myosotis* hybrid. Bottom left: *Nemesia* hybrid. Bottom right: *Nicotiana* × *sanderae* 'Crimson Rock'.

Annuals

Love-in-a-mist *Nigella damascena* L.

Ranunculaceae   30—50 cm   VII—VIII   ○ ◩

Origin: Mediterranean region. *Description:* Branching stem with finely cut leaves. Flowers up to 4 cm across, surrounded by filament-like bracts. *Requirements:* Will grow in practically any garden soil. *Cultivation:* Put grown-on plants outside in May. *Propagation:* Sow under glass in late March, or outdoors in flowering position at end of April. *Uses:* In annual beds. Cut flowers last 6 days in water. *Varieties:* Cultivated in a mixture of colours, and also separate varieties such as 'Miss Jekyll' — azure blue. 'Persian Jewels' is a recommended mixed strain.

Corn Poppy *Papaver rhoeas* L.

Papaveraceae   30—80 cm   V—VI   ○ ◩

Origin: Central Europe and Asia. *Description:* Erect stem with finely cut leaves; when injured a white milky fluid oozes from the tissues. Flowers on long stalks. *Requirements:* Well-drained soil with plenty of nutrients. *Cultivation:* Does not tolerate transplanting. *Propagation:* Because it makes only a tap root, sow seed outside in permanent site in April, and thin early so that plants are not unduly weak. *Uses:* Because of its brief flowering period it should be used chiefly in places where a bright colour effect is desired at a specific time. Not good for cutting. *Varieties:* The type species has scarlet flowers with black centre; usually offered in a mixture of colours including white, pale pink, copper, scarlet, carmine and purple in various shades.

Opium Poppy *Papaver somniferum* L.

Papaveraceae   50—90 cm   VI—VIII   ○ ◩

Origin: Unknown; grows wild in practically all parts of the world. *Description:* Blue-green, smooth leaves, large flowers. *Requirements, cultivation, propagation* and *uses:* As for the preceding species. *Varieties:* Practically all colours except yellow and blue. The most widely grown for ornamental purposes is var. *paeoniaeflorum,* double, available in mixed colours as well as in separate colours.

Beard Tongue *Penstemon* hybrids

Scrophulariaceae   30—90 cm   VI—IX   ○ ◩

Origin: Mexico. *Description:* Erect plants with ground rosette of longish ovate leaves. Long panicles of bell-shaped flowers. *Requirements:* Well-drained soil, a warm and sheltered situation. *Cultivation:* Put out grown-on seedlings in the second half of April. *Propagation:* Sow in boxes in February, prick out into small pots as soon as possible. *Uses:* In annual beds. Cut flowers last about 6 days in water. *Varieties:* Usually offered in a mixture of red, violet, blue, yellow, white and bi-coloured varieties.

Top left: *Nigella damascena.* Top right: *Papaver rhoeas.* Bottom left: *Papaver somniferum.* Bottom right: *Penstemon* hybrid.

Annuals

Petunia hybrids

Solanaceae 20—70 cm VI—IX   ○ ◩

Origin: Argentina and Brazil. *Description:* Branching stems, erect or pendent; leaves small, ovate, entire, hoary. Trumpet-shaped flowers varying in size and colouration. *Requirements:* Very adaptable plants with no special needs apart from liberal watering. *Cultivation:* Put outdoors in the second half of May, not before. Apply liquid compound fertilizer once every two weeks; remove faded flowers regularly. *Propagation:* Sow in boxes in the greenhouse in February. Seeds usually germinate within 10 days. Prick out, preferably in pots plunged in soil in a frame, when the second leaf appears. *Uses:* In beds, window-boxes and flower bowls. *Varieties:* A great many varieties have been developed during the past 150 years. They differ in habit, colour and shape of the flower, profusion of flowers, hardiness and other characteristics, and for purposes of selection are divided into the following groups:

"Nana Compacta"—compact habit, 20 to 30 cm high, profusion of small, entire flowers. Fairly resistant to unfavourable weather and therefore used in bedding schemes.

"Pendula"—branched, trailing stems, 40 to 70 cm long. Flowers about 7 cm across with entire margin. Stand up fairly well to rainy as well as very hot weather.

"Grandiflora Nana"—only 20 to 35 cm high, branched habit. Flowers about 8 cm across, somewhat less hardy. Varieties: 'Mariner F_1'—violet; 'Polynesia F_1'—brick-red; 'Radost'—carmine-red.

"Grandiflora Fimbriata"—25 to 35 cm high, flowers 7 to 9 cm across, frilled margin. Require a sheltered site. Used chiefly in window-boxes, especially varieties 'Red Cloud' and 'Blue Cloud'.

"Grandiflora Superbissima"—40 to 70 cm high. Flowers up to 12 cm across with ruffled margin and conspicuously veined throat. Fairly tender, so grown chiefly in boxes in sheltered situations; must be tied to pea-sticks. Usually offered in a mixture of colours.

"Flore Pleno"—double petunias 25 to 40 cm high, with flowers small or large, but heavy and thus less tolerant of unfavourable weather. Grown in variegated mixtures, but also offered on the market are newly developed varieties such as 'F_1 Caprice'—vivid pink, large-flowered; 'F_1 Cardinal'—scarlet; 'F_1 Cherry Tart'—carmine with white; 'F_1 Nocturne'—dark blue, large-flowered; 'F_1 Rhapsodie'—purple, large-flowered; 'F_1 Allegro'—dark salmon-pink; 'F_1 Lyric'—salmon-pink; 'F_1 Strawberry Tart'—scarlet-white.

Top left: *Petunia* hybrid Grandiflora Fimbriata (white). Top right: *Petunia* hybrid Grandiflora Nana 'Mariner F_1'. Bottom left: *Petunia* hybrid Grandiflora Nana 'Polynesia F_1'. Bottom right: *Petunia* hybrid Grandiflora Nana 'Radost'.

California Bluebell   *Phacelia campanularia* A. GRAY

Hydrophyllaceae   15 — 30 cm   VI — IX   ○ □

Origin: North America. *Description:* Plants covered with light down, leaves deeply notched. *Requirements:* Will grow where other flowers do not thrive. *Cultivation:* Great attraction for bees. *Propagation:* Sow in pinches in permanent site, spaced 20 × 20 cm, in early April. Thin as soon as possible. *Uses:* In smaller or larger masses in annual beds. Also in place of bulbs after they have finished flowering and died back. *Varieties:* P. campanularia A. GRAY — gentian-blue, bell-like flowers, about 25 mm across with conspicuous white stamens.

Runner Bean   *Phaseolus coccineus* L. *(P. multiflorus* LAM.*)*

Leguminosae   200 — 400 cm   VII — IX   ○ ◪

Origin: South America. *Description:* Stem twining spirally upward from right to left, heart-shaped leaves arranged three to a stalk. Loose clusters of red, white or bi-coloured flowers. *Requirements:* Nourishing, well-drained soil, and a warm situation. *Cultivation:* Plants require a support up which to climb. *Propagation:* Sow in pots in a frame in mid-April or outdoors in permanent site in mid-May. *Uses:* As a vegetable; also to cover pergolas, fences, etc. Also in boxes and on a terrace. *Varieties:* Available in a great many varieties with edible fruits.

Phlox drummondii HOOK.

Polemoniaceae   15 — 60 cm   VI — IX   ○ ◪

Origin: Mexico. *Description:* Sparsely branched stems with sessile, pointed leaves and clusters (cymes) of flowers up to 3 cm across. *Requirements:* A warm, sunny situation and good garden soil. *Cultivation:* Put outdoors at the end of April. *Propagation:* Sow in boxes in February or in a frame in March. Prick out into small pots. *Uses:* In annual beds. Tall varieties for cutting, low varieties in boxes. *Varieties:* Offered as a mixture as well as in separate colours. 'Twinkle Dwarf Star Mixed' is a popular compact strain.

Sun Plant, Rose Moss   *Portulaca grandiflora* HOOK.

Portulacaceae   10 — 15 cm   VI — IX   ○ □

Origin: Argentina and Brazil. *Description:* Prostrate, fleshy stems with narrow, rod-like leaves. Flowers up to 2 cm across, single or double. *Requirements:* Well-drained soil and a warm situation. In excessively rich and heavy soil it bears few flowers. *Cultivation:* Does not tolerate frost, therefore plant out in the second half of May, spaced 20 × 20 cm. *Propagation:* Sow in boxes in late February, then prick out and grow on in pots plunged in soil in a frame. *Uses:* As coloured carpets in annual bedding schemes, in flower boxes and bowls. Also in a rock garden or dry wall after bulbs have faded. *Varieties:* Usually cultivated in a mixture of colours including white, yellow-pink, carmine, scarlet and violet.

Top left: *Phacelia campanularia.* Top right: *Phaseolus coccineus.* Bottom left: *Phlox drummondii.* Bottom right: *Portulaca grandiflora.*

Annuals

Coneflower, Blackeyed Susan   *Rudbeckia hirta* L.

Compositae   50—100 cm   VII—X   ○ ☑

Origin: North America. *Description:* Branching plant with hoary, longish lanceolate leaves. Flowers about 12 cm across with striking protruding centre. *Requirements:* Does best in heavier soil. *Cultivation:* Put outdoors in mid-May. *Propagation:* Sow under glass in March, later prick out and harden off seedlings before planting outdoors. *Uses:* Singly or in smaller groups among annuals and perennials. Cut flowers last up to 12 days in water. *Varieties:* Most widely cultivated are the varieties 'Kelvedon Star'—yellow-zoned, orange and brown; 'My Joy'—golden-yellow with almost black centre.

Trumpet Flower   *Salpiglossis sinuata* RUIZ et PAV. *(S. variabilis* HORT.*)*

Solanaceae   30—100 cm   VII—IX   ○ ☑

Origin: Chile. *Description:* Branching stems with longish, hoary, toothed leaves. Large, trumpet-shaped flowers. *Requirements:* Well-drained, nourishing soil and a sheltered situation. *Cultivation:* Put out in beds in the second half of May. *Propagation:* Sow under glass in late March, then prick out into small pots. *Uses:* In annual beds and in larger bowls. Cut flowers last about 7 days in water. *Varieties:* Usually grown in a mixture of colours including white, yellow, pink, red, purple, violet, blue and brown—all have conspicuous dark veining.

Scarlet Sage   *Salvia splendens* SELLO ex NEES

Labiatae   15—50 cm   V—X   ○ ☑

Origin: Brazil. *Description:* Erect, branching stems. Opposite, heart-shaped leaves with serrate margins. Labiate flowers arranged in spikes. *Requirements:* Good nourishing soil. *Cultivation:* Put out in mid-May, not before. Regular removal of faded flowers promotes continuous flowering. *Propagation:* Sow in boxes in January, and prick out into pots plunged in soil in a frame in March. *Uses:* In beds in parks and gardens, on graves, in boxes and bowls. *Varieties:* Those with brilliant scarlet flowers are generally cultivated, e.g. 'Fireball'—35 cm high; 'Blaze of Fire'—25 cm high; 'Scarlet Pigmy'—20 cm high. White, blue-violet, pink and salmon varieties are also offered.

Creeping Zinnia   *Sanvitalia procumbens* LAM.

Compositae   10—25 cm   VI—X   ○ ☑

Origin: Mexico. *Description:* Prostrate, felted stems with ovate-lanceolate leaves. *Requirements:* Rather light, nourishing soil and a warm situation. *Cultivation:* Put out after all danger of frost is past. *Propagation:* Sow under glass in late March and then prick out. *Uses:* On sunny slopes, as edging. Also in rock gardens after bulbs have faded. *Varieties:* The type species has yellow flowers with striking purple-black centres.

Top left: *Rudbeckia hirta* 'My Joy'. Top right: *Salpiglossis sinuata*. Bottom left: *Salvia splendens*. Bottom right: *Sanvitalia procumbens*.

Annuals

Schizanthus wisetonensis hybrids   *(S.* × *wisetonensis* LOW*)*

Solanaceae   25—40 cm   VII—IX   ○ ◪

Origin: Chile. *Description:* Many-branched plant with finely cut leaves. *Requirements:* A warm and sunny situation, good garden soil. *Cultivation:* Put out in mid-May, not before, spaced 25 to 30 cm apart. *Propagation:* Sow under glass in the second half of March or outdoors in the permanent site in April. *Uses:* In mixed beds, in boxes and for cutting. *Varieties:* Usually offered only in a mixture of colours—white, pink, red, purple to violet. 'Hit Parade' and 'Dwarf Bouquet' are two modern strains.

Setaria italica P. BEAUV.

Gramineae   30—100 cm   VII—VIII   ○ □ ◪

Origin: South-East Asia. *Description:* Stems are terminated by a panicle-like spike about 3 cm wide. *Requirements:* A rather warm situation and good garden soil. *Cultivation:* In medieval times it was widely grown as a grain crop in southern Europe. *Propagation:* Sow in April or May in its permanent site. *Uses:* Singly or in groups in turf or among low-growing annuals and perennials; it may also serve as winter decoration in a vase. *Varieties:* Only the type species is cultivated.

Catchfly   *Silene coeli-rosa* GODR. *(Viscaria oculata* LINDL.*)*

Caryophyllaceae   30—80 cm   VI—VIII   ○ ◪

Origin: Southern Europe. *Description:* Dense clump of hoary stems with longish lanceolate leaves and long-stalked flowers about 3 cm across. *Requirements:* Will grow in almost any soil. *Cultivation:* If cut back after flowering it will put out new shoots and flower a second time later the same year. *Propagation:* Sow under glass in March, or outdoors in the permanent site in early April. *Uses:* In annual beds, in boxes and bowls. *Varieties:* Usually cultivated only in a mixture of colours including white, pink, red, purple and blue.

African Marigold   *Tagetes erecta* L.

Compositae   20—120 cm   VII—IX   ○ ◪

Origin: North America. *Description:* Erect stems with odd-pinnate leaves. Flowers composed of ray and tubular petals. *Requirements:* Adaptable plants, fairly easy to grow. *Cultivation:* Put outdoors in May, not before, as they do not tolerate spring frosts. *Propagation:* Sow sparsely under glass in March. *Uses:* In ornamental beds in parks and gardens. Low-growing varieties also in window-boxes, on balconies and terraces, and in bowls. *Varieties:* The many varieties are divided into several groups, such as:
"Chrysanthemum-flowered"—with narrower, longer, curving petals;
"Carnation-flowered"—with broader ray petals variously frilled and notched on the margin; e.g. 'Golden Age' and many modern F_1 hybrids. Newer varieties include 'Moonshot'—dwarf, deep yellow; 'Apollo'—very dwarf, double, orange; 'Red Seven Star'—red-brown.

Top left: *Schizanthus wisetonensis* hybrid. Top right: *Setaria italica.* Bottom left: *Silene coeli-rosa.* Bottom right: *Tagetes erecta.*

Annuals

Mexican Sunflower *Tithonia rotundifolia* S. F. BLAKE
(T. speciosa GRISEB.*)*

Compositae   100—150 cm   VIII—X   ○ ▨

Origin: Mexico. *Description:* Many-branched plant with fairly large, soft, felted leaves. Flowers about 15 cm across which close in the evening. *Requirements:* A site sheltered from wind. *Cultivation:* Does not tolerate frost and should therefore not be put outdoors before the second half of May. *Propagation:* Sow under glass in March, then prick out into pots. *Uses:* Singly or in smaller groups. Also to mask unattractive areas in the garden. Cut flowers last up to 10 days in water. *Varieties:* The type species has scarlet flowers with yellow tips and central disc.

Nasturtium   *Tropaeolum majus* L.

Tropaeolaceae   40—300 cm   VI—X   ○ ◕ □ ▨

Origin: South America. *Description:* Many-branched plants with fleshy stems and rounded leaves. Flowers up to 5 cm across. *Requirements:* Well-drained soil that is not unduly rich. *Cultivation:* Climbing varieties should be provided with a support. *Propagation:* Sow in pots plunged in soil in a frame in mid-April. May be sown outdoors in permanent site in May. *Uses:* Low-growing varieties in beds, flower-boxes and bowls. Tall varieties beside fences or other constructions. *Varieties:* Tall climbing or pendent varieties include 'Lucifer'—brilliant scarlet with dark foliage; 'Luteum'—golden-yellow; and 'Golden Gleam'. Low shrubby varieties are about 40 cm high, of which the most widely grown are 'Golden King'—yellow; 'Empress of India'—carmine-pink with dark foliage; 'Theodor'—blackish red with dark foliage.

Ursinia anethoides N. E. BR.

Compositae   25—30 cm   VI—IX   ○ ▨

Origin: South Africa. *Description:* Many-branched plant with finely cut leaves and flowers up to 5 cm across. *Requirements:* A sunny situation and well-drained soil. *Cultivation:* Put out grown-on seedlings in mid-May. *Propagation:* Sow under glass in March, or directly in flowering position in mid-April. *Uses:* In annual beds. *Varieties:* The type species is orange-yellow with a purplish red ring round the central disc.

Namaqualand Daisy, Monarch of the Veldt
Venidium fastuosum STAPF

Compositae   20—80 cm   VI—X   ○ ▨

Origin: South Africa. *Description:* Erect, branching stems with lobed to elongate leaves. Flowers up to 10 cm across; they close in the evening. *Requirements:* Well-drained, nourishing soil. *Cultivation:* Grown-on plants may be put out in early May. *Propagation:* Sow under glass at beginning of April. *Uses:* In mixed beds. Cut flowers last about 6 days in water. *Varieties:* Cultivated varieties are orange or white with a dark violet ring round the central disc.

Top left: *Tithonia rotundifolia.* Top right: *Tropaeolum majus.* Bottom left: *Ursinia anethoides.* Bottom right: *Venidium fastuosum.*

Annuals

Vervain *Verbena rigida* SPRENG. *(V. venosa* GILL. et HOOK.*)*

Verbenaceae   25 — 40 cm   VI — X   ○ ▣

Origin: America. *Description:* Erect stems with notched, hoary leaves. Thick heads of small flowers. *Requirements:* Rather light, well-drained soil that is sufficiently moist. *Cultivation:* Put outdoors in mid-May, not before. *Propagation:* Sow in boxes in February or in a frame in March. Prick out into pots. *Uses:* In mixed beds, in boxes and in bowls. Cut flowers last about a week in water. *Varieties:* The type species has narrow leaves and blue-violet flowers.

Pansy, Viola *Viola wittrockiana* hybrids

Violaceae   10 — 35 cm   III — VI   ○ ◐ ▣

Origin: Europe. *Description:* Single flowers on long stalks growing from the leaf axils. *Requirements:* Intolerant of full sun. *Cultivation:* Put out in beds in late August. Cover with evergreen twigs before the onset of frosts. *Propagation:* Sow sparsely under glass in late June. *Uses:* In flower boxes and bowls, on graves and in beds. *Varieties:* The many varieties are divided into a number of groups, such as "Hiemalis", "Pirna", "Erfurt", "Swiss Giants", "Quedlinburg Giants", "Roggli Giants", "Aalsmeer Giants", etc., each of which includes white, yellow, blue, violet and sometimes also bi-coloured varieties. There are also many new F$_1$ hybrids.

Zinnia elegans JACQ.

Compositae   30 — 120 cm   VI — IX   ○ ▣

Origin: Mexico. *Description:* Stiff stems with rough, longish ovate leaves. Flowers either single or double. *Requirements:* Good, nourishing soil, liberal watering, and a sheltered situation. *Cultivation:* Put outdoors in late May, not before. Larger blooms may be obtained by pinching out side shoots. *Propagation:* Sow sparsely under glass in March. *Uses:* In beds. Cut flowers last up to 10 days in water. *Varieties:* Intensive breeding has yielded a great number of attractive varieties which come in white, cream, yellow, orange, buff, rose, red, carmine, purple and violet. They are divided into the following groups according to habit of growth and form, and fullness of the blooms:
"Dahlia-flowered" — about 90 cm high, flowers up to 15 cm across with saucer-shaped, curved-in petals.
"California Giants" — also 90 cm high, flowers flat, up to 15 cm across, with overlapping petals.
"Giant Cactus" — about 80 cm high, petals curved and pointed.
"Scabious-flowered" — 60 to 80 cm high, flowers about 8 cm across, with raised petals in the centre encircled by several rows of broad ray petals.
"Pumila" — 60 to 70 cm high, flowers about 7 cm across, dense, double, semi-globular.
"Lilliput" — only 30 to 40 cm high, with a great profusion of flowers. Flowers 3 to 5 cm across, double, on slender but firm stems, Many new F$_1$ hybrids are also available.

Top left: *Verbena rigida.* Top right: *Viola wittrockiana* hybrid. Bottom left: *Zinnia elegans.* Bottom right: *Zinnia elegans* "Scabious-flowered".

Perennials

Bear's Breeches *Acanthus longifolius* POIR. *(A. balcanicus* HEY. et RICH.*)*

Acanthaceae   80 — 100 cm   VI — VII   ○ ☐

Origin: Dalmatia. *Description:* Plant with both decorative foliage and flowers. Clumps of long, green, beautifully cut leaves. Large spikes of purplish-pink, hooded flowers. *Requirements:* A sunny situation and ordinary to rather heavy soil. Tolerates dry conditions better than wet. *Cultivation:* Put out in spring or autumn, 60 cm apart. *Propagation:* By seed sown under glass in spring, by division in spring, or by root cuttings in winter. *Uses:* Singly or in small groups in natural settings. Also in larger rock gardens. *Varieties:* Normally only the type species is grown.

Milfoil, Yarrow *Achillea filipendulina* LAM.

Compositae   100 — 150 cm   VII — VIII   ○ ☐

Origin: Caucasus. *Description:* Erect, stiff stems, grey-green, attractively cut leaves with toothed margin. Small, golden-yellow flowers arranged in large, plate-like heads. *Requirements:* Easy to grow, best in light soil and a dry, sunny situation. *Cultivation:* Put out in spring or autumn, 40 cm apart. *Propagation:* By division in spring or autumn, or by cuttings in spring. *Uses:* In mixed borders, free-style groupings, or singly. Also for cutting and drying. *Varieties:* 'Coronation Gold' — early-flowering, low; 'Goldplate' — large heads; 'Parker' — late-flowering, more robust.

Milfoil, Yarrow *Achillea ptarmica* L.

Compositae   60 — 70 cm   VII — VIII   ○ ◪

Origin: Europe, Asia, North America. *Description:* Erect stems with narrow, dark green, serrate leaves. The stems are branched and terminated by loose heads of white, double flowers up to 10 to 15 mm across. Makes off-shoots. *Requirements:* Garden soil and sun. *Cultivation:* Put out in spring or autumn, 40 cm apart. Cut back after flowering. *Propagation:* By division or cuttings in spring. *Uses:* In mixed borders and for cutting. *Varieties:* 'Perry's White' — more robust, earlier-flowering, taller; 'The Pearl' and 'Nana Compacta' — lower, more compact, make fewer offshoots.

Agapanthus Headbourne hybrids

Liliaceae   50 — 120 cm   VII — VIII   ○ ◪

Origin: By crossing several South African species. *Description:* Perennial, tuber-like root; dark green, longish, flat leaves; flower stem with umbel of bell-like flowers. *Requirements:* May be overwintered in the open only in a temperate climate; good cover in winter is a must. *Cultivation:* Put out with a pot in May in a sunny position. Before the onset of the first frosts return into a cold greenhouse or other suitable place. *Propagation:* By division of larger clumps. If raised from seed, it flowers only after 3 to 6 years. *Uses:* Good for growing in larger containers or in sheltered places in the garden. Also for cutting. *Varieties:* Most varieties have blue flowers; var. 'Alice Gloucester' has white flowers.

Top left: *Acanthus longifolius.* Top right: *Achillea filipendulina.* Bottom left: *Achillea ptarmica* 'Perry's White'. Bottom right: *Agapanthus* Headbourne hybrid.

Perennials

Windflower *Anemone hupehensis* var. *japonica* BOWLES et STEARN

Ranunculaceae   60—100 cm   VIII—X

Origin: China; varieties are hybrids from *A. vitifolia. Description:* Leaves trifoliate, stems sparsely branched; flowers large, single or double, white, pink to red. *Requirements:* Humus-rich, lime-free soil, plenty of moisture, partial shade. *Propagation:* By root cuttings in spring. *Uses:* In partial shade together with rhododendrons and ferns. *Varieties:* 'Alice'—pink, 100 cm; 'Honorine Jobert'—white, 100 cm; 'Königin Charlotte'—pink, semi-double; 'Prinz Heinrich'—dark red, semi-double, 60 cm; 'Bressingham Glow'—deep pink, 60—80 cm.

Windflower *Anemone sylvestris* L.

Ranunculaceae   30—40 cm   V

Origin: Europe to Siberia. *Description:* Compact clumps, palmate leaves; creamy-white flowers on long stalks. Spreads by underground rhizomes. *Requirements:* Well-drained, rather dry soil with a little lime; a sunny to partly shaded situation. *Cultivation:* Put out in spring or autumn, 30 to 40 cm apart. *Propagation:* By division in spring or early autumn, or by seed sown under glass in March. *Uses:* In mixed borders, free-style groupings, larger rock gardens. *Varieties:* 'Elisa Fellmann'—double, with slightly smaller flowers than the type species.

Columbine *Aquilegia* hybrids

Ranunculaceae   50—80 cm   V—VI

Origin: Varieties originated from American species, chiefly *A. coerulea. Description:* Leaves divided into rounded sections, branching stems terminated by long-spurred flowers with sepals often a different colour from the petals. *Requirements:* Garden soil with plenty of moisture. *Cultivation:* Put out in spring or autumn, 40 to 50 cm apart. *Propagation:* Only by means of top-quality seed, sown under glass in March and then pricked out into pots. *Uses:* In mixed borders and free-style groupings. *Strains* (seed): 'Crimson Star'—red and white; 'Edelweiss'—white; 'Snow Queen'—white; 'Monarch'—mixed.

Michaelmas Daisy *Aster amellus* L.

Compositae   50—70 cm   VIII—IX

Origin: Europe to Siberia. *Description:* Leaves elongate, rough, grey-green, stems erect, branching; flowers single, pink, blue, violet. *Requirements:* Nourishing, well-drained soil in a warm situation. *Cultivation:* Put out in spring, 40 to 50 cm apart; remove faded flowers. *Propagation:* By seed sown under glass in March, varieties by division in spring. *Uses:* In mixed borders, free-style groupings. *Varieties:* 'Dr. Otto Petschek'—pale blue-violet, 70 cm; 'Lady Hindlip'—pink, 60 cm; 'Heinrich Seibert'—pale pink, 60 cm; 'Sternkugel'—lavender, 50 cm; 'Veilchenkönig'—violet, 50 cm.

Top left: *Anemone hupehensis* var. *japonica.* Top right: *Anemone sylvestris.* Bottom left: *Aquilegia* hybrid 'Crimson Star'. Bottom right: *Aster amellus.*

Perennials

Michaelmas Daisy *Aster novi-belgii* L.

Compositae   80—100 cm   IX—X   ○ ☑

Origin: Eastern North America. *Description:* Leaves elongate, glabrous, dark green; flowers single to semi-double on branching stems, white, pink, red, blue, violet. *Requirements:* Good garden soil, atmospheric moisture. *Cultivation:* Put out in spring, 40 to 50 cm apart. *Propagation:* By division in spring or by cuttings. *Uses:* In mixed borders and free-style groupings. *Varieties:* 'Blandie'—white, semi-double, 80 cm; 'Fellowship'—pale pink, 100 cm; 'Mary Ballard'—pale blue, semi-double, 80 cm; 'Royal Blue'—blue-violet, 100 cm; 'Winston Churchill'—red, semi-double, 70 cm.

Aster tongolensis FRANCH.

Compositae   40—50 cm   VI—VIII   ○ ☑

Origin: Himalayas. *Description:* Ground rosette of deep green, broadly oval leaves; flowers borne singly on firm stems, blue with orange centre. *Requirements:* Nourishing, well-drained soil that does not dry out. *Cultivation:* Put out in spring or late summer, 30 cm apart. *Propagation:* By division in spring. *Uses:* In larger rock gardens, free-style groupings, and for cutting. *Varieties:* 'Berggarten'—broad, pale blue-violet ray petals; 'Herrenhausen'—narrow, pale blue-violet ray petals; 'Napsbury'—lavender blue, good for cutting.

False Goat's Beard *Astilbe arendsii* hybrids

Saxifragaceae   50—80 cm   VII—VIII   ◐ ● ☑ ■

Origin: Varieties are chiefly crosses between the East Asian species *A. astilboides* and *A. davidii*. *Description:* Leaves divided 2 to 3 times; fine, feathery clusters of small flowers coloured white, pink, violet to red. *Requirements:* Humus-rich, non alkaline, fairly moist soil. *Cultivation:* Put out in spring, 40 to 50 cm apart. *Propagation:* By division in spring. *Uses:* In borders and free-style groupings in partial shade; good with rhododendrons and ferns. *Varieties:* 'Cattleya'—violet, 80 cm; 'Diamant'—white, 80 cm; 'Fanal'—deep red, 50 to 60 cm; 'Finale'—pale pink, 50 cm; 'Amethyst'—lilac-pink, 50 to 60 cm; 'Red Sentinel'—intense brick red spikes.

Bellflower *Campanula glomerata* L.

Campanulaceae   40—60 cm   VI—VII   ○ ◐ □ ☑

Origin: Europe to the Caucasus and Iran. *Description:* Erect, unbranched stems with rough, hairy, lanceolate leaves; deep violet, bell-like flowers arranged in several whorls on the top and in the leaf axils. Spreads by underground rhizomes. *Requirements:* Easy to grow in both damp and dry conditions. *Cultivation:* Put out in spring or autumn, 40 cm apart. *Propagation:* By division in spring or autumn. *Uses:* In borders, free-style groupings and for cutting. *Varieties:* 'Acaulis'—only 20 to 30 cm high, does not make underground stems; 'Superba'—profusion of large flowers; 'Alba'—white, only about 40 cm high.

Top left: *Aster novi-belgii* 'Winston Churchill'. Top right: *Aster tongolensis*. Bottom left: *Astilbe arendsii* hybrid. Bottom right: *Campanula glomerata*.

Perennials

Bellflower   *Campanula persicifolia* L.

Campanulaceae 60—80 cm VI—VII		○◑▣

Origin: Europe to Siberia. *Description:* Ground rosette of narrow, lanceolate leaves from which rise leaved stems terminating in loose clusters of broad blue or white bells. *Requirements:* Any good garden soil. *Cultivation:* Put out in spring or autumn, 50 cm apart. *Propagation:* By division in spring or autumn, or by seed sown under glass in spring. *Uses:* In borders, free-style groupings and for cutting. *Varieties:* 'Alba'—white; 'Blue Belle'—blue, double; 'Moerheimii'—white, double. Both double forms are propagated only by division.

Cornflower   *Centaurea dealbata* WILLD.

Compositae 70—90 cm VI—VII		○▣

Origin: Asia Minor, Caucasus. *Description:* Upright habit, leaves pinnate, white-felted on the underside; sparsely branched stems with pale carmine flowers. *Requirements:* Any good garden soil and a sunny situation. *Cultivation:* Put out in spring or late summer, 40 to 50 cm apart. *Propagation:* By division of clumps in spring or after flowering in late summer. *Uses:* In free-style perennial groupings, in borders and for cutting. *Varieties:* Most widely cultivated is the variety 'Steenbergii', which has larger, deep carmine flowers.

Chrysanthemum coccineum WILLD.   *(Pyrethrum roseum* BIEB.*)*

Compositae 60—80 cm VI—VII		○▣

Origin: Mountain meadows in the Caucasus. *Description:* Compound leaves finely bipinnate, stems sparsely leaved; daisy-like flowers from vivid red, pink to white borne singly on each stem. *Requirements:* Good, moist garden soil; a sunny situation. *Propagation:* By seed sown under glass in spring or by division in spring or autumn—chiefly the double forms. *Uses:* In mixed borders, but mainly for cutting: the flowers are long-lived. *Varieties:* 'Eileen May Robinson'—pink; 'Kelway's Glorious'—crimson; 'Evenglow'—salmon-scarlet.

Shasta Daisy   *Chrysanthemum maximum* RAM.

Compositae 50—100 cm VI—VII		○▣

Origin: Pyrenees. *Description:* Leaves elongate, toothed, dark green; stems sparsely leaved, terminating in single or semi-double, white, daisy-like flowers with yellow centres. *Requirements:* Good, nourishing, moist garden soil; plenty of sun. *Cultivation:* Put out either in early autumn or in spring, 50 to 60 cm apart; after 2 to 3 years divide and plant separately. *Propagation:* By seed sown under glass in spring, varieties by division. *Uses:* In mixed borders and for cutting. *Varieties:* 'Wirral Pride'—semi-double, 90 cm; 'Bishopstone'—single white; 'September Snow'—double white.

Top left: *Campanula persicifolia.* Top right: *Centaurea dealbata.* Bottom left: *Chrysanthemum coccineum* 'Yvonne Cayeux'. Bottom right: *Chrysanthemum maximum.*

Perennials

Chrysanthemum × *hortorum* L. H. BAILEY

Compositae   40—100 cm   IX—X   ○ ◨

Origin: Garden forms are derived chiefly from the species *C. indicum, C. koreanum* and *C. rubellum.* In general practice they are divided according to height and the shape of the flower into three main groups: (1) single and semi-double, (2) double, (3) low, double. *Description:* Erect plants with branching stems and dark green, lobed leaves. Blooms are single or double and come in many different colours ranging from white through pink, red, yellow and orange to violet. After asters they are the most important perennials for autumn flowering. *Requirements:* These are fairly demanding plants, needing loose, nourishing reasonably moist soil and a warm, sheltered, sunny situation; in winter dry conditions are preferable, and in harsher climates a light protective cover. *Cultivation:* Put out in spring or early autumn, 40 to 50 cm apart. Cut back to the ground after flowering. *Propagation:* By division of clumps in spring, or by cuttings: take cuttings about 5 cm long from the tips of shoots, and insert in sand under glass in a frame. When they put out roots, which is quite soon, transfer to—and grow on in—small pots until it is time to plant outdoors. *Uses:* In mixed borders and free-style perennial groupings. Chrysanthemums are important and rewarding perennials for cutting as blooms are very long-lived in water. In more severe climates early-flowering and mid-season varieties are recommended as later-flowering varieties may be damaged by early frosts. Polythene sheeting provides good protection for chrysanthemums grown for cutting, as not only are plants protected against early frosts but also the blooms develop more fully. *Varieties:* There are a great many varieties of single and double, and late- and early-flowering chrysanthemums; these are best selected from local specialist nurseries.

Tickseed   *Coreopsis verticillata* L.

Compositae   50—70 cm   VII—VIII   ○ ◨ □

Origin: North America. *Description:* Erect plant with thin, but firm, sparsely branching stems, finely laciniate (fringed), pale-green leaves and masses of bright yellow flowers produced over a long period. *Requirements:* Very easy to grow, doing well in any garden soil, tolerant of dry conditions, fond of sun. *Cultivation:* Put out in spring or autumn, 40 to 50 cm apart. *Propagation:* By division of clumps in spring or autumn. *Uses:* In mixed borders and free-style groupings. *Varieties:* 'Grandiflora'—deep yellow; 'Badengold'; 'Goldfink'—dwarf 30 cm.

Top left: *Chrysanthemum* × *hortorum* 'Krasavice'. Top right: *Chrysanthemum* × *hortorum* 'Mixture'. Bottom left: *Chrysanthemum* × *hortorum* 'Rayonante'. Bottom right: *Coreopsis verticillata*.

Perennials

Delphinium hybrids

Ranunculaceae   130 — 180   VI — VII   ○ ◩

Origin: Varieties are derived chiefly from *D. elatum. Description:* Erect stems and palmate leaves; towering spikes of single or semi-double flowers coloured white or blue to violet. *Requirements:* Good, nourishing, reasonably moist garden soil. *Cultivation:* Put out in spring or autumn, 60 cm apart; water in dry weather. Cut back after flowering. *Propagation:* By division in spring, or by cuttings taken when growth starts. *Uses:* In borders, free-style groupings, and also for cutting. *Varieties:* There is a wide assortment of strains and hybrids, including 'Large-flowered' and 'Belladonna'; there are also some new red, scarlet and orange hybrids from Holland.

Bleeding Heart   *Dicentra spectabilis* LEM.

Papaveraceae   60 — 80 cm   V   ◐ ◩

Origin: Eastern Asia. *Description:* Fragile, fleshy stems with grey-green leaves divided as much as three times; pink and white heart-shaped flowers on arching stems. Dies back after flowering. *Requirements:* Good, well-drained, moist garden soil. *Cultivation:* Put out in spring, 50 to 60 cm apart. *Propagation:* By division of clumps in spring, or by cuttings. Take cuttings with heel, and put to root in pots in a frame. *Uses:* In mixed perennial borders and free-style groupings of flowers. *Varieties:* A white form exists.

Burning Bush   *Dictamnus albus* L.

Rutaceae   60 — 100 cm   VI — VII   ○ ☐

Origin: Central Europe to Eastern Asia. *Description:* Erect stems, leaves grey-green, odd-pinnate; flowers 5-merous, white or pink with darker veining, borne in loose spikes. The entire plant is aromatic, and an inflammable vapour is given off from the seed-pods. *Requirements:* Nourishing soil containing lime, and a sunny, dry situation. *Cultivation:* Put out in spring or autumn, 50 to 60 cm apart. *Propagation:* By seed, sown under glass as soon as harvested. Young plants are grown in pots. *Uses:* Singly and in free-style groupings in natural sections of the garden. *Varieties:* 'Caucasicus' — deep pink; 'Albiflorus' — white.

Foxglove   *Digitalis purpurea* L.

Scrophulariaceae   80 — 150 cm   V — VI   ○ ◩

Origin: Western Europe. *Description:* Ground rosette of dark green, roughly hairy, ovate-lanceolate leaves from which rises a stout, unbranched stem with a dense spike of thimble-shaped, purplish-pink flowers. *Requirements:* Well-drained garden soil that is moist, but not waterlogged. *Cultivation:* Put out in early autumn. Usually it does not live longer than two years, but if faded flowers are removed it may well last another year. *Propagation:* By seed sown under glass in May or June. *Uses:* In mixed borders, free-style groupings and for cutting. *Varieties:* 'Gloxiniaeflora' — mixture of white, pink and red.

Top left: *Delphinium* hybrid 'Mixture'. Top right: *Dicentra spectabilis.* Bottom left: *Dictamnus albus.* Bottom right: *Digitalis purpurea.*

Perennials

Leopard's Bane *Doronicum columnae* TEN.

Compositae   50—60 cm   V   ○ ◑ ▣

Origin: Southern Alps, the Balkans, Asia Minor. *Description:* Clumps of basal leaves, stalked, heart-shaped. Stems sparsely leaved, terminating in yellow, daisy-like, narrow-rayed flowers up to 7 cm across. *Requirements:* Nourishing, preferably fairly heavy, moist garden soil, sun or partial shade. *Cultivation:* Put out in late summer, 40 cm apart. Cut off faded flowers. *Propagation:* By division after flowering. *Uses:* In mixed borders with other spring flowers. Also good for cutting; easy to force. *Varieties:* Normally only the type species is grown.

Purple Cone Flower *Echinacea purpurea* MOENCH *(Rudbeckia purpurea* L.*)*

Compositae   70—100 cm   VII—VIII   ○ □ ▣

Origin: North America. *Description:* Erect, bushy plant with stiff, stout, branching stems. Leaves lanceolate, sharply toothed, roughly hairy. Large, pink to purplish daisy-petalled flowers with protruding prickly central cone. *Requirements:* Best in well-drained, rather dry garden soil and a sunny position. *Cultivation:* Put out in spring or autumn, 50 to 60 cm apart. *Propagation:* By seed sown under glass in March, or by division in spring or early autumn. *Uses:* In mixed borders, though most often in free-style groupings; also for cutting. *Varieties:* 'Abendsonne'—bright pink; 'Earliest of All'—earlier-flowering; 'The King'—large, dark purple flowers.

Fleabane *Erigeron* hybrids

Compositae   50—80 cm   VI—VIII   ○ ▣

Origin: Most varieties are derived from *E. speciosus. Description:* Erect plants with branching stems; leaves longish-lanceolate, glabrous. The finely-rayed flowers, coloured blue, violet or pink, resemble asters. *Requirements:* Good, nourishing, reasonably moist soil, plenty of sun. *Cultivation:* Put out in spring, 50 to 60 cm apart. Staking is recommended as they are easily bent to the ground. If cut back in time they will often flower again. *Propagation:* Mostly by division in spring. *Uses:* In mixed borders, free-style groupings, and also for cutting. *Varieties:* 'Adria'—deep violet, semi-double; 'Rote Schönheit'—dark pink; 'Wuppertal'—silvery violet.

Sea Holly *Eryngium bourgatii* GOUAN

Umbelliferae   30—40 cm   VII—VIII   ○ □

Origin: Spain, Pyrenees. *Description:* Low bushes, stiff, much divided leaves with prominent white veins. Stiff stems, sparsely leaved, branched in the upper part; small, thimble-like, blue flowers with spiny bracts. *Requirements:* Rather light, preferable fairly dry soil, sun. *Cultivation:* Put out in spring, 30 cm apart. *Propagation:* By seed sown under glass in spring. Young plants are grown in pots. *Uses:* In natural settings, chiefly steppe gardens, and in larger rock gardens. Also for cutting and drying. *Varieties:* Only the type species is grown at present.

Top left: *Doronicum columnae.* Top right: *Echinacea purpurea.* Bottom left: *Erigeron* hybrid 'Rote Schönheit'. Bottom right: *Eryngium bourgatii.*

Perennials

Sea Holly   *Eryngium giganteum* M.B.

Umbelliferae   80 – 100 cm   VII – VIII   ○ □

Origin: Caucasus. *Description:* Rosette of grey-green, leathery, heart-shaped leaves from which rises a branching stem carrying thimble-shaped flowers with wide, spiny, grey-green bracts. Though a biennial it seeds itself freely. *Requirements:* Easy to grow, but soil should be well-drained, rather dry, and the situation sunny. *Cultivation:* Put out in late summer, 60 cm apart. *Propagation:* By seed sown outdoors as soon as it is ripe. Young plants are grown in pots. *Uses:* In free-style, natural groupings. Excellent for cutting and drying. *Varieties:* Only the type species is grown at present.

Spurge   *Euphorbia epithymoides* L. (*E. polychroma* KERNER)

Euphorbiaceae   40 – 50 cm   V – VI   ○ □

Origin: Eastern and south-eastern Europe. *Description:* Compact, nearly spherical clumps with oval, fine-haired leaves. The terminal leaves turn yellow during the flowering period; flowers are insignificant. *Requirements:* Well-drained soil containing lime; sun. *Cultivation:* Put out in spring or autumn, 50 to 60 cm apart. Cut back for the winter. *Propagation:* By division in spring, or by cuttings after flowering. *Uses:* Mostly singly or in small groups in larger rock gardens and natural informal settings. *Varieties:* Only the type species is grown at present.

Meadowsweet   *Filipendula kamtschatica* MAXIM.

Rosaceae   150 – 200 cm   VII – VIII   ○ ◑ ◪

Origin: Manchuria, Kamchatka. *Description:* Erect plant with branching stems, pinnate leaves, terminal leaflets large, heart-shaped, with 3 to 5 lobes; large plumes of small white flowers. A very decorative plant. *Requirements:* Any good garden soil that is reasonably moist, a sunny to partly shaded situation. *Cultivation:* Put out in spring or autumn, 80 to 100 cm apart. *Propagation:* By division or by cuttings in spring. *Uses:* In larger gardens and parks in free-style, informal groupings. *Varieties:* 'Elegantissima'; 'Rosea'.

Meadowsweet, Queen of the Prairies   *Filipendula rubra* ROBINS.

Rosaceae   100 – 150 cm   VI – VII   ○ ◑ ◪

Origin: North America. *Description:* Erect plant with pinnate leaves, the terminal leaflets smaller; plumes of pink to red flowers. Very fragrant. *Requirements:* Any moist garden soil, sun or partial shade. *Cultivation:* Put out in spring, 60 to 80 cm apart. *Propagation:* By cuttings or division in spring. *Uses:* In mixed borders, but mainly in free-style perennial groupings. *Varieties:* 'Venusta' – dark pink; 'Venusta Magnifica' – large, carmine-pink flowers.

Top left: *Eryngium giganteum.* Top right: *Euphorbia epithymoides.* Bottom left: *Filipendula kamtschatica* 'Rosea'. Bottom right: *Filipendula rubra* 'Venusta Magnifica'.

Perennials

Meadowsweet   *Filipendula ulmaria* MAXIM.

Rosaceae   100–150 cm   VI–VII   ◐ ☑

Origin: Europe, Asia. *Description:* Erect plants with sparsely branched stems and dark-green, pinnate leaves. Loose heads of small creamy-white flowers. Grows wild in woodlands, chiefly in damp places. *Requirements:* Very easy to grow, does well in any soil that is reasonably moist. *Cultivation:* Put out in spring or autumn, 50 to 60 cm apart. *Propagation:* By division at any time of the year. *Uses:* Chiefly in natural settings, best of all close to water and in partial shade; also for cutting. *Varieties:* 'Plena'—double variety; 'Variegata'—leaves striped yellow.

Blanket Flower   *Gaillardia aristata* PURSH. (*G. grandiflora* HORT.)

Compositae   40–70 cm   VI–IX   ○ □

Origin: North and Central America. *Description:* Ground rosette of broadly lanceolate leaves with entire to coarsely toothed margins; whole plant is roughly hairy. Branching, sparsely leaved stems terminated in daisy-like flowers with wide, spreading ray petals and dark centres. Varieties come in yellow-red, bronze-orange to wine-red. This is a short-lived perennial, with a life span of 2 to 3 years. *Requirements:* Good, well-drained soil, on the dry rather than moist side, in a sunny situation. *Cultivation:* Put out from late summer till early autumn so that they root well before winter; spacing 40 to 60 cm, depending on the variety. Taller varieties need a support. Prompt removal of faded flowers prolongs the life of the plants. *Propagation:* Chiefly by seed, which should be of good quality. Sow in May under glass, put outside in September. *Uses:* Taller varieties in mixed borders and for cutting. Low, compact varieties as edging plants and in free-style perennial groupings. *Varieties:* 'Bremen'—yellow-red, 60 to 70 cm; 'Burgunder'—rich wine red, 60 to 70 cm; 'Mandarin'—bronze-orange, 60 to 70 cm; 'Kobold'—golden-red, low (30 to 40 cm high), very compact to globose; 'Wirral Flame'—dark, brownish-red; 'Croftway Yellow'—pure yellow.

Goat's Rue   *Galega officinalis* L.

Leguminosae   80–120 cm   VII–IX   ○ ☑

Origin: Italy, the Balkans to Asia Minor. *Description:* Stiff, branching stems, pinnate leaves; spikes of white or violet flowers borne in profusion over a long period. *Requirements:* Does best in deep, moist garden soil, and likes sun. *Cultivation:* Put out in spring or autumn, 60 cm apart. *Propagation:* By seed sown under glass in spring, by division or by cuttings in spring. *Uses:* Chiefly in natural sections of parks and gardens. *Varieties:* 'Albiflora'—white; 'Compacta'—of lower habit; 'Plena'—double; 'Geere Hartland'—blue-violet with paler margin.

Top left: *Filipendula ulmaria.* Top right: *Gaillardia aristata* 'Burgunder'. Bottom left: *Gaillardia aristata* 'Kobold'. Bottom right: *Galega officinalis* 'Geere Hartland'.

Perennials

Crane's Bill *Geranium platypetalum* FISCH. et MEY.

Geraniaceae   50—60 cm   VI—VII   ○◑□

Origin: From Caucasus to Iran. *Description:* Erect, with palmate leaves; entire plant is covered with fine hairs. Flowers large, vivid violet-blue; in autumn the leaves turn an attractive orange or red. *Requirements:* Well-drained garden soil; tolerates quite dry conditions. Likes sun but tolerates partial shade. *Cultivation:* Put out in spring or early autumn, 40 to 50 cm apart. *Propagation:* Chiefly by division in spring. *Uses:* A profusely flowering perennial for borders and free-style groupings in natural sections of the garden. *Varieties:* A number of closely related hybrids are in cultivation under *G.* × *magnificum* and *G.* × *ibericum.*

Avens *Geum coccineum* SIBTH. et SM.

Rosaceae   40—50 cm   V—VI   ○□◩

Origin: Mountain meadows in the Caucasus and Balkans. *Description:* Ground rosette of leaves, from which rise leaved, sparsely branched stems carrying vivid brick-red flowers. *Requirements:* Easy to grow; does best in moderately moist, well-drained soil, but tolerates dry conditions. *Cultivation:* Put out in spring or autumn, 30 to 40 cm apart. *Propagation:* By seed sown under glass in spring, or by division in spring or autumn. *Uses:* In mixed borders and free-style groupings, chiefly in natural sections of the garden where its brilliantly coloured flowers make a striking display. *Varieties:* 'Lady Stratheden'—deep yellow; 'Mrs Bradshaw'—brick red.

Baby's Breath *Gypsophila paniculata* L.

Caryophyllaceae   60—100 cm   VII—VIII   ○□

Origin: South-eastern Europe. *Description:* Strong, fairly long tap root, fragile, richly branched stem, the lower part covered with narrow grey-green leaves. Profusion of small white flowers. *Requirements:* Xerophilous plant for a well drained soil and a sunny site. *Cultivation:* Put out in spring, 80 to 100 cm apart; cut back in autumn. *Propagation:* Type species by seed sown under glass in spring, double varieties by grafting onto species rootstock. *Uses:* Singly or in large groups in natural settings. Excellent for cutting. *Varieties:* 'Flamingo'—larger flowers, double, pink; 'Bristol Fairy'—double, white.

Sneezeweed *Helenium* hybrids

Compositae   70—120 cm   VII—VIII   ○◩

Origin: Varieties are derived mainly from *H. autumnale* (Canada and eastern USA). *Description:* Erect plants, leaves longish, lanceolate; flowers daisy-like with almost globular central disc and wide ray petals in colours ranging from yellow to bronze-red. *Requirements:* Sufficiently moist garden soil, and sun. *Cultivation:* Put out chiefly in spring, 50 to 60 cm apart. Cut back after flowering. *Propagation:* Mostly by division in spring. *Uses:* In mixed borders and for cutting. *Varieties:* Many varieties, e.g. 'Bressingham Gold'—yellow; 'Mahogany'—bronze-red; 'Wyndley'—brown-red; 'Moerheim Beauty'—copper red; "Gold Fox"—tawny-orange.

Top left: *Geranium platypetalum.* Top right: *Geum coccineum.* Bottom left: *Gypsophila paniculata.* Bottom right: *Helenium* hybrid 'Moerheim Beauty'.

Perennials

Sunflower *Helianthus decapetalus* L.

Compositae   100—150 cm   VIII—IX   ○ ◪

Origin: North America. *Description:* Stout, fleshy rhizomes; firm, erect stems covered with thin, roughly hairy, oval-ovate leaves. Flowers large, with yellow centre and wide, golden--yellow ray petals. *Requirements:* Fairly deep garden soil with plenty of nutrients, sun. *Cultivation:* Put out in autumn or spring, 50 to 60 cm apart. Cut back after flowering. *Propagation:* By division, mainly in spring. *Uses:* In mixed borders, free-style groupings, also for cutting. *Varieties:* 'Capenock Star'—single, pale yellow; 'Meteor'—semi-double, wide ray petals; 'Soleil d'Or'—large, deep yellow flowers; 'Loddon Gold'—vivid deep yellow.

Sunflower *Helianthus salicifolius* A. DIETR.

Compositae   250—300 cm   IX—X   ○ ◪

Origin: North America. *Description:* Long, strong, unbranched stems thickly covered their entire length with long, narrow, arching leaves; terminal clusters of single yellow flowers. Main decorative features are the habit and foliage. *Requirements:* Good, well-drained, reasonably moist garden soil, plenty of sun. *Cultivation:* Put out in spring or autumn, 80 cm apart. Cut back for the winter. *Propagation:* By division in spring. *Uses:* Chiefly as a decorative, solitary specimen among groups of smaller flowers. *Varieties:* Normally only the type species is grown.

Orange Sunflower *Heliopsis helianthoides* SWEET

Compositae   100—150 cm   VII—VIII   ○ □

Origin: North America. *Description:* Erect plant, stems slightly branched at the top; leaves opposite, broadly lanceolate, toothed. Flowers golden-yellow, single or semi-double, resembling small sunflowers. *Requirements:* Thrives in any garden soil that is not soggy; a sunny situation. *Cultivation:* Put out in spring or autumn, 50 to 60 cm apart. Cut back after flowering. *Propagation:* By seed sown under glass in spring, or by division in spring or autumn (chiefly the varieties). *Uses:* In mixed borders and for cutting. *Varieties:* 'Scabra Patula'—larger, semi-double flowers; 'Goldgrünherz'—double, lower; 'Hohlspiegel'—semi-double, taller. Not widely cultivated in Britain.

Christmas Rose *Helleborus niger* L.

Ranunculaceae   30 cm   II—III   ◐ ◪

Origin: Eastern Alps and the Balkans. *Description:* Dark, stiff, evergreen leaves, cut into longish sections; large single flowers on slightly branching, leafless stems above the leaves. The type species is white. *Requirements:* Loose, moist, humus-rich soil containing lime; partial shade. *Cultivation:* Put out in spring or early autumn, 30 to 40 cm apart. Water in dry weather. *Propagation:* By seed sown under glass as soon as it is ripe; also by divison. *Uses:* In spring-flowering, partly shaded areas, and also in rock gardens. *Varieties:* 'Praecox'—very early flowering, white; 'Rosea'—delicate pink; 'Potter's Wheel'—very large, white.

Top left: *Helianthus decapetalus.* Top right: *Helianthus salicifolius.* Bottom left: *Heliopsis helianthoides.* Bottom right: *Helleborus niger.*

Perennials

Day Lily   *Hemerocallis* hybrids

Liliaceae   60—100 cm   VI—VIII   ○ ◪

Origin: The varieties commonly grown in gardens are derived from type species mostly of East Asian origin. *Description:* Fleshy, often spindle-shaped roots; leaves narrow, channelled, arching. In habit the plants resemble a robust grass, and are also decorative when not in flower. Stem branched at the top, carrying a profusion of buds that open in succession. Flowers 6-merous, trumpet-shaped, lily-like; individual flowers generally last only one day but new ones are constantly unfolding so that the plants are in flower for 5 to 6 weeks and even longer. Type species are mostly yellow to orange. Varieties, of which there are a great number thanks chiefly to American breeders, come in colours that were previously unknown, e.g. pink, red and violet; the flowers may also have differently coloured throats, stripes down the centre of the petals, or ruffled margins. *Requirements:* These comparatively demanding perennials do best in good, well-drained garden soil and a sunny situation. They tolerate dry conditions better than wet; in partial shade they grow well but produce fewer flowers. *Cultivation:* The best time for planting is in spring, though they may also be put out after flowering. Spacing: 60 to 80 cm. They appreciate an occasional application of feed. Faded flowers should be removed promptly. After three or four years the plants should be divided. *Propagation:* Garden varieties solely by vegetative means—by division, chiefly in spring. Also possible by seed, but the plants do not come true. *Uses:* In mixed borders, but best of all in free-style perennial groupings. Very good near water gardens, although they are not moisture-loving plants. *Varieties:* Type species mainly grown in gardens include: *H. citrina*—80 to,120 cm high, flowering period July—August, flowers long, narrow trumpets coloured lemon-yellow. *H. fulva*—90 to 120 cm high, flowering period July—August, leaves broad, flowers yellow-orange with red markings round the throat. *H. middendorfiana*—60 to 70 cm high, flowering period May—June, flowers orange. Varieties include: 'Alan'—70 to 90 cm, mid-season, bright red with yellow throat; 'Atlas'—100 cm, mid-season, flowers light greenish-yellow; 'Corky'—75 cm, mid-season, flowers smaller, warm yellow; 'Crimson Glory'—100 cm, mid-season, flowers carmine-red with yellow throat; 'Crimson Pirate'—70 to 80 cm, mid-season, flowers deep red, throat orange with dark markings; 'Earliana'—90 cm, very early, flowers bright yellow; 'Frans Hals'—70 cm, mid-season, flowers wide-mouthed, red inside, light orange outside; 'Golden Sceptre'—80 to 90 cm, mid-season, golden-yellow' 'Mary Guenther'—80 to 90 cm, early, orange outside, brownish-red inside; 'Pink Damask'—80 cm, mid-season, pink with greenish-yellow throat; 'Resplendent'—100 cm, mid-season, reddish-brown with striking yellow rays; 'Sammy Russel'—60 cm, mid-season, reddish-brown with orange throat, and many more.

Top left: *Hemerocallis* hybrid 'Atlas'. Top right: *Hemerocallis* hybrid 'Crimson Pirate'. Bottom left: *Hemerocallis* hybrid 'Frans Hals'. Bottom right: *Hemerocallis* hybrid 'Golden Sceptre'.

Perennials

Heracleum stevenii MANDEN. (*H. villosum* FISCH.)

Umbelliferae   200 – 300 cm   VI – VII   ○ ◐ ◪

Origin: Caucasus. *Description:* Biennial of huge, robust habit. Giant leaves, up to 1 metre across, palmate, deeply cut. Strong, hollow stem branching at the top and terminating in white flowers arranged in a cluster (cyme) up to 60 cm across. The main cluster is surrounded by several smaller ones. *Requirements:* Will grow in any situation, but best of all in moist soil. *Cultivation:* Put out in spring or autumn, 150 to 180 cm apart. Remove faded flowers to keep the plants in check. *Propagation:* By seed sown as soon as it is ripe into pots, also directly outdoors in permanent site. *Uses:* Singly in large gardens or parks. *Varieties:* None.
H. mantegazzianum is much more widely grown – an even more gigantic plant.

Coral Flower   *Heuchera sanguinea* ENGELM.

Saxifragaceae   40 – 80 cm   VI – VII   ○ ◐ ◪

Origin: North America. *Description:* Rosette of dark green, rounded heart-shaped leaves. Slender leafless stems terminate in loose panicles of small, bell-shaped flowers coloured pink to red. *Requirements:* Good, reasonably moist garden soil; partial shade, but also tolerates sun. *Cultivation:* Preferably put out in spring, 30 to 40 cm apart. *Propagation:* By cuttings with a small piece of root in spring, also by seed sown under glass in spring. *Uses:* In mixed borders, free-style groupings, in larger rock gardens and also for cutting. *Varieties:* 'Bressingham Blaze' – red; 'Gracillina' – small pink flowers; 'Red Spangles' – bright red flowers in dense panicles.

Plantain Lily   *Hosta sieboldiana* ENGL.

Liliaceae   40 – 60 cm   VI   ○ ◐ ◪

Origin: Japan. *Description:* Vigorously growing plant with large, ovate heart-shaped leaves more than 30 cm long, coloured grey-green with a bluish cast and with prominent veins on the upper side. Flowers funnel-shaped with slightly curving tips, pale violet, in slender spikes close above the leaves. The most decorative feature is the foliage. *Requirements:* Well-drained, loamy soil that is sufficiently moist and nourishing; likes partial shade but also tolerates sun. *Cultivation:* Put out in spring or autumn, 50 to 60 cm apart. *Propagation:* By division in spring or autumn. *Uses:* In natural, partially shaded sections near water. *Varieties:* 'Elegans' – particularly attractive foliage; 'Gold Edge' – striking, yellow leaf margins.

Chinese Trumpet Flower   *Incarvillea delavayi* BUR. et FRANCH.

Bignoniaceae   50 – 60 cm   VI – VII   ○ ◐ ◪

Origin: Western China. *Description:* Roots fleshy, white, branching; leaves dark green, odd-pinnate, roughly toothed. Firm stem terminates in a cluster of 3 to 10 trumpet-shaped flowers, rosy-red with yellowish troat. *Requirements:* Well-drained, nourishing, garden soil containing lime and sufficient moisture; a sunny or partly shaded situation. *Cultivation:* Put out in spring, at least 8 cm deep and 50 cm apart. *Propagation:* By seed sown under glass in spring. *Uses:* In mixed borders, free-style groupings. *Varieties:* 'Bee's Pink' – delicate pink.

Top left: *Heracleum stevenii*. Top right: *Heuchera sanguinea*. Bottom left: *Hosta sieboldiana*. Bottom right: *Incarvillea delavayi*.

Perennials

Bearded Iris *Iris barbata* hybrids *(I. germanica* L.*)*

Iridaceae   50—100 cm   V—VI   ○ □ ◪

Origin: The botanical species are rarely grown in gardens; they have been replaced by varieties that run into the thousands. Irises are widely cultivated and new varieties are constantly being offered. They are in great demand and as their popularity grows so does the price of newly developed varieties. American breeders are chiefly responsible for the many beautiful novelties. *Description:* Fleshy rhizomes with roots, leaves sword-like, flowers on firm, leafless, unbranched stems, six petals—three, larger, spreading or drooping 'falls' and three upright, usually narrower 'standards'—and a 'beard' which in some varieties is bright yellow or orange. Irises are divided according to height into three main sections: "Nana"—15 to 30 cm high, "Medial"—45 to 65 cm high, and "Elatior"—all varieties that are taller. The last group includes diploid varieties, which have smaller flowers but are very easy to grow, and tetraploid varieties with large, often magnificently coloured blooms, but which are far less floriferous and more demanding. *Requirements:* Nourishing, well-drained garden soil that is moderately moist, and a warm, sunny situation. Irises appreciate an occasional application of compound fertilizer. Too much nitrogen and a damp and shaded location make them susceptible to various diseases. *Cultivation:* Put out in spring or late summer, 30 to 40 cm apart. The rhizomes should not be put too deep; the correct depth is just below the surface. After two or three years the clumps should be lifted and divided and good, well-rotted compost added to the soil. *Propagation:* By division, best of all during August. Divide by cutting off sections of rhizomes with leaves. *Varieties:* The following are examples from the wide selection available: "**Nana**": 'Bright White'—15 to 25 cm, pure white; 'Cyanea'—15 to 20 cm, dark blue-violet; 'Path of Gold'—20 to 25 cm, golden yellow. "**Media**": 'Alaskan Gold'—50 to 60 cm, golden yellow to orange; 'Cloud Fluff'—40 cm, pure white, ruffled; 'Marine Wave'—45 to 55 cm, deep blue. "**Elatior**": 'Apricot Supreme'—100 cm, apricot with red beard; 'Cliffs of Dover'—80 to 100 cm, pure white, ruffled; 'Desert Song'—80 to 100 cm, light sandy-yellow; 'Goldfackel'—80 to 90 cm, deep yellow; 'Great Lakes'—90 to 100 cm, light blue; 'My Time'—80 to 90 cm, light rosy-violet and red-violet; 'Ola Kala'—100 to 110 cm, golden yellow; 'Orelio'—70 to 80 cm, dark reddish brown; 'Sable'—80 to 90 cm, dark violet; 'Royal Sovereign'—80 cm, orange-yellow, and many others.

Top left: *Iris barbata* hybrid 'Cliffs of Dover'. Top right: *Iris barbata* hybrid 'Great Lakes'. Bottom left: *Iris barbata* hybrid 'Kingdom'. Bottom right: *Iris barbata* hybrid 'Olympic Star'.

Perennials

Iris bucharica M. FOSTER

Iridaceae   40—60 cm   IV—V   ○ □

Origin: Southern parts of central Asia. *Description:* Fleshy, tuberous root; strong stem with alternate, large, fairly broad, grooved leaves. Flowers with white standards, yellow falls, and beards spotted dark-green. Dies back after flowering. *Requirements:* Nourishing, well-drained, rather dry soil, and a warm, sunny situation. *Cultivation:* Put out in spring or autumn, 30 to 40 cm apart. *Propagation:* Fairly easy from seed sown under glass in spring, also by division in summer—take care not to damage the fleshy roots. *Uses:* In larger rock gardens and in natural, steppe gardens. *Varieties:* Normally only the type species is grown.

Iris carthaliniae FOMIN

Iridaceae   100—150 cm   VI   ○ ☑

Origin: Eastern Caucasus. *Description:* Robust plant with grey-green leaves up to 3 cm wide. Flowers up to 11 cm across, about five to a stem. *Requirements:* No special needs. *Cultivation:* Should be left undisturbed for several years, otherwise it bears few flowers. *Propagation:* By division in spring or autumn, and also by seed, which has good powers of germination, in spring. *Uses:* In beds, particularly with perennials of dense habit, singly as a solitary specimen in expanses of grass, and for cutting as it is long-lived in water. *Varieties:* The type species has blue flowers with a golden-yellow stripe down the centre of each petal, and white markings.

Iris pallida LAM.

Iridaceae   80—100 cm   VI   ○ □

Origin: Southern Europe. *Description:* Fleshy rhizomes, leaves sword-shaped, flowers large, blue-violet, pleasantly scented. Only the variegated form with leaves striped lengthwise with yellow is grown in gardens. *Requirements:* Garden soil, preferably loamy and rather dry, and a sunny situation. *Cultivation:* Put out in spring or late summer, 40 cm apart. *Propagation:* By division in spring or after flowering. *Uses:* In free-style perennial groupings and near pools. *Varieties:* Most widely cultivated is the form 'Variegata' with yellow-striped leaves.

Beardless Iris   *Iris sibirica* L.

Iridaceae   60—100 cm   VI—VII   ○ □ ☑

Origin: Central Europe to Siberia. *Description:* Thick clumps of long, narrow leaves; slender stems, taller than leaves, bearing two or three flowers, with standards fairly narrow, pointed and erect, falls broader, downward-curving, with prominent veins. Blue, violet to white. *Requirements:* Garden soil that is reasonably moist, though it tolerates dry conditions; open situation. *Cultivation:* Put out in spring or autumn, 40 to 50 cm apart. *Propagation:* By division in spring or late summer. *Uses:* In natural sections and beside water. *Varieties:* 'Anniversary'—white; 'Mountain Lake'—blue; 'Blue King'—dark blue; 'Caesar's Brother'—violet; 'Emperor'—rich purple; 'Cambridge'—turquoise blue.

Top left: *Iris bucharica.* Top right: *Iris carthaliniae.* Bottom left: *Iris pallida.* Bottom right: *Iris sibirica.*

Perennials

Red Hot Poker, Torch Lily *Kniphofia* hybrids

Liliaceae   60 – 100 cm   VII – VIII   ○ ◨

Origin: Varieties derived from South African species are generally grown. *Description:* Dense yellow roots, rosette of narrow, green leaves from which rises a thick stem terminating in a spike of bell-shaped flowers coloured yellow, orange or red. *Requirements:* Well-drained, nourishing garden soil. *Cultivation:* Put out in spring, 50 to 60 cm apart. *Propagation:* By division, chiefly in spring. *Uses:* In borders, free-style groupings near water gardens, also for cutting.   *Varieties:* 'Alkazar' – orange-red; 'Buttercup' – canary yellow; 'Express' – light orange-red; 'Earliest of All' – orange and yellow; and others.

Perennial Pea *Lathyrus latifolius* L.

Leguminosae   100 – 200 cm   VII – VIII   ○ □

Origin: Southern Europe. *Description:* Large fleshy roots, long prostrate stems with tendrils which enable the plant to climb up a support; leaves even-pinnate, ashy-green. Clusters of red, pink and white flowers in leaf axils. *Requirements:* Will grow in practically any soil. *Cultivation:* Put out in spring or autumn, 100 to 150 cm apart. *Propagation:* By seed sown in spring. *Uses:* To cover banks and climb up fences, pergolas, arbours. *Varieties:* 'White Pearl' – white; 'Rose Queen' – pink, white eye.

Kansas Feather, Gay Feather *Liatris spicata* WILLD.

Compositae   60 – 100 cm   VII – VIII   ○ ◨

Origin: North America. *Description:* Flat, rounded tubers from which rise several thickly-leaved stems terminating in long spikes of fluffy pink flowers which open from the top downwards. Leaves dark-green, narrow. *Requirements:* Any normal garden soil and a sunny situation. *Cultivation:* Put out in spring or early autumn, 30 to 40 cm apart. *Propagation:* By division in spring, but chiefly by seed sown under glass in spring. *Uses:* In mixed borders, free-style perennial groupings; very good for cutting and may also be dried. *Varieties:* 'Kobold' – low, only about 40 to 50 cm high; 'Alba' – white.

Ligularia dentata HARA.   *(Senecio clivorum* MAXIM.*)*

Compositae   100 – 150 cm   VIII – IX   ◐ ◨

Origin: Japan and China. *Description:* Robust plant with erect, leaved stems branching in the upper part; leaves large, stalked, with rounded blade. Yellow to orange daisy-like flowers with large central disc and narrow ray petals, often curving downwards. *Requirements:* Humus-rich soil and a rather moist situation. *Cultivation:* Put out in spring or autumn, 60 to 80 cm apart. Water in dry weather. *Propagation:* By division in spring or autumn. *Uses:* In larger gardens and parks in free-style groupings in partial shade. *Varieties:* 'Orange Queen' – large, orange-yellow flowers; 'Desdemona' – of weaker habit, orange flowers, dark leaves.

Top left: *Kniphofia* hybrid. Top right: *Lathyrus latifolius.* Bottom left: *Liatris spicata.* Bottom right: *Ligularia dentata.*

Perennials

Sea Lavender *Limonium latifolium* O. KUNTZE

Plumbaginaceae   60 cm   VII—VIII   ○ □

Origin: Bulgaria, southern Russia. *Description:* Rosette of oval tongue-shaped leaves, up to 20 cm long, covered with light down. Sprays of tiny lavender-blue flowers on leafless, thickly branched stems. *Requirements:* Well-drained, rather dry soil containing lime, and a sunny situation. *Cultivation:* Put out in spring or autumn, 60 cm apart. *Propagation:* Only by seed sown under glass in spring. *Uses:* Mainly in dry, natural sections of the garden and for cutting; also for drying as everlastings. *Varieties:* 'Violetta'—dark blue; 'Blue Cloud'—pale blue-violet.

Flax *Linum perenne* L.

Linaceae   40—60 cm   VI—VII   ○ □

Origin: All temperate regions in the northern hemisphere. *Description:* Stiff, erect, slender stems, covered the entire length with small, narrow, pointed, grey-green leaves and terminating in a cluster of single, pale-blue flowers which open in succession over a fairly long period. *Requirements:* Fairly light soil that may even be rather poor, a sunny situation. It generally does not live longer than 3 to 4 years. *Cultivation:* Put out in spring or early autumn, 40 cm apart. *Propagation:* By seed sown under glass in spring. *Uses:* In mixed borders and free-style groupings. *Varieties:* 'Six Hills'—larger, rich blue flowers.

Lupin *Lupinus polyphyllus* hybrids

Leguminosae   100—120 cm   VI—VII   ○ ◪

Origin: Garden lupins are hybrids derived from several North American species. They are noted for their lovely colours and handsome spikes and are called Russell Lupins after the English breeder. *Description:* Robust plants with stalked, palmate leaves; stout, hollow, leaved stems terminate in long sturdy spikes crowded with flowers that come in a wide range of colours, some even bicoloured. *Requirements:* Lupins are fond of good, deep soil that does not have too much lime and is sufficiently moist, and a sunny situation. In light, sandy soil they are not as long-lived. *Cultivation:* Put plants out in spring or autumn, 60 to 80 cm apart. If flowerheads are removed as they fade there will be a second crop of blooms. *Propagation:* Original English varieties are increased by vegetative means, by cuttings from plants over-wintered in the greenhouse. Cuttings are taken with a piece of old rootstock; as they do not root readily a growth-stimulating agent should be applied. Varieties developed in recent years are reliable to the extent that the separate colours can be multiplied from seed. Sow seed in spring and grow the plants on in pots. *Uses:* Very decorative plants for the border as well as for free-style groupings and for cutting. *Varieties:* From seed: 'Fräulein'—white; 'Kastellan'—blue-white; 'Kronenleuchter'—yellow; 'Mein Schloss'—brick red. Multiplied by cuttings: 'Golden Queen'—yellow; 'Karneol'—red and yellow; 'Rita'—red; 'Sweetheart'—orange and pink; and others.

Top left: *Limonium latifolium.* Top right: *Linum perenne.* Bottom left: *Lupinus polyphyllus* hybrid 'Golden Queen'. Bottom right: *Lupinus polyphyllus* hybrid "Russel".

Perennials

Catchfly *Lychnis chalcedonica* L.

Caryophyllaceae 8 – 100 cm VI – VII	○ □ ■

Origin: Ukraine to Siberia. *Description:* Stout, unbranched stems covered with broadly lanceolate, hairy leaves, and terminating in thick heads of vivid vermilion flowers. *Requirements:* Fairly easy to grow: thrives in any garden soil, tolerates dry conditions, likes sun. *Cultivation:* Put out in spring or autumn, 50 to 60 cm apart. Cut back after flowering, as it will sometimes bear another crop of flowers. *Propagation:* By division in spring or autumn, also easily multiplied by seed sown under glass in spring. *Uses:* In mixed borders and for cutting. *Varieties:* Normally only the type species is grown.

Catchfly *Lychnis viscaria* L. *(Viscaria vulgaris* BERNH.*)*

Caryophyllaceae 30 – 40 cm V – VI	○ ■

Origin: Europe, Caucasus to Siberia. *Description:* Most commonly cultivated is the double variety, with a rosette of narrow, deep green leaves and stems terminating in clusters of double, vivid carmine-pink flowers. The stems have sticky bands. *Requirements:* Good, moist but not soggy garden soil, sun. *Cultivation:* Plant in spring or late summer, 30 to 40 cm apart; the plants should be divided after 3 years. *Propagation:* By division, preferably after flowering. *Uses:* In larger rock gardens, mixed borders and free-style perennial groupings. *Varieties:* Most widely cultivated is var. 'Splendens Plena'; 'Alba' – white.

Bergamot *Monarda* hybrids

Labiatae 70 – 120 cm VII – VIII	○ □

Origin: Only varieties derived from crosses between various North American species, chiefly *M. didyma* and *M. fistulosa,* are grown in gardens nowadays. *Description:* Erect plants with branching, square stems; leaves opposite, ovate-lanceolate, toothed, roughly hairy. Curiously shaped, labiate flowers with long, protruding stigmas arranged in thick whorls at the tips of the stems. *Requirements:* Does best in nourishing, well-drained soil and a warm, sunny situation. *Cultivation:* Put out in spring or autumn, 60 cm apart. *Uses:* Excellent in mixed borders and free-style, natural sections of the garden, where it makes an attractive display with its glowing colours. Also very good for cutting, as it is fairly long-lived. *Propagation:* Chiefly by division in spring or autumn, but also by cuttings in spring. *Varieties:* 'Cambridge Scarlet' – scarlet to vermilion, of weaker habit, 80 to 100 cm; 'Croftway Pink' – rosy-pink, taller, 120 to 130 cm; 'Mrs Perry' – vivid red, lower, 70 to 90 cm, early-flowering; 'Prairie Glow' – deep red, 110 to 120 cm; 'Prärienbrand' – dark red, 100 to 120 cm; 'Prairie Night' – violet, 110 to 120 cm; 'Snow Maiden' – white, 100 to 120 cm, late-flowering.

Top left: *Lychnis chalcedonica.* Top right: *Lychnis viscaria.* Bottom left: *Monarda* hybrid 'Croftway Pink'. Bottom right: *Monarda* hybrid 'Prairie Glow'.

Perennials

Peony   *Paeonia lactiflora* hybrids

Paeoniaceae   60—80 cm   VI   ○ ◨

Origin: The type species comes from northern China and Manchuria. The original varieties were developed in China and Japan; when they were introduced into Europe in the early 19th century it was mainly France and England that came up with new forms. In recent years they have been the subject of interest of American breeders, and they are making a comeback everywhere. *Description:* Roots fleshy, spindle-shaped; leaves stalked, 2- to 3-partite, with red veining. Flowers large, single, semi-double or double, white, pink or red, and also creamy-yellow. Varieties are divided into several groups according to the shape of the flowers. **Single**—with eight petals and many stamens; **Japanese**—either single or double but with unfertile stamens transformed into broad, yellow, twisted bands; **Anemone-flowered**—with a single row of normal petals and centre of short, broad petals; **Double**—with globular flowers. *Requirements:* A deep, loamy soil with sufficient humus, nutrients and moisture; likes sun but tolerates light partial shade. *Cultivation:* Put out in spring or late summer, 50 to 60 cm apart. Tubers should be put no deeper than 5 cm below the surface (to the depth of the eyes on the tubers) —if planted at a greater depth they flower poorly. Adding well-rotted compost to the soil is recommended before planting. In ensuing years feed regularly, best of all with compound fertilizer in liquid form, mainly in spring. *Propagation:* By division of the tuberous roots, best of all at the beginning of September. When dividing roots make sure that each has at least two eyes: tubers without eyes are worthless. *Uses:* In mixed borders and free-style perennial groupings. Invaluable also for cutting: cut stems with buds that already show colour, which will open in the vase and last a long time. *Varieties:* **Single:** 'Clairette'—pure white; 'Frans Hals'—purplish-red; 'Rembrandt'—vivid red; 'Thoma'—lilac-pink. **Japanese:** 'Ginkgo-nishiki'—white striped with purple; 'Meigetsu-ko'—pale lilac-red; 'Tsingtau'—pink. **Anemone-flowered:** 'Laura Dessert'—outside petals flesh-red, inside petals creamy; 'Mme de Pompadour'—deep carmine; 'Philomele'—outside petals pinkish-red, inside petals yellow. **Double:** 'Avalanche'—white with orange tinge; 'Augustin d'Hour'—bright violet-red; 'Bunker Hill'—crimson; 'Königin Wilhelmine'—light pink; 'Marie Lemoine'—creamy white; 'Solange'—delicate beige-pink, and many others.

Top left: *Paeonia lactiflora* hybrid 'Nancy'. Top right: *Paeonia lactiflora* hybrid 'Königin Wilhelmine'. Bottom left: *Paeonia lactiflora* hybrid 'Bunker Hill'. Bottom right: *Paeonia lactiflora* hybrid 'Celebration'.

Perennials

Iceland Poppy   *Papaver nudicaule* L.

Papaveraceae   30—40 cm   V—VII   ○ □

Origin: Mountains of interior Asia. *Description:* Biennial. Ground rosette of longish leaves from which rise many slender, hairy stems each bearing a single large flower; colours include white, pink, orange, yellow and red. The bright flowers are borne in great profusion over a long period. *Requirements:* Well-drained, rather dry soil, and sun. *Cultivation:* Put out in late summer, 30 to 40 cm apart. *Propagation:* Only by seed, sown in pots at the end of May and then thinned. Young plants are grown on in pots. *Uses:* In borders and low mixed groups, also in larger rock gardens. *Varieties:* Many strains available from seed.

Poppy   *Papaver orientale* L.

Papaveraceae   60—100 cm   V—VI   ○ ◪

Origin: Asia Minor, Caucasus. *Description:* Robust plant, leaves pinnatisect, coarsely toothed, dark green, hairy. Stems stout, bristly, each carrying a single, large flower, usually red or pink, sometimes also white. Dies back after flowering and begins growth anew in spring. *Requirements:* Deep, nourishing, sufficiently moist soil and a sunny situation. *Cultivation:* Planted out mainly in spring, 50 to 60 cm apart. *Propagation:* Varieties by root cuttings; young plants are grown in pots. *Uses:* In mixed borders and free-style groupings. *Varieties:* 'Juliane'—white with pink edge; 'Marcus Perry'—orange-scarlet; 'Salmon Glow'—deep salmon; 'Rosenpokal'—carmine-pink; 'Goliath'—rich red.

Phlox paniculata L.

Polemoniaceae   60—100 cm   VII—VIII   ○ ◪

Origin: Eastern North America. *Description:* Erect plants with stiff, unbranched stems covered their entire length with opposite, longish lanceolate leaves. Some varieties have reddish foliage. Flowers scented pleasantly, arranged in dense terminal clusters, they come in various shades of white, pink, red to violet. Some have an eye of a different colour. *Requirements:* Loose, well-drained, humus-rich soil that is nourishing and moist; sun to partial shade. Water in dry weather. Eelworm is a common and damaging pest. *Cultivation:* Put out in spring or early autumn, 40 to 50 cm apart. *Propagation:* By division in spring or autumn, also by soft terminal or root cuttings in spring. *Uses:* Excellent for mixed borders and free-style groupings, where it is most effective in larger masses; also for short-term decoration and for cutting. *Varieties:* 'Aida'—80 cm, carmine-red; 'Dorffreude'—120 cm, pinkish-lilac; 'Fanal'—100 cm, vivid red; 'Jules Sandeau'—60 cm, pink with pale eye; 'Frauenlob'—120 cm, pale pink; 'Frührosa'—100 cm, pink with red eye; 'Kirmesländer'—100 cm, white with red eye; 'Orange'—80 cm, vermilion-red; 'Pastorale'—90 cm, rosy-pink; 'Pax'—90 cm, all white; 'Rosendom'—90 cm, pale pink; 'Spitfire'—70 cm, bright vermilion with red eye; 'Wilhelm Kesselring'—70 cm, reddish-violet with white eye; 'Würtembergia'—60 cm, pink; 'Norah Leigh'—ivory-variegated leaves; there are many more.

Top left: *Papaver nudicaule.* Top right: *Papaver orientale* 'Salmon Glow'. Bottom left: *Phlox paniculata* 'Frührosa'. Bottom right: *Phlox paniculata* 'Pastorale'.

Perennials

Chinese Lantern, Cape Gooseberry *Physalis alkekengii* L.
(Physalis franchetii MAST.*)*

Solanaceae   60—80 cm   IX—X fruits   ○◑◨

Origin: Japan. *Description:* Erect, unbranched stems covered with ovate to rounded triangular leaves. Insignificant, whitish flowers borne in the leaf axils in July. More ornamental are the fruits — red berries enclosed in a showy, five-sided, inflated seed bag coloured vermilion and shaped like a lantern. Spreads rapidly by underground rhizomes. *Requirements:* Ordinary soil with some lime and sufficient moisture, sun. *Cultivation:* Put out in spring or autumn, 40 to 50 cm apart. *Propagation:* By division in spring. *Uses:* In free-style groupings, but mostly grown for the fruits and stems, which are dried. *Varieties:* Normally only the type species is grown.

Obedient Plant *Physostegia virginiana* BENTH.

Labiatae   80—100 cm   VII—VIII   ○◨

Origin: North America. *Description:* Erect plant with branching, four-sided stems covered with stiff, narrow-lanceolate, toothed leaves. Dense, four-sided spikes of labiate flowers coloured white, pink to red. *Requirements:* Good garden soil that is sufficiently moist, and a warm situation. *Cultivation:* Put out in spring, 50 to 60 cm apart. *Propagation:* By division in spring. *Uses:* In mixed borders and free-style groupings. Good for cutting, as flowers are borne over a long period. *Varieties:* 'Bouquet Rose' — deep pink; 'Vivid' — violet-red; 'Summer Snow' — pure white.

Poke Weed, Red Ink Plant *Phytolacca americana* L.

Phytolaccaceae   100—150 cm   VII—VIII   ○◑□◨

Origin: North America. *Description:* Robust plant with turnip-like root and erect, branching stems covered with longish-ovate leaves with prominent veins. Small white flowers, borne in upright clusters, are followed in late summer by dark red berries. The seeds are poisonous. *Requirements:* Any garden soil, sun or partial shade. *Cultivation:* Put out in spring, 80 cm apart. *Propagation:* By seed, best sown as soon as it is ripe. *Uses:* In informal natural settings or as a solitary specimen. *Varieties:* Normally only the type species is grown.

Balloon Flower *Platycodon grandiflorum* A.DC.

Campanulaceae   40—70 cm   VII—VIII   ○◨

Origin: Eastern Asia. *Description:* Fleshy, white roots, stems sturdy, moderately branched, covered with dark green, lanceolate, finely toothed leaves. Large, wide-belled flowers in blue, white or pale pink; buds inflated hollow globes. *Requirements:* Good garden soil that is moist but not soggy. *Cultivation:* Put out in spring or autumn, 40 cm apart. *Propagation:* By seed sown under glass in spring. *Uses:* In mixed borders, free-style groupings and for cutting. *Varieties:* 'Album' — white; 'Mariesii' — blue, shorter, profusely flowering; 'Perlmutterschale' — pale pink.

Top left: *Physalis alkekengi* var. *franchetii*. Top right: *Physostegia virginiana*. Bottom left: *Phytolacca americana*. Bottom right: *Platycodon grandiflorum*.

Perennials

Knotweed, Fleece Flower *Polygonum campanulatum* HOOK. F.

Polygonaceae   60—80 cm   VIII—X

Origin: Himalayas. *Description:* Plant of prostrate habit with ascending stem tips; leaves lanceolate to ovate. Spikes of pink, bell-shaped flowers. Valued for its late and lengthy flowering. *Requirements:* Ordinary garden soil that is reasonably moist, light partial shade. *Cultivation:* Put out in spring or autumn, 50 to 60 cm apart. *Propagation:* Chiefly by division in spring. *Uses:* Best of all in natural settings near pools and streams. *Varieties:* Normally only the type species is grown.

Bronzeleaf *Rodgersia aesculifolia* BATAL.

Saxifragaceae   70—100 cm   VII—VIII

Origin: Central China. *Description:* Robust plant with large horse chestnut-like leaves; airy, thickly branched pyramidal sprays of small white flowers. *Requirements:* Nourishing, moist (but not soggy) humus-rich soil, partial shade. *Cultivation:* Put out in spring, 80 to 100 cm apart. *Propagation:* Chiefly by division in spring. *Uses:* Excellent as a solitary specimen in partly shaded places in larger gardens and parks. Very effective near water. *Varieties:* Normally only the type species is grown.

Coneflower *Rudbeckia fulgida* var. *sullivantii* CRONQ.

Compositae   50—70 cm   VIII—IX

Origin: North America. *Description:* Firm, compact, erect plant with branching stems covered with broadly lanceolate, roughly haired leaves. Flowers deep yellow with dark brown to black centre, borne in great profusion. *Requirements:* Any good garden soil that is reasonably moist, a sunny situation. *Cultivation:* Put out in spring or autumn, 50 to 60 cm apart. *Propagation:* By division in spring or autumn, also by seed sown under glass in spring. *Uses:* One of the most valuable perennials for summer decoration, mixed borders, free-style groupings, singly and for cutting. *Varieties:* 'Goldsturm'—vivid yellow, black centres; and others.

Coneflower *Rudbeckia* hybrid

Compositae   80—100 cm   VII—X

Origin: North America, probably derived from *R. hirta*. *Description:* Erect plant with branching, hairy stems covered with pale-green, lanceolate, hairy leaves. Flowers large, single to semi-double, yellow, yellow-red to brownish-red with brown centre, borne in great profusion over a long period. *Requirements:* Ordinary garden soil, preferably on the dry side, sun. In moist soil it is short-lived. *Cultivation:* Put out in spring or early autumn, 70 to 80 cm apart. *Propagation:* Chiefly by seed sown under glass in spring—it flowers the same year. *Uses:* In mixed borders and free-style groupings; also very good for cutting. *Varieties:* Usually annual strains raised from seed—'Gloriosa Daisy'.

Top left: *Polygonum campanulatum.* Top right: *Rodgersia aesculifolia.* Bottom left: *Rudbeckia fulgida* var. *sullivantii.* Bottom right: *Rudbeckia* hybrid 'Gloriosa Daisy'.

Perennials

Coneflower *Rudbeckia laciniata* L.

Compositae   180—200 cm   VII—IX   ○ ▣

Origin: Eastern North America. *Description:* Tall, erect plant with branching stems covered with three-lobed, deeply cut leaves. Flowers double, golden-yellow, borne in great profusion; easily bent by the wind. *Requirements:* Any garden soil, a sunny situation. *Cultivation:* Put out in spring or autumn, 60 cm apart. *Propagation:* By division in spring or autumn. *Uses:* Taller groups in large gardens and parks. *Varieties:* 'Goldball'—only about 150 cm high; 'Goldquelle'—sturdy, only 80 cm high.

Coneflower *Rudbeckia nitida* NUTT.

Compositae   180—210 cm   VIII—IX   ○ ● ▣

Origin: Southern North America. *Description:* Tall plant with sturdy, branching stems; grows without a support. Leaves ovate-lanceolate, smooth, glossy; large flowers with pale green central cone and a single row of yellow downward-curving petals. *Requirements:* Ordinary garden soil that is reasonably moist, sun or light partial shade. *Cultivation:* Put out in spring or autumn, 70 to 80 cm apart. *Propagation:* By division in spring or autumn. *Uses:* At the back of the border and in free-style groupings; long-lived in the vase. *Varieties:* 'Herbstone' —tall, 210 cm.

Sage *Salvia nemorosa* L.

Labiatae   40—80 cm   VI—VII   ○ □

Origin: South-eastern Europe to north-western Asia. *Description:* Shorter perennial with erect stems, leaves deep green, lanceolate, hairy. Dense spikes of purplish-violet flowers. *Requirements:* Rather dry, well-drained soil, sun. *Cultivation:* Put out in spring or autumn, 30 to 40 cm apart. *Propagation:* By division or by cuttings in spring. *Uses:* In mixed borders and free-style natural groupings. *Varieties:* 'Lubeca'—deep violet with carmine calyx; 'Mainacht'—vivid blue; 'Superba'—violet-blue, calyx and bracts red.

Scabious *Scabiosa caucasica* BIEB.

Dipsacaceae   60—100 cm   VI—IX   ○ ▣

Origin: Caucasus. *Description:* Erect plant with branching stems, pinnatisect leaves; flowers delicate, outer florets large and wavy, light blue, violet or white. *Requirements:* Nourishing, well-drained soil with lime, a warm, sunny situation. *Cultivation:* Put out in spring or early autumn, 40 to 50 cm apart. *Propagation:* By division or by cuttings in spring, also by seed sown under glass in spring. *Uses:* In mixed borders and for cutting—the flowers are long-lasting. *Varieties:* 'Clive Greaves'—pale lavender; 'Miss Willmott'—white; 'Stäfa'—dark violet.

Top left: *Rudbeckia laciniata* 'Goldball'. Top right: *Rudbeckia nitida*. Bottom left: *Salvia nemorosa* 'Superba'. Bottom right: *Scabiosa caucasica*.

Perennials

Stoke's Aster *Stokesia laevis* GREENE

Compositae   30 — 40 cm   VIII — IX   ○ ▧

Origin: North-eastern United States. *Description:* Airy rosette of stalked, lanceolate, entire, glabrous leaves. Flowers up to 10 cm across, on upright branching stems, resemble China asters; lilac-blue with paler centre. *Requirements:* Well-drained, slightly moist, sandy-loamy soil; does not tolerate soggy conditions. *Cultivation:* Plant in spring, 30 cm apart. A protective cover for the winter is recommended. *Propagation:* By division in spring or by seed. *Uses:* In larger rock gardens, borders, and for cutting. *Varieties:* 'Blue Moon' — deep blue; 'Blue Star' — light blue.

Meadow Rue *Thalictrum aquilegifolium* L.

Ranunculaceae   80 — 130 cm   V — VI   ◑ ▧

Origin: From Europe through Siberia to Japan. *Description:* Erect plant with sturdy, branching stems covered with divided leaves resembling Maidenhair Fern. Delicate flowers with prominent stamens, densely packed in panicles coloured creamy-white, pink to pale violet. *Requirements:* Garden soil that is sufficiently moist, partial shade. *Cultivation:* Put out in spring or autumn, 50 to 60 cm apart. *Propagation:* By division in spring, also by seed sown under glass in spring. *Uses:* In partly shaded borders and free-style groupings. *Varieties:* 'Album' — white.

Spiderwort *Tradescantia andersoniana* hybrids

Commelinaceae   40 — 60 cm   VI — IX   ○ ◑ ▧

Origin: Varieties derived from American species, chiefly *T. virginiana*. *Description:* Erect plants, leaves narrow and grooved, with sheaths encircling the stems; flowers three-petalled in terminal clusters, white, pink and blue. *Requirements:* Garden soil that is sufficiently moist, sun to partial shade. *Cultivation:* Put out in spring or autumn, 40 to 60 cm apart. *Propagation:* Chiefly by division in spring. *Uses:* In mixed borders, free-style groupings, near pools and streams. *Varieties:* 'Blue Stone' — vivid blue; 'L'Innocence' — white; 'Karminglut' — carmine red; 'Zwannenburg' — dark blue-violet; 'Osprey' — white; 'Purple Dome' — purple.

Wake Robin, Trinity Flower *Trillium grandiflorum* SALISB.

Liliaceae   30 to 40 cm   IV — V   ◑ ▧

Origin: Eastern and central parts of North America. *Description:* Short tuberous root. Leaves broadly ovate, wavy, in a whorl at tip of stem. Rising from the centre of the leaves are short-stalked, three-petalled flowers with broadly elliptic, curved petals coloured white, passing to pink when fading. Plants die back in summer. *Requirements:* Moist, humus-rich soil, partial shade. Protective cover for the winter. *Cultivation:* Put out in spring, 30 to 40 cm apart. *Propagation:* By division of tubers, but chiefly by seed sown freely in dishes in autumn; it takes 3 to 4 years for the plants to develop fully. *Uses:* In rock gardens and natural sections of the garden in partial shade. *Varieties:* 'Roseum' — rose pink; 'Flore-Pleno' — double white.

Top left: *Stokesia laevis.* Top right: *Thalictrum aquilegifolium.* Bottom left: *Tradescantia andersoniana* hybrid. Bottom right: *Trillium grandiflorum.*

Perennials

Globe Flower   *Trollius* hybrids

Ranunculaceae   60—80 cm   V—VI   ○◑◪

Origin: Varieties derived from European and Asiatic species. *Description:* Sturdy, erect plants with palmate leaves; stems sparsely branched, terminating in single to double globe flowers coloured yellow to orange. *Requirements:* Moderately moist garden soil, sun to light partial shade. *Cultivation:* Put out in spring or autumn, 40 to 50 cm apart. *Propagation:* Varieties by division in spring or autumn, species by seed sown in autumn. *Uses:* In mixed borders, free-style groupings, particularly near pools and streams. *Varieties:* 'Aetna' — orange; 'Earliest of All' — golden yellow, early-flowering; 'Goldquelle' — dark yellow, late-flowering; 'Prichard's Giant' — orange; 'Byrne's Giant' — late, yellow.

Speedwell   *Veronica incana* L.

Scrophulariaceae   40—50 cm   VI—VII   ○◑◪

Origin: South-eastern Europe to northern Asia. *Description:* Ground rosette of broadly lance-olate leaves, erect, moderately branching stems terminating in dense spikes of deep blue flowers. The entire plant is white-felted. *Requirements:* Well-drained, moist garden soil, sun to light partial shade. *Cultivation:* Put out in spring or autumn, 30 to 40 cm apart. *Propagation:* By division in spring or autumn. *Uses:* In borders and informal natural sections of the garden. *Varieties:* 'Rosea' — pink; 'Wendy' — more vigorous, blue.

Horned Violet   *Viola cornuta* L.

Violaceae   10—20 cm   V—IX   ○◪

Origin: Pyrenees. *Description:* Cushions of branching stems covered with longish ovate leaves. The flowers, resembling small pansies, come in various colours, chiefly shades of blue and violet, and are borne over a long period. *Requirements:* Good, moist garden soil, an open situation but not full sun. *Cultivation:* Plant in spring or late summer, 30 to 40 cm apart. *Propagation:* By division in spring or cuttings in summer, some varieties also by seed. *Uses:* In larger rock gardens and free-style perennial groupings. *Varieties:* 'Admirace' — deep violet; 'Altona' — creamy-yellow; 'Hansa' — blue; 'White Superior' — white, and others.

Adams Needle   *Yucca filamentosa* L.

Liliaceae   100—120 cm   VI—VIII   ○□

Origin: Southern North America. *Description:* Large rosette of slender, stiff, grey-green leaves from which rises a stout branching stem with a profusion of nodding, creamy-white, bell-shaped flowers. Thick underground rhizomes. *Requirements:* Good, well-drained garden soil, a warm, sunny situation; tolerates parched conditions. *Cultivation:* Put out in spring, 80 to 100 cm apart. *Propagation:* By division of clumps and rhizomes in spring. *Uses:* Splendid as a solitary specimen, and also in free-style groupings in steppe and xerophilous sections of the garden. *Varieties:* Some clones exist with white or pale pink flowers.

Top left: *Trollius* hybrid. Top right: *Veronica incana.* Bottom left: *Viola cornuta.* Bottom right: *Yucca filamentosa.*

Grasses

Tall Oat Grass *Arrhenatherum elatius* ssp. *bulbosum* HYL.

Gramineae 30 — 40 cm   ○ □

Origin: Europe, Africa, western Asia. *Description:* Most widely grown is the variegated form, with grey-green leaves striped longitudinally with white; stems about 50 cm high topped by small spikes. Flat, roundish underground roots. Leaves die back in summer. *Requirements:* Does best in rather dry, well-drained soil and sunny situation. *Cultivation:* Put out in spring, 30 cm apart. *Propagation:* By division in spring before the plants start putting out leaves. *Uses:* In steppe and heather gardens, in free-style groupings, and also for edging. *Varieties:* 'Variegatum'—white striped.

Wild Oat *Avena sempervirens* VILL. *(Helictotrichon sempervirens* PILG.*)*

Gramineae 40 — 60 cm   spikes 100 cm   ○ □

Origin: Temperate regions of the northern hemisphere. *Description:* Beautiful spreading clumps of narrow, grey-blue leaves. Spikes on long stems are produced in late May. *Requirements:* Sandy, rather poor, dry soil, a sunny situation. *Cultivation:* Put out in spring, 50 to 60 cm apart. Cut back hard to the ground in early spring and the plants will rapidly make new growth. The clumps should be divided after 3 or 4 years. *Propagation:* By division in spring. *Uses:* Lovely as a solitary specimen in rock gardens, natural informal settings, heath and steppe gardens. *Varieties:* Normally only the type species is grown.

Pampas Grass *Cortaderia selloana* ASCHERS. et GRAEBN.

Gramineae 80 — 100 cm   spikes up to 220 cm   from IX   ○ ◧ □

Origin: Argentina, Brazil. *Description:* Large clumps of narrow, grey-green leaves. From late summer onward it produces large, silky, silvery spikes on long stems. One of the loveliest of all grasses. *Requirements:* A warm, sheltered situation, deep, well-drained, nourishing soil. Ample moisture in spring, dry conditions in winter. *Cultivation:* Put out in spring, 100 to 150 cm apart. In colder regions give a good protective cover for the winter. Cut back in spring. *Propagation:* By division in spring; young plants are grown in earthenware pots. *Uses:* Splendid as a solitary specimen and in grass and steppe sections of the garden. *Varieties:* 'Pumila'—very compact; 'Sunningdale Silver'—very graceful.

Tufted Hair Grass *Deschampsia cespitosa* P. BEAUV.

Gramineae 40 cm   spikes 80 cm   from VII   ○ ◕ □ ◧

Origin: Europe, Asia, America. *Description:* Lovely spreading clumps of narrow, dark green leaves. Profusion of dainty, loose, yellowish spikes that remain on the plant until late autumn. *Requirements:* Easy to grow, doing well in practically any situation; flowers most abundantly in sun. *Cultivation:* Put out in spring or late summer, 50 to 60 cm apart; it will grow for a long time in the same place. Cut back to the ground in early spring. *Propagation:* By division in spring or autumn. *Uses:* Singly in larger rock gardens, but chiefly in steppe and heath gardens. *Varieties:* 'Bronze Veil'—brightly coloured.

Top left: *Arrhenatherum elatius* ssp. *bulbosum.* Top right: *Avena sempervirens.* Bottom left: *Cortaderia selloana.* Bottom right: *Deschampsia cespitosa.*

Grasses

Fescue *Festuca glauca* LAM.

Gramineae   15—20 cm   ○ □

Origin: Alps. *Description:* Low-growing, compact, tufted grass with stiff, very narrow, silvery-blue leaves. Small spikes borne in late May. Loveliest of the low-growing grasses. *Requirements:* Rather dry, poor, sandy soil and a sunny situation. *Cultivation:* Put out in spring or late summer, 20 to 30 cm apart. Divide and separate clumps after 2 or 3 years. *Propagation:* By division in spring or autumn. *Uses:* In rock gardens, natural settings, heath gardens and various flat flower schemes. *Varieties:* Normally only the type species is grown.

Miscanthus sinensis ANDERSS.

Gramineae   160—180 cm   ○ □ ◪

Origin: Southern and eastern Asia. *Description:* Robust grass with decorative leaves and habit of growth. Leaves are broad or narrow, green or differently coloured, depending on the variety. *Requirements:* Deep, well-drained, moist, nourishing soil, a sunny situation; preferably dry conditions in winter. *Cultivation:* Put out in spring, 80 to 150 cm apart; scatter fallen leaves over the plants to protect them for the winter. Cut back in spring. Starts growth late. *Propagation:* By division in spring. *Uses:* Splendid as a solitary specimen and in informal, natural settings. *Varieties:* 'Gracillimus' — lovely spreading tufts with narrow green leaves; 'Zebrinus' — austere habit, wider leaves, striped horizontally with yellow.

Reed Canary Grass   *Phalaris arundinacea* L.

Gramineae   60—80 cm   VI—VIII   ○ ◕ ◪

Origin: Europe. *Description:* Only variegated varieties, with leaves striped longitudinally with white, are cultivated. The dense spikes are also ornamental when in flower. Spreads by rhizomes, often to an unwelcome degree. *Requirements:* Very demanding plant, doing best in a moist situation. *Cultivation:* Put out in spring or autumn, 40 to 50 cm apart. *Propagation:* Very easy by division in spring or autumn. *Uses:* In borders, natural sections of the garden, and also beside water. *Varieties:* 'Picta' — leaves pink at first, later striped with white; 'Tricolor' — leaves striped with red, violet and white.

Spartina pectinata LINK.

Gramineae   150—170 cm   ○ ◕ ◪

Origin: North America. *Description:* Huge tufts of narrow leaves arching to the ground; dense spikes in summer. Spreads by its stout, pale rhizomes but is not invasive. *Requirements:* Good garden soil which is reasonably moist, particularly in spring during growth. A sunny or partially shaded situation. *Cultivation:* Put out in spring, 60 to 80 cm apart. Cut back top parts in spring. *Propagation:* By division in spring. *Uses:* Splendid as a solitary specimen in natural, informal sections of the garden. *Varieties:* The type species has all-green leaves; the variety 'Aureomarginata' has yellow-edged leaves.

Top left: *Festuca glauca.* Top right: *Miscanthus sinensis* 'Gracillimus'. Bottom left: *Phalaris arundinacea.* Bottom right: *Spartina pectinata.*

Kingcup, Marsh Marigold   *Caltha palustris* L.

Ranunculaceae   20—30 cm   IV—V   ○◐◪

Origin: Entire temperate zone. *Description:* Leaves kidney-shaped, deep glossy green; flowers vivid yellow. Spreads by rhizomes. The double form is most widely grown in gardens. *Requirements:* Moisture-loving plant requiring even submersion in water for a time; does well in any soil, best of all in partial shade, but tolerates sun. *Cultivation:* Put out in spring or late summer, 30 cm apart. *Propagation:* By division in spring or early autumn. *Uses:* Beside pools and streams, and also in rock gardens. *Varieties:* 'Multiplex' — double; 'Alba' — white, single.

Water Hyacinth   *Eichhornia crassipes* SOLMS *(E. speciosa* KUNTH*)*

Pontederiaceae   20—30 cm   VI—VII   ○◪

Origin: Central and South America. *Description:* Floating aquatic plant. Roots long, fibrous, bluish; rosette of heart-shaped leaves supported by swollen, spongy stalks. Lilac-coloured flowers in spikes on short stems. *Requirements:* Thermophilous plant, which in colder regions must be overwintered in frost-free premises. *Cultivation:* Put out in pools from late May onwards. *Propagation:* By seed sown as soon as it is ripe, in pots standing in water; overwinter in the greenhouse. *Uses:* To brighten the vegetation in garden pools. *Varieties:* 'Aurea' — yellow flowers.

Hippuris vulgaris L.

Hippuridaceae   30—50 cm   VI—VII   ○■

Origin: Europe, western Asia, North America, Australia. *Description:* Erect stems rising above the water's surface, covered with delicate linear leaves resembling horse-tail grass or a coniferous plant. Tiny, insignificant flowers. *Requirements:* Any soil; a sunny situation is best as it tends to flop in shade. Best depth of submersion is 10 to 20 cm. *Cultivation:* Put out in spring before growth starts. In smaller pools it should be put in submerged containers as otherwise it spreads too much. *Propagation:* Very easy by division. *Uses:* In pools. *Varieties:* Normally only the type species is grown.

Iris pseudacorus L.

Iridaceae   80—100 cm   V—VI   ○◪■

Origin: Europe. *Description:* Long, relatively wide, deep green leaves; yellow flowers with narrow standards and wide falls opening gradually on branched stems. *Requirements:* Grows equally well in shallow water and in moist soil. *Cultivation:* Put out in spring or autumn; may be left in one place for many years. *Propagation:* By division of clumps. Plants raised from seed usually flower in the second year. *Uses:* In shallow pools, near ponds and brooks. Not only the flowers are used for cutting but also the fruits, which should be cut before having ripened. *Varieties:* The species has golden-yellow flowers, var. *pallidiflora* is cream-yellow.

Top left: *Caltha palustris* 'Plena'. Top right: *Eichhornia crassipes.* Bottom left: *Hippuris vulgaris.* Bottom right: *Iris pseudacorus* var. *pallidiflora.*

Aquatic and Bog Plants

Water Lily *Nymphaea* hybrids

Nymphaeaceae   VI−IX   ○ ■

Origin: Cultivated varieties are derived mostly from European and American species. *Description:* Large, fleshy rootstock; leaves long-stalked, with large rounded blades floating on the water. Flowers semi-double to double with prominent stamens in a wide range of colours — white, cream, yellow, pink, red, orange and coppery bronze. *Requirements:* Lime-free, fairly heavy, nourishing soil, a warm, sunny situation and still water. Optimum depth depends on the species and variety; generally between 40 and 60 cm, for miniature varieties 20 to 30 cm. *Cultivation:* Plant in spring, between late April and June. There are various methods of growing: in containers, which are lifted in the autumn and the plants overwintered in a cellar, or directly in soil on the bottom of the pool, where they may remain submerged for the winter if there is no danger of the construction cracking, or with the water drained off and a layer of leaves spread over the bottom. In shallow pools the required depth may be obtained by making pockets in which the water lilies are planted. If kept in containers the plants should be removed every 2 to 3 years and given new, nourishing soil; they are also divided at this time. *Propagation:* By division in spring. *Uses:* In man-made or natural pools. *Varieties:* Very wide range, e. g. 'Marliacea Albida' — white; 'Graziella' — orange-red; 'Indiana' — coppery-orange; 'James Brydon' — cherry red; 'Helvola' — yellow; and many more.

Pickerel Weed *Pontederia cordata* L.

Pontederiaceae   50−60 cm   VI−VIII   ○ ■

Origin: North America. *Description:* Leaves long-stalked, heart-shaped ovate, glossy green; flowers blue, arranged in erect spikes. *Requirements:* A sunny situation, depth of submersion 10 cm. *Cultivation:* Plant in spring (April−May). Cover with a layer of leaves for the winter after water has been drained from the pool. *Propagation:* By division in spring, or by seed sown in April into pots standing in water. *Uses:* In boggy sections and shallow pools. *Varieties:* 'Angustifolia' — has narrower leaves and bright blue flowers.

Arrow-head *Sagittaria sagittifolia* L.

Alismataceae   40−70 cm   VI−VII   ○ ■

Origin: Europe. *Description:* Aquatic plant with arrow-shaped leaves; flowers white with a purple patch at the base, arranged in whorls on a leafless stem. *Requirements:* Non-alkaline, fairly heavy soil, depth of submersion 10 to 20 cm, and a sunny situation. *Cultivation:* Plant in spring in bogs and pools; in deeper pools put in containers and stand these on bricks or stones at the required depth. *Propagation:* Chiefly by division in spring. *Uses:* In the water or bog garden. *Varieties:* Besides the type species, also var. *leucopetala* — pure white, and var. *plena* — double, white.

Top left: *Nymphaea* hybrid 'Marliacea Albida'. Top right: *Nymphaea* hybrid 'Indiana'. Bottom left: *Pontederia cordata*. Bottom right: *Sagittaria sagittifolia*.

132

Ferns

Hard Fern *Blechnum spicant* ROTH

Polypodiaceae   12—25 cm

Origin: Europe, Asia Minor, Caucasus to Japan. *Description:* Evergreen plant. The fronds are of two kinds: sterile fronds are deep green, narrow, up to 20 cm long, deeply cut, arranged in a rosette; fertile fronds are longer, with brown stalk and numerous brown spores on the underside. *Requirements:* A sour, coniferous humus containing peat is best, with plenty of moisture, semi-shade to shade. *Cultivation:* Plant in spring, 26 cm apart. *Propagation:* By division in spring. *Uses:* In shaded parts of the rock garden, shady and damp areas of the garden. *Varieties:* Normally only the type species is grown.

Male Fern *Dryopteris filix-mas* SCHOTT

Polypodiaceae   80—150 cm

Origin: Forests on plains or mountains throughout the world. *Description:* Robust fern with large, pinnate fronds arranged to form a funnel. Short rhizomes covered with rusty down. *Requirements:* Fairly easy to grow, in soil that is not unduly dry and sandy; prefers partial shade, but tolerates sun if provided with sufficient moisture. *Cultivation:* Plant in spring, best of all when growth starts, 50 to 60 cm apart. *Propagation:* By division in spring. *Uses:* In partially shaded sections of the garden. *Varieties:* 'Barnesii'—fronds bipinnate; 'Cristata'—fronds narrow, bipinnate, with forked tips; 'Linearis'—fronds very narrow, with narrow sections.

Ostrich Fern *Matteucia struthiopteris* TODARO

Polypodiaceae   80—100 cm

Origin: Europe to northern Asia. *Description:* Sterile pinnate fronds form a large funnel, from the centre of which rise the fertile fronds, about 40 cm long, olive-green at first, later changing to brown. Scaly rhizome forms many off-shoots by which the plant rapidly spreads. *Requirements:* Lime-free, humus-rich, moist soil; prefers partial shade but tolerates a more open situation. *Cultivation:* Plant in spring when growth begins, 50 to 60 cm apart. *Propagation:* By division, root cuttings. *Uses:* In natural, partly shaded sections of gardens and parks. *Varieties:* Normally only the type species is grown.

Hart's Tongue Fern *Phyllitis scolopendrium* NEWM. *(Asplenium scolopendrium)*

Polypodiaceae   20—40 cm

Origin: Europe. *Description:* Creeping rhizome thickly covered with reddish-brown scales. Leaves are short-stalked, broadly lanceolate, entire, with auricles at the base, pale green in youth, later a darker green; linear spores on the underside. *Requirements:* Damp, humus-rich soil, shade. *Cultivation:* Plant in spring, 25 to 30 cm apart. *Propagation:* By leaf cuttings or division in spring; also by spores sown in peat in a cold greenhouse in shade as soon as they are ripe. *Uses:* To make low masses in damp, shaded parts of the garden. *Varieties:* 'Capitatum'—frilled leaves; 'Crispum'—wavy leaves.

Top left: *Blechnum spicant.* Top right: *Dryopteris filix-mas.* Bottom left: *Matteucia struthiopteris.* Bottom right: *Phyllitis scolopendrium.*

Pheasant's Eye   *Adonis vernalis* L.

Ranunculaceae   15—25 cm   IV—V   ○ □

Origin: Warmer regions of Europe. *Description:* Leaves delicate, filamentous, on unbranched stems; flowers large, single, vivid yellow. Dies back in late spring. *Requirements:* Well-drained, rather dry soil containing lime, and a warm, sunny situation. *Cultivation:* Plant in early spring or after it has died back, 25 to 30 cm apart. *Propagation:* By division, but chiefly by seed harvested before it is ripe and sown immediately. Young plants are very slow to develop at first. *Uses:* In rock gardens and natural settings, chiefly in steppe gardens. *Varieties:* Normally only the type species is grown.

Bugle   *Ajuga reptans* L.

Labiatae   10—20 cm   V—VI   ○ ◑ ◪

Origin: Europe. *Description:* Leaves dark, obovate; flowers small, blue, in whorls on short, leaved stems. Most decorative is the foliage, which differs in colouration according to the variety. Makes low, dense masses and spreads rapidly. *Requirements:* Reasonably moist garden soil, sun or partial shade. *Cultivation:* Plant any time, 20 to 25 cm apart. *Propagation:* Readily by division. *Uses:* In damper, partly shaded parts of rock gardens, near water, and as a substitute for turf. *Varieties:* 'Atropurpurea'—leaves brownish-red; 'Multicolor'—leaves brownish-red splashed with yellow; 'Variegata'—leaves green splashed with white.

Alopecurus lanatus SIBTH. et SM.

Gramineae   10—15 cm   VII   ○ □

Origin: High mountains of Asia Minor. *Description:* Low-growing grass with silvery-grey, felted, lanceolate leaves; flowers are small insignificant spikes. *Requirements:* Will grow in almost pure sand with a small amount of peat added. Needs good drainage, dry and sunny situation. *Cultivation:* Plant in spring 10 to 15 cm apart. Cover with glass to protect against winter damp. *Propagation:* By division in spring. *Uses:* Chiefly for those who collect unusual plants—in rock gardens and rock crevices. *Varieties:* Normally only the type species is grown.

Alyssum saxatile L.

Cruciferae   20—30 cm   IV—V   ○ □

Origin: Europe to Asia Minor. *Description:* Cushion of longish, grey-green leaves; small golden-yellow flowers in dense panicles. Flowers profusely. *Requirements:* Quite undemanding, but does best in well-drained, lime-rich soil and a sunny situation. *Cultivation:* Put out in spring or autumn, 40 cm apart. *Propagation:* By seed in spring; young seedlings are grown in pots. *Uses:* For drier spots and natural settings, in rock gardens and dry walls. *Varieties:* 'Citrinum'—pale green; 'Compactum'—lower, more compact.

Top left: *Adonis vernalis.* Top right: *Ajuga reptans.* Bottom left: *Alopecurus lanatus.* Bottom right: *Alyssum saxatile.*

Mount Atlas Daisy *Anacyclus depressus* BALL

Compositae   10 — 15 cm   V — VI   ○ □

Origin: High mountains of Morocco. *Description:* Prostrate plant with deeply cut, hairy leaves. Flowers small, white, daisy-like, in short-stalked clusters. Buds pink. *Requirements:* A sunny situation, well-drained soil with some lime. *Cultivation:* Plant in spring, 20 cm apart. *Propagation:* By seed sown as soon as ripe in light, gravelly soil in the greenhouse; young plants are grown in pots. Also by cuttings in spring. *Uses:* In smaller rock gardens and in pockets. *Varieties:* Normally only the type species is grown.

Rock Jasmine *Androsace alpina* LAM.

Primulaceae   3 — 5 cm   VI — VII   ○ ◪

Origin: Higher altitudes of the Central Alps. *Description:* High mountain plant forming loose cushions to carpets of small grey-green rosettes; leaves elongate, pointed, covered with light down. Flowers pink or white, borne singly, pressed close on the leaf rosettes. Flowers profusely, mainly at higher altitudes. *Requirements:* Well-drained, stony soil that is sufficiently moist, a light, open situation. *Cultivation:* Plant in spring, 15 cm apart; at lower altitudes provide a winter cover. *Propagation:* By detaching rooted rosettes. *Uses:* In dainty parts of rock gardens between stones, and in stone rubble where there is plenty of moisture. *Varieties:* Normally only the type species is grown.

Rock Jasmine *Androsace hirtella* DUF.

Primulaceae   5 — 10 cm   VII — VIII   ○ ◕ □

Origin: Pyrenees. *Description:* Tiny shrubs or small cushions of dense, bluntly elongate, dark-green to brownish leaves covered with light down. Flowers white, about 4 mm across. *Requirements:* Well-drained, best of all sandy, humus-rich soil without lime; an open situation, preferably with an eastern aspect. *Cultivation:* Plant in spring, 10 cm apart. Provide a light cover in winter. *Propagation:* By seed sown as soon as it is ripe in dishes under glass; young plants are grown in pots. *Uses:* Chiefly in crevices in daintier parts of rock gardens. *Varieties:* Normally only the type species is grown.

Dwarf Marguerite, Chamomile *Anthemis nobilis* L.

Compositae   15 — 25 cm   VII — VIII   ○ □

Origin: Europe. *Description:* Only the double form is grown in gardens. It makes a loose clump with finely cut leaves; the double flowers are white, without a central disc, up to 15 mm across. It spreads rapidly and makes a good ground cover, and is also prized for its late flowering. *Requirements:* No special needs — any garden soil that is sufficiently moist, and a sunny situation. *Cultivation:* Plant in spring or late summer, 30 cm apart. *Propagation:* By division, best done in spring. *Uses:* In larger rock gardens as a flat element; also as a substitute for turf. *Varieties:* 'Flore Pleno' — double, white.

Top left: *Anacyclus depressus.* Top right: *Androsace alpina.* Bottom left: *Androsace hirtella.* Bottom right: *Anthemis nobilis* 'Flore Pleno'.

Columbine *Aquilegia discolor* LEVIER et LEVESCHE

Ranunculaceae   12—15 cm   V   ○◑■

Origin: Spain. *Description:* Small shrub, leaves twice divided into rounded sections; short, sparsely branched stems with pale blue and white flowers. *Requirements:* Does best in good, well-drained, reasonably moist soil, in light partial shade. *Cultivation:* Plant in spring or late summer, 20 cm apart. *Propagation:* By seed sown under glass in spring; young plants are grown in pots. *Uses:* In rock gardens, planted singly or in small groups. *Varieties:* Normally only the type species is grown.

Rock Cress *Arabis caucasica* SCHLECHTEND. *(Arabis albida* STEV. ex FISCH.*)*

Cruciferae   15—20 cm   IV—V   ○◑■

Origin: East Mediterranean region to the Caucasus. *Description:* Thick tufts of grey-green, spatulate leaves; slender, practically leafless stems terminating in clusters of white flowers. *Requirements:* Any garden soil, in sun or partial shade. *Cultivation:* Plant in spring or autumn, 25 to 30 cm apart. *Propagation:* By division or cuttings. *Uses:* In larger rock gardens, as flat masses in natural sections of the garden, for edging, in dry walls. *Varieties:* 'Plena' — double; 'Schneehaube' — single, white, profusely flowering; 'Variegata' — leaves splashed with white.

Rock Cress *Arabis procurrens* WALDST. et KIT.

Cruciferae   10—30 cm   IV—V   ○◑■

Origin: Carpathians, the Balkans. *Description:* Short, very dense masses of glossy, deep green leaves; slender stems about 20 cm high carry small panicles of tiny white flowers. Profusion of flowers, vigorous growth, good ground cover, evergreen. *Requirements:* Well-drained, reasonably moist garden soil, in sun or partial shade. *Cultivation:* Plant in spring or late summer, 20 to 30 cm apart. *Propagation:* Readily by division in spring or late summer. *Uses:* In larger rock gardens, dry walls and as a substitute for turf, even on larger areas. *Varieties:* Normally only the type species is grown.

Thrift *Armeria caespitosa* BOISS.

Plumbaginaceae   5—10 cm   V   ○□

Origin: Pyrenees. *Description:* Compact cushions of short, narrow, dark green, grass-like leaves. Almost stemless, round heads of pink flowers close above the leaves. *Requirements:* Likes sun in moderation, and sandy, humus-rich, well-drained soil; does not tolerate soggy soil, particularly in winter. *Cultivation:* Plant in spring, 15 to 20 cm apart. *Propagation:* By cuttings in July or August under glass; young plants are grown in pots. *Uses:* In daintier parts of rock gardens, best of all in rock crevices; also in dry walls. *Varieties:* 'Suendermannii' — hardier with larger flowers; 'Variabilis' — paler pink; 'Bevans Var' — deep pink.

Top left: *Aquilegia discolor.* Top right: *Arabis caucasica* 'Variegata'. Bottom left: *Arabis procurrens.* Bottom right: *Armeria caespitosa.*

Wormwood *Artemisia nitida* BERTOL.

Compositae 10—20 cm VII—VIII ○ □

Origin: South-eastern Alps, Dolomites. *Description:* Low, thick masses with finely cut, silvery-grey foliage—the plant's most decorative feature. Flowers insignificant. *Requirements:* Well-drained, stony, rather dry soil with lime, sun. Does not tolerate soggy soil. *Cultivation:* Plant in spring, 20 cm apart. *Propagation:* By division or cuttings under glass in spring; young plants are grown in pots. *Uses:* In rock gardens of all kinds, in crevices as well as flat spaces; also in dry walls, heath and steppe gardens. *Varieties:* Normally only the type species is grown.

Aster alpinus L.

Compositae 15—20 cm V—VI ○ □

Origin: Interior of Asia, Europe, North America. *Description:* Compact shrubs or cushions of elongate, entire leaves. Violet-blue flowers with yellow centres are borne singly on almost leafless stems; varieties also come in white and pink. *Requirements:* Well-drained, rather dry soil with some lime, sun. *Cultivation:* Plant in spring or late summer, 30 cm apart. *Propagation:* By division, cuttings or seed sown under glass in spring. *Uses:* In rock gardens and dry walls. *Varieties:* 'Albus'—white; 'Rex'—shorter with large blue flowers; 'Roseus Superbus'—pink.

False Goat's Beard *Astilbe chinensis* var. *pumila* ANON.

Saxifragaceae 15—25 cm VIII—IX ○ ◑ □ ◪

Origin: Spain. *Description:* Low masses with twice- to thrice-divided leaves. Flowers small, lilac pink, in thin, dense, upright spikes. *Requirements:* Non-alkaline, humus-rich soil, light partial shade or sun; tolerates rather dry soil. *Cultivation:* Plant in spring or late summer, 25 to 30 cm apart. *Propagation:* By division, preferably in spring. *Uses:* In rock gardens in larger or smaller masses; good as ground cover.

Purple Rock Cress *Aubrieta* hybrids

Cruciferae 5—10 cm IV—V ○ □ ◪

Origin: Type species native to the region between the Balkans and Asia Minor. *Description:* Thick, evergreen cushions composed of rosettes of small spatulate leaves covered with light down. During the flowering period smothered with blossoms coloured blue, violet, pink or red, depending on the variety. *Requirements:* Good, well-drained soil containing lime, a sunny situation. *Cultivation:* Plant in spring or late summer, 20 to 30 cm apart. *Uses:* In rock gardens to form continuous masses, also in dry walls. *Varieties:* 'Barker's Double'—purple, double; 'H. Marshall'—pale bluish-violet; 'The Queen'—deep red.

Top left: *Artemisia nitida.* Top right: *Aster alpinus* 'Roseus Superbus'. Bottom left: *Astilbe chinensis* var. *pumila.* Bottom right: *Aubrieta* hybrid.

Pig Squeak   *Bergenia cordifolia* hybrids

Saxifragaceae   40−50 cm   IV−V   ○ ◑ □ ◪

Origin: Korea. *Description:* Robust evergreen plant with large, rounded, entire, glossy, deep green leaves. Sprays of pink, white or red flowers on stout stems above the leaves. Spreads by thick rhizomes. *Requirements:* Well-drained, moderately moist soil; tolerates dry conditions. Sun to semi-shade. *Cultivation:* Plant in spring or autumn, 40 cm apart. *Propagation:* By division or by cuttings under glass in spring. *Uses:* Singly in larger rock gardens, near water, and in free-style groupings. *Varieties:* 'Abendglut'−dark red; 'Morgenröte'−vivid pink; 'Silberlicht'−white, later changing to pink.

Bellflower   *Campanula carpatica* JACQ.

Campanulaceae   15−25 cm   VI−VII   ○ ◑ ○

Origin: Limestone screes in the Carpathians. *Description:* Tufts to cushions of heart-shaped, ovate leaves, flowers fairly large, cup-shaped bells coloured blue or white. *Requirements:* Well-drained soil, preferably on the dry side, containing lime; sun or light partial shade. *Cultivation:* Plant in spring or autumn, 30 to 40 cm apart. *Propagation:* The type species by seed sown under glass in spring, varieties by division in spring. *Uses:* In rock crevices, flat spaces in rock gardens, and in dry walls. *Varieties:* 'Alba'−white; 'Isabel'−pale violet; 'Karpatenkrone'−wide-open, blue bells; 'White Star'−large white bells.

Bellflower   *Campanula poscharskyana* DEGEN

Campanulaceae   20 cm   VI−VIII   ○ ◑ □ ◪

Origin: Dalmatia. *Description:* Prostrate stems covered with heart-shaped, coarsely toothed leaves. Bells wide open, star-shaped, lilac-blue. Lovely trailing plant which flowers for a long time. *Requirements:* Undemanding; will grow in practically any soil, in sun or partial shade. *Cultivation:* Plant in spring or autumn, 30 to 40 cm apart. *Propagation:* By division in spring. *Uses:* In rock gardens of all kinds. Trails attractively over stones in rock gardens and dry walls. *Varieties:* 'Stella'−flowers darker, more deeply cut.

Snow-in-Summer   *Cerastium tomentosum* var. *columnae* ARCANG.

Caryophyllaceae   15 cm   V−VI   ○ □

Origin: Apennines, Sicily. *Description:* Dense cushions of narrow, lanceolate, white-felted leaves; white flowers borne in profusion on slender stems. *Requirements:* Does best in well-drained, rather dry soil with lime, and a sunny situation. *Cultivation:* Plant in spring or autumn, 20 to 25 cm apart. *Propagation:* By division or cuttings, mostly in spring; young plants are grown in pots. *Uses:* In flat spaces in rock gardens of all kinds and in dry walls. Grows attractively over stones. *Varieties:* Normally only this variety is grown.

Top left: *Bergenia cordifolia.* Top right: *Campanula carpatica.* Bottom left: *Campanula poscharkyana.* Bottom right: *Cerastium tomentosum* var. *columnae.*

Rock Garden Plants

Chrysanthemum arcticum L.

Compositae   15—25 cm   VIII—IX   ○ ◑ ◪

Origin: Alps. *Description:* Low masses of grey-green notched leaves; daisy-like flowers, white or pink, on short stems. *Requirements:* Well-drained, humus-rich soil, reasonably moist, containing lime; a sunny or partly shaded situation. Valuable species for its late flowering. *Cultivation:* Plant in spring or autumn, 20 to 30 cm apart. *Propagation:* By division or by cuttings under glass in spring. *Uses:* For larger as well as smaller spaces in rock gardens. *Varieties:*'Roseum'—a pink-flowering variety.

Lily-of-the-Valley   Convallaria majalis L.

Liliaceae   15—20 cm   V—VI   ○ ◑ ◪

Origin: Europe, North America, and temperate regions of Asia. *Description:* Leaves smooth, elliptic-lanceolate, deep green. Stems with clusters of white, bell-like flowers, pleasantly scented. In congenial conditions it sometimes spreads excessively. *Requirements:* Good, well-drained garden soil which is moderately moist, semi-shade to full sun. *Cultivation:* Plant in spring or late summer, 30 cm apart. *Propagation:* By division and by detaching rhizomes. *Uses:* In partly shaded sections of larger rock gardens, also for underplanting trees and shrubs; very good for cutting. *Varieties:*'Rosea'—pale pink flowers.

Slipper Orchid   Cypripedium calceolus L.

Orchidaceae   40—50 cm   V—VI   ◑ ◪

Origin: Broad-leaved woodlands of foothills in Europe. *Description:* Stems covered with oval-lanceolate, prominently veined leaves. Flowers, borne one to three on a stem, with brownish-red petals, pouch yellow with red markings at the base. Starts growth late in spring. *Requirements:* Well-drained, humus-rich soil, with lime and sufficient moisture; partly shaded situation. *Cultivation:* Plant in spring, 30 to 40 cm apart. *Propagation:* Mostly by detaching the separate pseudo-bulbs in spring when it begins growth. May be multiplied from seed, but this is a lengthy process. *Uses:* In moist, partly shaded sections of larger rock gardens. *Varieties:* Normally only the type species is grown.

Pink   Dianthus alpinus L.

Caryophyllaceae   10—15 cm   V—VI   ○ □

Origin: Eastern Alps. *Description:* Low, dense tufts of elongate leaves, flowers large, flat, carmine-pink with darker ring round the centre, borne singly on short stalks. *Requirements:* Does well in a mixture of sandy leaf-mould, rotted turves and limestone rubble with good drainage in a sunny, east-facing position. *Cultivation:* Plant in spring, 20 cm apart. *Propagation:* By seed sown under glass in spring; young plants are grown in pots. *Uses:* Chiefly in rock crevices in rock gardens. *Varieties:*'Albus'—a white-flowering variety.

Top left: *Chrysanthemum arcticum* 'Roseum'. Top right: *Convallaria majalis.* Bottom left: *Cypripedium calceolus.* Bottom right: *Dianthus alpinus.*

Rock Garden Plants

Maiden Pink   *Dianthus deltoides* L.

Caryophyllaceae   15—25 cm   VI—VII   ○ □

Origin: Europe, Asia. *Description:* Dense clumps of slender, prostrate stems covered with small, narrow leaflets. Small, single flowers, coloured white, pink or red, on slender stems. *Requirements:* Well-drained, preferably drier soil with lime, sun. *Cultivation:* Plant in spring or late summer, 25 to 30 cm apart. *Propagation:* By cuttings after flowering, and by seed sown under glass in spring. *Uses:* In rock gardens, dry walls, and to make flat spreading sheets, primarily in natural parts of the garden. *Varieties:* 'Albus' — white with carmine eye; 'Brillant' — carmine-pink; 'Splendens' — dark carmine flowers, brownish-green leaves.

Pink   *Dianthus gratianopolitanus* VILL.

Caryophyllaceae   15—25 cm   V—VI   ○ □

Origin: Europe. *Description:* Dense cushions of narrow, stiff, grey-green leaves. Flowers fairly large, single or semi-double, white, pink or red, one colour or with an eye. *Requirements:* Best of all is a loamy soil with lime, sun and preferably dry conditions. *Cultivation:* Plant in spring or late summer, 30 to 40 cm apart. *Propagation:* By cuttings in late summer or by seed sown under glass in spring. *Uses:* In rock gardens, dry walls and sunny natural sections of the garden. *Varieties:* 'Fanal' — vivid carmine with dark eye; 'Rotglut' — deep red, semi-double; 'Nordstjernen' — pink, and others.

Shooting Star, American Cowslip   *Dodecatheon meadia* L.

Primulaceae   30—40 cm   V—VI   ◑ ◪

Origin: North America. *Description:* Ground rosette of oval leaves from which rises a leafless stem terminating in a cluster of cyclamen-shaped flowers. Dies back after flowering. *Requirements:* Loamy, humus-rich, reasonably moist soil, light partial shade. *Cultivation:* Plant in spring or after the plants have died back, 25 to 30 cm apart. *Propagation:* By seed sown under glass in spring, or by division when plants begin growth. *Uses:* In groups in rock gardens. *Varieties:* 'Albiflorum' — white; 'Splendens' — larger, deep pink flowers.

Whitlow Grass   *Draba aizoides* L.

Cruciferae   5—10 cm   IV—V   ○ □

Origin: Alps and Carpathians. *Description:* Deep green tufts composed of firm rosettes of short, linear leaves from which rise short, slender stems with clusters of small, bright yellow flowers. *Requirements:* Rather dry, well-drained soil with stone rubble, sun. *Cultivation:* Plant in spring or by cuttings in August. *Uses:* In rock crevices and small spaces in rock gardens, and also in dry walls. *Varieties:* Normally only the type species is grown.

Top left: *Dianthus deltoides*. Top right: *Dianthus gratianopolitanus*. Bottom left: *Dodecatheon meadia*. Bottom right: *Draba aizoides*.

Rock Garden Plants

Edraianthus pumilio A. DC.

Campanulaceae   4—6 cm   IV—V   ○ □

Origin: Mountains of southern Europe. *Description:* Dense cushions of stiff, needle-like leaves covered with light greyish down. Flowers upward-facing bells coloured blue-violet, with prominent pistils. *Requirements:* Well-drained, stony soil with lime; does not tolerate too much moisture. *Cultivation:* Plant in spring 20 cm apart. *Propagation:* By seed sown under glass in spring; seedlings are planted directly in small pots. Older plants cannot be transplanted. *Uses:* Best of all in rock crevices and in pockets in tuff. Also good for dry walls. *Varieties:* Normally only the type species is grown.

Spurge   *Euphorbia myrsinites* L.

Euphorbiaceae   10—20 cm   V—VI   ○ □

Origin: Mediterranean region. *Description:* Stout, prostrate stems thickly covered with greyish blue-green, overlapping leaves. Stems topped by small yellow flowers; the leaves just below the flowers also turn yellow during the flowering period. *Requirements:* Well-drained soil with stone rubble, dry conditions, sun. *Cultivation:* Plant in spring or early autumn, 30 to 40 cm apart. *Propagation:* By division, by cuttings, but most readily by seed sown as soon as it is ripe directly into pots; young plants are grown in pots. *Uses:* In sunny spots in rock gardens, and in xerophilous natural sections of the garden. Seeds itself freely. *Varieties:* Normally only the type species is grown.

Gentian   *Gentiana clusii* PERR. et SONG.

Gentianaceae   5—10 cm   V   ○ ◪

Origin: Alps to Carpathians. The garden hybrids, which resemble the species but have better characteristics, are usually grown. *Description:* Leaves dark green, elliptic to lanceolate. Flowers large, bell-like, upright, stemless or on short stems; they are deep blue, sometimes with a paler throat. *Requirements:* Loamy, stony soil with sufficient lime and moisture, sun. *Cultivation:* Plant in spring or late summer, 20 to 30 cm apart. It appreciates an application of feed from time to time. *Propagation:* By division after flowering, or by seed sown in dishes in autumn. *Uses:* In flat spaces in rock gardens, in dry walls. *Varieties:* Normally only the type species is grown.

Gentian   *Gentiana septemfida* PALL.

Gentianaceae   20—25 cm   VII—VIII   ○ ◐ ◪

Origin: Asia Minor to Iran, Turkestan, Altai. *Description:* Prostrate stems thickly covered with deep-green, ovate leaves, terminating in clusters of 6 to 8 bell-like flowers with deeply cut petals, deep blue, the throat pale with darker spots. *Requirements:* Any well-drained, reasonably moist garden soil, sun to light partial shade. *Cultivation:* Plant in spring or late summer, 30 to 40 cm apart. *Propagation:* By division in autumn, or by seed sown under glass in spring. *Uses:* In any kind of rock garden, in dry walls. *Varieties:* Var. *lagodechiana* KUSN. —more compact, flowers with green-spotted throat.

Top left: *Edraianthus pumilio.* Top right: *Euphorbia myrsinites.* Bottom left: *Gentiana clusii.* Bottom right: *Gentiana septemfida.*

150

Globe Daisy *Globularia cordifolia* L.

Globulariaceae   10 — 15 cm   V — VI   ○ □

Origin: Southern Alps to the Carpathians. *Description:* Rosette of oval-elongate leaves, leafless stems terminating in pale violet, globose heads of flowers. *Requirements:* A well-drained soil with lime and a sunny situation; very easy to grow. *Cultivation:* Plant in spring or late summer, 20 to 30 cm apart. *Propagation:* By division in August, or by seed sown under glass in spring. *Uses:* In rock gardens in rock crevices, flat spaces and stone rubble. *Varieties: G. trichosantha* spreads more rapidly by runners and bears a profusion of vivid blue flowers.

Strawflower *Helichrysum milfordiae* KILLICK

Compositae   5 — 7 cm   VI — VII   ○ □

Origin: South Africa. *Description:* Cushions composed of small rosettes of silvery-grey, elliptic leaves. Flowers are pink in bud, white when fully open, on short stems. *Requirements:* Well-drained, sandy soil with lime; does not tolerate soggy soil. A sunny, east-facing position in the rock garden. *Cultivation:* Plant in spring, 15 to 20 cm apart. *Propagation:* By division or cuttings in late summer. *Uses:* In daintier parts of rock gardens, best of all in crevices or in pockets in tuff. *Varieties:* Normally only the type species is grown.

Hepatica nobilis MILL.

Ranunculaceae   10 — 15 cm   III   ◐ ◪

Origin: Europe. *Description:* Low plant with smooth, evergreen, three-lobed leaves. Flowers single or double, blue, pink, red or white. *Requirements:* Well-drained, humus-rich, reasonably moist soil, partial shade. *Cultivation:* Plant in spring or early autumn, 25 to 30 cm apart; it takes some time after planting to grow to a reasonable size. *Propagation:* Chiefly by division after flowering. *Uses:* In partly shaded, moister parts of rock gardens; also as underplanting for trees or shrubs and in free-style groupings with plants of similar requirements. *Varieties:* 'Plena' — blue, double; 'Rosea Plena' — pink, double; 'Rubra Plena' — red, double; 'Rosea' — pink, single.

Hutchinsia alpina R.BR.

Cruciferae   5 — 10 cm   V — VI   ◐ ◪

Origin: Pyrenees, central Europe, Carpathians. *Description:* Dainty plant forming thick tufts of dark-green, pinnatifid leaves. Dense clusters of small, white flowers on short, leafless stems. *Requirements:* Humus-rich soil with stone rubble and sufficient moisture; light partial shade. *Cultivation:* Plant in spring, 15 to 20 cm apart. *Propagation:* By division in late summer or by seed sown in dishes as soon as it is ripe. *Uses:* In rock crevices and in smaller spaces in rock gardens. *Varieties: H. auerswaldii* WILLK. of Spain, which makes denser tufts and bears larger flowers, is frequently cultivated.

Top left: *Globularia cordifolia.* Top right: *Helichrysum milfordiae.* Bottom left: *Hepatica nobilis.* Bottom right: *Hutchinsia alpina.*

Rock Garden Plants

St John's Wort *Hypericum olympicum* L.

Guttiferae   20—30 cm   VI—VII   ○ □

Origin: South-eastern Europe, Syria, Asia Minor. *Description:* Low shrub with erect stems covered with small, lanceolate, blue-green, spotted leaves. Flowers quite large, yellow, with prominent stamens. *Requirements:* Well-drained, preferably rather dry soil, a sunny situation. *Cultivation:* Plant in spring or early autumn, 30 cm apart. *Propagation:* By division or cuttings in late summer, or by seed sown under glass in early spring. *Uses:* In dry and sunny spots in rock gardens, dry walls and natural sections of the garden. *Varieties:* 'Citrina' — pale yellow.

Candytuft *Iberis saxatilis* L.

Cruciferae   5—10 cm   IV—V   ○ ◪

Origin: Pyrenees to southern Europe. *Description:* Dwarf, prostrate, evergreen plant with narrow, lanceolate, dark green leaves. Flowers in dense, flat panicles, white changing to pale pink as they fade, borne in profusion. *Requirements:* Well-drained, humus-rich soil, a sunny situation. *Cultivation:* Plant in spring, 20 cm apart; growth is quite slow and young plants should be pinched at first to make them thicker. *Propagation:* By cuttings after flowering, although they do not root readily. *Uses:* In daintier parts of rock gardens, chiefly in crevices, and also in dry walls. *Varieties:* Normally only the type species is grown.

Iris *Iris pumila* L.

Iridaceae   15—20 cm   IV—V   ○ □

Origin: Type species from central Europe to Central Asia. More widely grown are varieties obtained by crosses between the type species and taller species belonging to the *Iris chamaeiris* group. *Description:* Resembles other irises, but is short with comparatively large flowers. *Requirements:* Ordinary, well-drained, rather dry soil, a sunny situation. *Cultivation:* Plant either in April or after flowering, 30 cm apart. The plants should be lifted and divided after two years. *Propagation:* By division, best of all in July or late summer. *Uses:* In rock gardens and in low-growing groups in natural parts of the garden. *Varieties:* 'Bright White' — white; 'Cyanea' — dark blue-violet; 'Citraea' — pale yellow; 'Orchid Flare' — bright violet; and others.

Bitter-root *Lewisia cotyledon* ROBINS.

Portulacaceae   25—30 cm   V—VI   ○ □

Origin: California. *Description:* Fairly large, evergreen rosettes of radiating, narrow, stiff leaves; branching stems, with an abundance of flowers coloured white to pink with darker stripes. *Requirements:* Well-drained, sandy, humus-rich soil without lime. Open, but not parched, situation. Intolerant of soggy soil, particularly in winter. *Cultivation:* Plant in spring, 20 to 25 cm apart. In spring it needs moisture and an occasional feed, in winter a protective cover. *Propagation:* By seed sown under glass in early spring; young plants are grown in pots. *Uses:* Chiefly in an east-facing position in rock gardens, in slanting or vertical rock crevices, and in dry walls. *Varieties:* Normally only the type species is grown.

Top left: *Hypericum olympicum*. Top right: *Iberis saxatilis*. Bottom left: *Iris pumila* 'Citraea'. Bottom right: *Lewisia cotyledon*.

Bitter-root *Lewisia rediviva* PURSH

| Portulacaceae | 10 cm | VII | ○ □ |

Origin: Western North America. *Description:* Root fleshy, carrot-like; leaves elongate, in loose rosettes, begin to die back at end of flowering. Flowers large, pink, borne singly close above the leaves. A fairly tender species for the more experienced gardener. *Requirements:* Intolerant of damp, particularly in winter; lime-free, sandy soil with humus. Sun or light semi-shade. *Cultivation:* Plant in spring, 15 cm apart, provide good drainage and protection against winter damp. *Propagation:* By seed sown shortly after it has ripened; young plants are grown in pots. *Uses:* In daintier parts of rock gardens in an east-facing position. *Varieties:* Normally only the type species is grown.

Bitter-root *Lewisia tweedyi* ROBINS.

| Portulacaceae | 20 – 25 cm | V – VI | ○ □ |

Origin: North America. *Description:* Leaves obovate, dark green, die back after flowering. Flowers large, 3 or 4 to a stem, peach-pink with silky sheen. *Requirements:* Well-drained, sandy, humus-rich, lime-free soil; an open, east-facing position. Protect against winter damp. *Cultivation:* Plant in spring in crevices between stones so that water does not collect round the neck. *Propagation:* By seed sown as soon as it is ripe; young plants are grown in pots. *Uses:* In daintier parts of rock gardens. *Varieties:* Different colour forms of the flowers are available.

Loosestrife *Lysimachia nummularia* L.

| Primulaceae | 5 – 10 cm | V – VII | ○ ◑ ◨ |

Origin: Europe. *Description:* Prostrate stems covered with opposite, oval leaves. Flowers flat, pure yellow, in the leaf axils. In congenial conditions it spreads rapidly by means of rooting runners. *Requirements:* Very easy to grow; does best in damp soil both in sun and in partial shade. *Cultivation:* Plant any time, 30 cm apart. *Propagation:* Readily by division and by detaching rooted shoots. *Uses:* Excellent for making a dense carpet near water; trails attractively over stones. *Varieties:* 'Aurea' – yellow-leaved.

Musk *Mimulus cupreus* D'OMBRAIN

| Scrophulariaceae | 10 – 15 cm | VI – IX | ○ ◑ ◨ |

Origin: Chile. *Description:* Low, thick clumps of prostrate, rooting stems covered with hairy, sticky, ovate-lanceolate leaves. Flowers are coppery orange, passing to yellow. *Requirements:* Damp, well-drained, humus-rich soil, an open to partly shaded situation. *Cultivation:* Put out in spring, 25 cm apart. In regions with harsher climates provide a protective cover for winter. *Propagation:* By cuttings in August; young plants should be covered for the winter. *Uses:* Beautiful plant, invaluable for damp places in rock gardens and by the sides of pools or streams. *Varieties:* 'Roter Kaiser' – scarlet; 'Whitecroft Scarlet' – brilliant red.

Top left: *Lewisia rediviva.* Top right: *Lewisia tweedyi.* Bottom left: *Lysimachia nummularia.* Bottom right: *Mimulus cupreus.*

Evening Primrose *Oenothera missouriensis* SIMS

Onagraceae   20—25 cm   VI—IX   ○ □

Origin: Southern North America. *Description:* Massive roots and prostrate, branching stems covered with narrow, willow-like leaves. Starts growth late. Flowers large, sulphur-yellow, bell-like; long-flowering. *Requirements:* Any soil, tolerates dry conditions, likes sun. *Cultivation:* Plant in spring or autumn, 60 cm apart. *Propagation:* Readily by seed sown under glass in spring. Young plants are grown in pots. *Uses:* In larger rock gardens, in informal perennial sections, excellent as a cover plant for places planted with bulbs. *Varieties:* Normally only the type species is grown.

Prickly Pear *Opuntia rhodantha* K. SCHUM.

Cactaceae   20 cm   VI—VII   ○ □

Origin: Colorado, Nebraska, Utah. *Description:* Stem segments (pads) longish-oval, about 10 cm long. Brownish spines in clumps of 2 to 3 with darker tips, barbed hairs (glochids). Flowers about 8 cm across, carmine-red. *Requirements:* A warm, sunny situation and sandy to moderately heavy soil. Dry conditions, particularly in winter, when a protective cover is also needed. *Cultivation:* Plant only in spring, 25 to 30 cm apart. *Propagation:* Place detached pads flat on well-drained soil in boxes in a warm place; they will soon put out roots. *Uses:* In rock gardens as one of the xerophilous plants. *Varieties:* Normally only the type species is grown in cool glasshouse conditions.

Marjoram *Origanum vulgare* L.

Labiatae   30—40 cm   VIII—IX   ○ □

Origin: Dry, calcareous meadows from Europe to western Asia. *Description:* Small, dense shrubs to continuous masses. Stems covered with opposite, oval, grey-green, pubescent leaves. The entire plant is aromatic. Flowers are small, purplish-pink, in dense panicles at the tops of the stems. *Requirements:* Very undemanding; does best in rather dry, well-drained soil with lime, in a warm, sunny situation. *Cultivation:* Plant in spring or autumn, 30 to 40 cm apart. *Propagation:* Readily by division or by cuttings in late spring. *Uses:* Most widely grown in gardens are the varieties of lower, compact habit or with coloured foliage. Rewarding plants for their late and lengthy flowering as well as decorative foliage. Used in larger rock gardens, dry walls and informal, natural parts of the garden. *Varieties:* 'Compactum'—only about 15 to 20 cm high, makes good thick masses; 'Aureum'—about the same height but with golden-yellow leaves, insignificant flowers (this variety should not be sprayed in sun as the leaves turn brown).

Top left: *Oenothera missouriensis.* Top right: *Opuntia rhodantha.* Bottom left: *Origanum vulgare.* Bottom right: *Origanum vulgare* 'Aureum'.

Rock Flame   *Phlox subulata* L.

Polemoniaceae   10—15 cm   IV—V   ○ □ ◪

Origin: Eastern North America. *Description:* Dense evergreen clumps or cushions; prostrate, branching stems covered with narrow, stiff, bristle-like leaves. Flowers borne in profusion, white, pink, red or lilac-blue. The shape and colour of the flower varies depending on the variety. *Requirements:* Good, well-drained, slightly moist garden soil, a sunny situation. *Cultivation:* Plant in spring or late summer, 30 cm apart. A light cover of evergreen twigs is recommended as protection against severe frost. *Propagation:* By division or by cuttings after flowering. *Uses:* Good for covering smaller or larger spaces in rock gardens; also in dry walls, as edging, as a substitute for turf, and in informal perennial areas. *Varieties:* 'Atropurpurea' — purple with dark eye; 'Blue Eyes' — dark lilac-blue; 'Daisy Hill' — salmon-pink with red eye; 'G. F. Wilson' — flowers star-like, pale lilac; 'Leuchtstern' — compact, pink with dark eye; 'Maischnee' — flowers rounded, white; 'Morgenstern' — flowers large, pink with striking eye; 'Temiscaming' — vivid purplish red; 'Vivid' — deep salmon-pink; and others.

Phyteuma comosum L.

Campanulaceae   5—10 cm   VI—VII   ○ ◪

Origin: Limestone Alps. *Description:* Low plants with grey-green, coarsely toothed leaves interspersed with short-stalked, dense heads of light blue, bottle-shaped flowers with long, protruding stigmas. *Requirements:* Well-drained, humus-rich soil containing lime and fine gravel; open, east-facing position. *Cultivation:* Plant in spring, 15 cm apart in crevices between stones. Protect against snails. *Propagation:* By seed sown in well-drained soil in the greenhouse in August or September; young plants are grown in pots. *Uses:* In daintier parts of rock gardens. *Varieties:* Normally only the type species is grown.

Knotweed, Fleece Flower   *Polygonum affine* D. DON

Polygonaceae   15—25 cm   VIII—IX   ○ ◐ □

Origin: Himalayas. *Description:* Evergreen plant with creeping, woody shoots and narrow lanceolate, glossy deep green leaves turning red to brown in autumn. Sparsely leaved stems terminate in dense spikes of small pink flowers which change to red when in bloom. *Requirements:* Well-drained, rather poor soil, sun or partial shade. *Cultivation:* Plant in spring or late summer, 25 cm apart. *Propagation:* By division in spring. *Uses:* In larger spaces in rock gardens and in natural, informal areas of the garden. *Varieties:* Var. *superbum* — longer spikes; 'Darjeeling Red' — deep pink; 'Donald Lowndes' — pink.

Top left: *Phlox subulata* 'Morgenstern'. Top right: *Phlox subulata* 'Temiscaming'. Bottom left: *Phyteuma comosum*. Bottom right: *Polygonum affine*.

Alpine Auricula *Primula auricula* L.

Primulaceae   10—15 cm   IV—V   ○ □

Origin: Europe, limestone Alps, Apennines to western Carpathians. *Description:* Ground rosette of obovate or round, stiff, glabrous leaves, leafless stems terminating in one-sided cymes of broad, funnel-shaped, fragrant yellow flowers. *Requirements:* Well-drained, loamy, preferably rather dry soil with lime, and a sunny situation. *Cultivation:* Plant in spring, 20 to 25 cm apart. *Propagation:* By seed sown under glass in spring. *Uses:* In rock gardens, in rock crevices as well as open spaces; it is lovely combined with spring gentians. *Varieties:* 'Blairside Yellow' — miniature yellow flowers.

Primrose *Primula* × *bullesiana* BEES

Primulaceae   40—50 cm   VI—VII   ◐ ▧

Origin: A cross between *P. beesiana* and *P. bulleyana*. *Description:* Leaves broadly lanceolate, irregularly toothed. Flowers yellow, orange, red, lilac and violet, borne in a succession of whorls on a long stem. *Requirements:* Rather damp, humus-rich soil, partial shade. *Cultivation:* Plant in spring or late summer, 30 to 40 cm apart. *Propagation:* By seed sown under glass in March; young plants are grown in pots. *Uses:* In moist, partly shaded areas in larger rock gardens, and among groups of perennials, particularly near water. *Varieties:* Seedling strains available.

Primrose *Primula cortusoides* L.

Primulaceae   15—25 cm   IV—V   ◐ ▧

Origin: Urals and Altai. *Description:* Ground rosettes of round to elongate leaves, from which rise several stems carrying dense clusters of pink flowers with yellow centres. The whole plant is covered with light down. *Requirements:* Sufficiently moist, humus-rich soil, light semi-shade. *Cultivation:* Plant in spring or late summer, 25 to 30 cm apart. *Propagation:* Mainly by seed sown under glass in March, but also by division. *Uses:* In small groups in rock gardens, and in free-style perennial groupings, often together with other primroses. *Varieties:* Normally only the type species is grown.

Primrose *Primula denticulata* SM.

Primulaceae   20—25 cm   III—IV   ◐ ▧

Origin: Central and western Asia. *Description:* Rosette of longish lanceolate leaves, slightly rough, with finely toothed margin. Leafless stems terminating in round heads of lilac-blue flowers. Some varieties are white, pink, red or violet. *Requirements:* Sufficiently moist, good garden soil, sun to semi-shade. *Cultivation:* Plant in spring or early autumn, 30 cm apart. *Propagation:* By division, root cuttings, or by seed sown under glass in March. *Uses:* In rock gardens singly or in groups, also in areas planted with spring-flowering perennials. *Varieties:* 'Alba' — white; 'Atroviolacea' — deep violet; 'Delicata' — pale pink; 'Rubin' — deep red.

Top left: *Primula auricula*. Top right: *Primula* × *bullesiana*. Bottom left: *Primula cortusoides*. Bottom right: *Primula denticulata* 'Alba'.

Oxlip *Primula elatior* HILL.

Primulaceae   25—30 cm   IV—V   ○ ◐ ◪

Origin: Europe to central Asia. *Description:* Leaves longish-ovate, roughly hairy on the under-side. Flowers large, flat, carried on leafless stems; cultivated mostly in white, pink, red, violet and yellow. *Requirements:* Good, nourishing, reasonably moist garden soil, light partial shade. *Cultivation:* Plant in spring or early autumn, 30 to 40 cm apart. *Propagation:* By division in late summer, but chiefly by seed sown under glass in March. *Uses:* In larger rock gardens, among groups of perennials, and also for cutting. *Varieties:* Varieties are listed by their colour; 'Pacific Giant'—American primrose with exceptionally large flowers.

Primrose *Primula* × *pubescens* JACQ.

Primulaceae   20—30 cm   IV—V   ○ ◐ ◪

Origin: Cross between *P. auricula* and *P. hirsuta. Description:* Smooth, round leaves as in *P. auricula,* flowers larger, in various colours such as violet, red, pink, yellow, with yellow centres, velvety surface and paler margins. *Requirements:* Well-drained, preferably loamy, slightly moist soil; sunny situation, but tolerates partial shade. *Cultivation:* Plant in spring or late summer, 30 to 35 cm apart. *Propagation:* By division in summer or by seed sown under glass in spring. *Uses:* In larger rock gardens and among groups of perennials. *Varieties:* 'Alba'—white.

Primrose *Primula sieboldii* E. MORR.

Primulaceae   15—20 cm   V—VI   ◐ ◪

Origin: Japan, Korea, Manchuria. *Description:* Leaves up to 10 cm long, ovate to elongate, hairy. Flowers large, in cymose panicles, white, pink, red or pinkish-violet. *Requirements:* Humus-rich, sufficiently moist soil, semi-shade. *Cultivation:* Plant in spring or late summer, 25 to 30 cm apart. *Propagation:* Chiefly by division or by cuttings after flowering. *Uses:* In moist and partly shaded spots in rock gardens, in groups of spring-flowering perennials and near water. *Varieties:* 'Daphnis—bright pinkish-red; 'Miss Nelly Bernard'—carmine-red; 'Queen of the Whites'—pure white; 'Robert Herold'—pinkish violet.

Common Primrose *Primula vulgaris* HUDS.

Primulaceae   10—15 cm   III—IV   ◐ ◪

Origin: Europe. *Description:* Leaves obovate, softly downy. Flowers borne singly on slender stems close above the leaves so that they form cushions; white, pink, red, yellow or blue with yellow eye. One of the loveliest and most important of the primroses. *Requirements:* Loose, nourishing, humus-rich, reasonably moist soil, light semi-shade. *Cultivation:* Plant in spring or autumn, 30 to 40 cm apart. *Propagation:* By seed sown under glass in March or by division after flowering. *Uses:* In rock gardens among groups of spring-flowering perennials; can also be used for forcing. *Varieties:* Rarely double and unusual forms are available.

Top left: *Primula elatior.* Top right: *Primula pubescens.* Bottom left: *Primula sieboldii.* Bottom right: *Primula vulgaris.*

Pasque Flower *Pulsatilla vulgaris* ssp. *grandis* ZAMELS

Ranunculaceae   15—20 cm   IV—V   ○□

Origin: Europe, grows in the wild in rather dry, sunny meadows on a limestone substratum, chiefly in warmer steppe regions. *Description:* Basal leaves long-stalked, finely divided, begin to grow after flowering. Buds downy, both stalks and outer petals; stems leafless, sepals also divided and downy. Flowers large, six-petalled with a great many golden-yellow stamens; the type species is violet, garden varieties white, pink or red. Flowers are followed by heads of downy seeds which are also a decorative feature until they ripen and are dispersed by the wind. Leaves that develop after flowering last until autumn. *Requirements:* Does best in a sunny situation, in well-drained soil containing lime, though it tolerates fairly dry conditions and light semi-shade. A very rewarding plant and fairly easy to grow. *Cultivation:* Plant in spring or late summer, 30 to 40 cm apart. Put out only young (one- or two-year-old) plants grown on in pots. Older plants which have been in the same place for more than 3 years cannot be moved, and gradually die if transplanted; the life span is 4 to 6 years. *Propagation:* By seed, best sown as soon as it is ripe so that it germinates by autumn. In spring prick out young plants and grow on in small pots; they will be ready for putting outdoors by autumn. Varieties differing in colour from the type species should be grown separately because they cross-breed readily and then generally do not come in the desired form. This applies chiefly to the red and white varieties. *Uses:* In rock gardens, either singly in an important place or in smaller groups. It is also lovely in steppe gardens together with pheasant-eye, thyme and various grasses, chiefly fescue. *Varieties:* Besides the type species, with violet flowers, also cultivated are the varieties 'Alba'—white; 'Mrs van der Elst'—delicate pink; 'Rubra'—purplish red.

Pulsatilla halleri ssp. *slavica* ZAMELS

Ranunculaceae   20—25 cm   IV   ○□

Origin: Carpathians. *Description:* One of the loveliest of pulsatillas. Leaves more coarsely divided, flowers large, pale violet-blue, covered with dense grey down on the reverse. Flowers larger and appearing earlier than those of *P. grandis*. *Requirements:* Does best in well-drained, rather dry soil with lime, and a sunny situation. *Cultivation:* Plant in spring or late summer, 30 to 40 cm apart. *Propagation:* Only by seed, sown either shortly after gathering or in early spring; young plants are grown in pots. *Uses:* Splendid plant for any kind of rock garden and for natural sections, particularly steppe gardens. *Varieties:* Normally only the type species is grown.

Top left: *Pulsatilla vulgaris* ssp. *grandis*. Top right: *Pulsatilla vulgaris* ssp. *grandis* 'Alba'. Bottom left: *Pulsatilla vulgaris* ssp. *grandis* 'Rubra'. Bottom right: *Pulsatilla halleri* ssp. *slavica*.

Crowfoot *Ranunculus illyricus* L.

Ranunculaceae   30—40 cm   V—VI   ○ □

Origin: Europe, Asia. *Description:* Rhizomes with short, tuber-like roots. Leaves long-stalked, trilobate, with longish lanceolate lobes, deep green. Flowers 2 to 3 cm across, on sparsely branching stem, vivid yellow, glossy inside. Whole plant covered with light grey down. *Requirements:* Preferably rather dry, well-drained soil, and sun. *Cultivation:* Plant in spring or late summer, 30 cm apart. *Propagation:* By division or by seed sown in dishes as soon as it is ripe. *Uses:* In larger rock gardens, natural sections and heath gardens. *Varieties:* Normally only the type species is grown.

Crowfoot *Ranunculus parnassifolius* L.

Ranunculaceae   5—10 cm   VI   ○ ◪

Origin: Pyrenees, Alps. *Description:* Leaves entire, heart-shaped to ovate, bluish-green, downy on the margin. Flowers white, often reddish on the outside, on short stems. *Requirements:* Loamy soil with stone rubble, sufficient moisture. Fairly tender at lowland altitudes. *Cultivation:* Plant in spring 15 to 20 cm apart. *Propagation:* By division after flowering, or by seed sown as soon as it is ripe; young plants are grown in pots. *Uses:* In daintier parts of rock gardens, best of all beside pools and streams where there is plenty of moisture. *Varieties:* Normally only the type species is grown.

Lavender Cotton *Santolina chamaecyparissus* L.

Compositae   30—40 cm   VII—VIII   ○ □

Origin: Western Mediterranean region. *Description:* Evergreen, semi-woody plant with small, silvery grey, thread-like leaves. Flowers double, button-like, yellow. The whole plant is aromatic. *Requirements:* A warm, sunny situation, rather dry, sandy soil. In moist soil easily damaged by frost. *Cultivation:* Plant in spring, 30 to 40 cm apart; generally planted as a solitary specimen. *Propagation:* Chiefly by cuttings in summer; young plants are grown in pots. *Uses:* In rock gardens, and singly or in groups in drier, natural sections of the garden. *Varieties:* 'Nana'—more compact.

Soapwort *Saponaria × olivana* WOCKE

Caryophyllaceae   5—10 cm   VI—VIII   ○ □ ◪

Origin: Cross between *S. caespitosa* and *S. pumila*. *Description:* Dense, firm cushions of small dark green, lanceolate leaves. Flowers rather large, stemless, pink, borne in great profusion. *Requirements:* Fairly easy to grow; does best in well-drained, humus-rich soil and a sunny situation. *Cultivation:* Plant in spring, 20 cm apart. *Propagation:* By cuttings in June or July. *Varieties:* 'Bressingham'—mauve-pink flowers with white eye and brownish-red calyx, long-flowering.

Top left: *Ranunculus illyricus*. Top right: *Ranunculus parnassifolius*. Bottom left: *Santolina chamaecyparissus*. Bottom right: *Saponaria × olivana*.

Rockfoil   *Saxifraga* × *arendsii* hybrids

Saxifragaceae   10 — 15 cm   V — VI

Origin: Hybrids descended chiefly from *S. caespitosa. Description:* Thick carpets of small rosettes composed of divided leaflets. Flowers on slender stems, white, pink or red. *Requirements:* Well-drained, humus-rich, reasonably moist soil; semi-shade; generally do not tolerate full sun. *Cultivation:* Plant in spring, 15 to 20 cm apart; they will soon form a continuous mass. Dry patches will appear after a few years, and should be repaired by putting out newly divided plants. *Propagation:* By division in spring. *Uses:* As flat masses in rock gardens. *Varieties:* 'Bees Pink' — carmine-pink; 'Schneeteppich' — white; 'Schwefelblüte' — sulphur-yellow; 'Triumph' — dark red; and others.

Bell Saxifrage   *Saxifraga grisebachii* DEG. et DORFL.

Saxifragaceae   10 — 20 cm   IV — V

Origin: The Balkans. *Description:* Large rosettes of stiff, narrow, tongue-shaped, grey-green leaves, from which rise hairy stems topped by curving clusters of flowers coloured carmine-red with striking red bracts. One of the most attractive saxifrages of the Engleria section. *Requirements:* Fairly heavy, well-drained soil with peat and stone rubble; an open situation to light semi-shade. *Cultivation:* Plant in spring, 15 cm apart. Provide a light protective cover for the winter. *Propagation:* By cuttings and by detaching side rosettes. *Uses:* In rock gardens in narrow cracks, and in tuff. *Varieties:* 'Wisley Variety' — of more vigorous habit and with more intensely coloured flowers.

Rockfoil   *Saxifraga longifolia* LAPEYR.

Saxifragaceae   flower spikes up to 70 cm   VII

Origin: Pyrenees. *Description:* Within a number of years the plant forms a huge star-like rosette of stiff, narrow, tongue-shaped lanceolate, grey-green leaves. It does not flower until the 4th to 6th year and dies after the seeds have ripened. Flowers white, sometimes spotted with red, borne in long spikes. It does not make side rosettes and must be replaced by new plants. *Requirements:* Well-drained soil with lime, an open, east-facing position. *Cultivation:* Plant in spring. *Propagation:* By seed taken from isolated plants, because it cross-breeds easily, and sown in the greenhouse in winter. *Uses:* In rock crevices and in dry walls. *Varieties:* Normally only the type species is grown.

Rockfoil   *Saxifraga oppositifolia* L.

Saxifragaceae   3 — 5 cm   III — IV

Origin: Europe, Siberia, Greenland and the Arctic regions of North America. *Description:* Prostrate plant with creeping stems covered with small, stiff, oval, dark green leaves. Flowers large, deep pink, open and practically stemless. *Requirements:* Good, well-drained soil containing peat, good compost and stone rubble; sufficient moisture. *Cultivation:* Plant in spring, 15 to 20 cm apart. *Propagation:* By division or cuttings in autumn. *Uses:* In cracks between stones in the east-facing side of rock gardens; does well in tuff. *Varieties:* 'Latino' — glistening pink; 'Vaccariniana' — carmine red.

Top left: *Saxifraga* × *arendsii* hybrid. Top right: *Saxifraga grisebachii*. Bottom left: *Saxifraga longifolia*. Bottom right: *Saxifraga oppositifolia*.

Rock Garden Plants

Stonecrop *Sedum acre* L.

Crassulaceae   5—10 cm   VI   ○ □

Origin: Europe, Asia. *Description:* Low, thick carpets of short stems covered spirally with broadly ovate, fleshy leaves. Flowering stems somewhat higher, teminating in a cluster of vivid yellow star-like flowers borne in great profusion. *Requirements:* Quite undemanding; does best in rather dry, sandy soil in sun. *Cultivation:* Plant in spring or late summer, 20 cm apart. *Propagation:* Readily by division. *Uses:* In any kind of rock garden as a flat element, also in natural xerophilous schemes. *Varieties:* Normally only the type species is grown.

Stonecrop *Sedum kamtschaticum* FISCH. et MEY.

Crassulaceae   10—15 cm   VI—VII   ○ □ ◩

Origin: Eastern Siberia to northern China. *Description:* Low plants with branching stems covered with deep green, broadly ovate, fleshy leaves. Flowers orange-yellow, borne in clusters at the ends of the stems. *Requirements:* Well-drained soil and a sunny situation; tolerates light partial shade. *Cultivation:* Plant in spring or autumn, 25 to 30 cm apart. *Propagation:* By division or cuttings in spring or summer. *Uses:* In flat spaces in rock gardens, in dry walls and in informal perennial schemes. *Varieties:* Besides the type species with green leaves, the yellow variegated form 'Variegatum' is also available.

Stonecrop *Sedum spur um* M.B.

Crassulaceae   10—15 cm   VII—VIII   ○ ◕ □

Origin: Caucasus. *Description:* Prostrate, rooting stems covered with opposite, short-stalked, broadly obovate, fleshy leaves with toothed margin. Flowers pink, carried in dense, flat clusters at the ends of the stems. *Rquirements:* Well-drained garden soil, sun to partial shade. *Cultivation:* Plant in spring or autumn, 30 cm apart. *Propagation:* By division or cuttings in spring. *Uses:* In any kind of rock garden, in dry walls and in informal perennial schemes. *Varieties:* 'Album Superbum'—white flowers; 'Purpurteppich'—flowers dark red, leaves brownish-red; 'Schorbuser Blut'—leaves dark, flowers deep carmine.

Stonecrop *Sedum telephium* L.

Crassulaceae   40—60 cm   VIII—IX   ○ ◩

Origin: Europe to Siberia. *Description:* Clumps of stout, unbranched stems covered with fleshy, oval, coarsely toothed, grey-green leaves. Small, purplish-pink flowers densely packed in large, wide heads. *Requirements:* Well-drained, nourishing, reasonably moist garden soil. *Cultivation:* Put out in spring or early autumn, 40 to 60 cm apart. *Propagation:* By division or terminal cuttings in spring. *Uses:* In larger rock gardens, mixed borders and free-style groupings. *Varieties:* 'Herbstfreude'—brownish-red flowers that turn brownish-purple when spent; 'Munstead Dark Red' reddish-brown flowers, brownish-red leaves.

Top left: *Sedum acre.* Top right: *Sedum kamtschaticum.* Bottom left: *Sedum spurium* 'Schorbuser Blut'. Bottom right: *Sedum telephium.*

Rock Garden Plants

Houseleek   *Sempervivum* hybrids

Crassulaceae   10 — 25 cm   VII   ○ □

Origin: Europe. *Description:* Firm, round rosettes of fleshy, rigid, stiffly-tipped leaves of various colours—green, brown to brownish-red, some even bicoloured. Scaly-leaved stem terminating in a cluster of flowers differing in colour according to the variety. Spreads by means of side rosettes. *Requirements:* Rather poor, well-drained soil, a sunny and dry situation. *Cultivation:* Plant in spring or late summer, 20 cm apart. *Propagation:* By detaching the side rosettes. *Uses:* Chiefly in rock crevices and dry walls. *Varieties:* 'Smaragd'—leaves vivid green with red tips, flowers pink; 'Alpha'—leaves pale brown, flowers pink; 'Topas'—leaves dark red, flowers carmine, and others.

Soldanella carpatica VIERH.

Primulaceae   5 — 10 cm   V — VI   ◕ ▨

Origin: Carpathians. *Description:* Low clumps of stalked, kidney-shaped, deep green, glabrous leaves. Flowers violet-blue, bell-like, finely fringed, on leafless stems, *Requirements:* Well-drained, humus-rich soil with lime and sufficient moisture; light partial shade. *Cultivation:* Plant in spring, 20 cm apart. *Propagation:* By division in July or August, or by seed sown in dishes under glass in early spring. *Uses:* In rock gardens in larger cracks, in moist stone rubble and in daintier, informal sections. *Varieties:* Normally only the type species is grown.

Stachys officinalis TREV.

Labiatae   30 — 60 cm   VII — VIII   ○ □ ▨

Origin: Europe to Asia Minor. *Description:* Leaves stalked, longish ovate, with toothed margin. Pale violet, labiate flowers borne in racemes at the ends of erect, sparsely leaved stems. Entire plant covered with light down. *Requirements:* Any garden soil that is reasonably moist; although it also tolerates dry conditions; an open situation is preferred. *Cultivation:* Plant in spring or autumn, 25 to 30 cm apart. *Propagation:* By division in spring or autumn. *Uses:* In larger rock gardens, perennial borders and free-style groupings. *Varieties:* 'Rosea'—a pink-flowering variety.

Stachys olympica POIR.   *(Stachys lanata* JACQ. non CRANTZ*)*

Labiatae   15 — 25 cm   VI — VII   ○ □

Origin: Caucasus, Iran. *Description:* Low mass of longish ovate, white-felted leaves which are the main decorative feature. Small pink flowers in several whorls on erect, leaved stems. Spreads rapidly by offshoots. *Requirements:* Quite undemanding, though most vividly coloured in a dry, sunny situation; tends to rot in damp. *Cultivation:* Plant in spring or autumn, 30 to 40 cm apart. Remove flower stems as they add little to the plant's attractiveness. *Propagation:* Readily by division at any time. *Uses:* In larger rock gardens, also in free-style perennial schemes to form a thick ground cover. *Varieties:* 'Silver Carpet'—non flowering prostrate form.

Top left: *Sempervivum* hybrid 'Alpha'. Top right: *Soldanella carpatica.* Bottom left: *Stachys officinalis* 'Rosea'. Bottom right: *Stachys olympica.*

Rock Garden Plants

Thyme *Thymus serpyllum* L.

Labiatae   3 — 5 cm   VI — VII   ○ □

Origin: Europe, Asia, North Africa. *Description:* A creeping plant which makes carpets of small, dark green, oval leaves, smothered with small clusters of tiny, purplish-pink labiate flowers. There are also white and red varieties. *Requirements:* Well-drained, rather dry, preferably poor soil and full sun. *Cultivation:* Plant in spring or early autumn, 20 to 25 cm apart. *Propagation:* Very easy by division. *Uses:* As a flat element in the rock garden, also between paving stones and as a substitute for lawn. *Varieties:* 'Albus' — white; 'Coccineus' — carmine-red; 'Purpurteppich' — scarlet-red; 'Splendens' — carmine.

Townsendia parryi D.C.

Compositae   5 — 15 cm   V   ○ ◑ □

Origin: North America. *Description:* From the long tap-root grows a low rosette of longish leaves. The short-stalked flowers have yellow centres and small, violet-pink, tongue-shaped sepals. *Requirements:* Does best in warm stands in sandy, well-drained soil mixed with rubble. *Cultivation:* Put out in spring. Cover with polythene sheets for the winter. *Propagation:* By seed sown in spring or autumn; prick out the seedlings into small pots. May be propagated also by offshoots. *Uses:* In dry slopes, in screes or among stones; also in crevices in small rock gardens. *Varieties:* Normally only the type species is grown.

Tunica saxifraga SCOP. *(Petrorhagia saxifraga* LINK*)*

Caryophyllaceae   15 — 25 cm   VI — IX   ○ □

Origin: Southern Europe, Asia Minor, Caucasus. *Description:* Low, thickly branched plant covered with small, narrow, pointed leaves. Profusion of small, pale pink flowers. The type species seeds itself freely, sometimes excessively. *Requirements:* Undemanding plant, does best in well-drained, rather dry soil with lime, and in sun. *Cultivation:* Plant in spring, 25 cm apart. *Propagation:* The type species readily by seed, double varieties by cuttings; young plants are grown in pots. *Uses:* In rock gardens, dry walls and natural sections of the garden. *Varieties:* 'Alba Plena' — shorter, white, double; 'Rosette'-pink, double.

Umbilicus spinosus DC. *(Orostachys spinosa* SWEET*)*

Crassulaceae   inflorescence up to 25 cm   V — VI   ○ □

Origin: Siberia, Manchuria, Mongolia. *Description:* Fairly large rosettes resembling houseleeks; leaves grey-green with long white spines. Yellow inflorescence on a long stem. The rosette dies after flowering. *Requirements:* Does best in rather dry, sandy soil and an open situation, but not in full sun. *Cultivation:* Plant in spring, 15 cm apart. Provide a light cover for the winter. *Propagation:* By detaching side rosettes in late summer; these, however, are few in number. Also by seed. *Uses:* Chiefly in crevices in rock gardens. *Varieties:* Normally only the type species is grown.

Top left: *Thymus serpyllum.* Top right: *Townsendia parryi.* Bottom left: *Tunica saxifraga.* Bottom right: *Umbilicus spinosus.*

Rock Garden Plants

Merry Bells *Uvularia grandiflora* SM.

Liliaceae 30 cm IV—VI ◐●▨

Origin: Eastern North America. *Description:* Erect stems covered with longish leaves with pointed tips and fine down on the underside. Flowers slender, yellow, up to 4 cm long. *Requirements:* Does best in semi-shade or shade, in humus-rich soil that does not have too much lime and is sufficiently moist. *Cultivation:* Plant in spring or early autumn, 25 to 30 cm apart. *Propagation:* Chiefly by division in late summer. *Uses:* In larger rock gardens and in shaded natural sections of the garden. *Varieties:* Normally only the type species is grown.

Speedwell *Veronica prostrata* L.

Scrophulariaceae 10—15 cm VI ○▢

Origin: Europe, Asia. *Description:* Prostrate, mound-forming plants. Stems covered with opposite, longish-lanceolate, serrate leaves; clusters of small blue flowers in leaf axils. *Requirements:* Rather dry, well-drained soil, a sunny situation. *Cultivation:* Put out in spring or late summer, 30 cm apart. *Propagation:* By division in spring or autumn. *Uses:* In rock gardens, dry walls, as a carpeting plant in free-style groupings. *Varieties:* 'Alba'—white; 'Rosea'—pink.

Periwinkle *Vinca minor* L.

Apocynaceae 10—15 cm IV—V ○◐▢▨

Origin: Europe. *Description:* Evergreen plant with long, prostrate, branching stems that put out roots. Leaves opposite, oval, stiff, dark green; flowers blue. Grows rapidly and makes a good ground cover. *Requirements:* Easy to grow; it does best in partial shade in humus-rich soil that is reasonably moist, but also tolerates dry conditions. *Cultivation:* Plant in spring or autumn, 30 cm apart. *Propagation:* Readily by division or cuttings. *Uses:* In larger rock gardens in partial shade, excellent as an underplanting to trees and shrubs. *Varieties:* 'Rubra'—red; 'Variegata'—yellow variegated leaves.

Viola lutea HUDS.

Violaceae 15—20 cm VI—VIII ◐○▨

Origin: Europe. *Description:* Leaves roundish to ovate, flowers on slender stems, pure yellow with black markings near the centre. Borne in profusion for a comparatively long time. *Requirements:* Well-drained, reasonably moist garden soil, a partly shaded to open situation. *Cultivation:* Plant in spring, 20 cm apart. *Propagation:* By seed sown under glass in spring. *Uses:* In rock gardens, in larger cracks as well as in flat spaces, and in dry walls. *Varieties:* Normally only the type species is grown.

Top left: *Uvularia grandiflora.* Top right: *Veronica prostrata.* Bottom left: *Vinca minor.* Bottom right: *Viola lutea.*

178

Bulbs

Acidanthera bicolor HOCHST.

Iridaceae   60—100 cm   VII—X   ○ ◨

Origin: Ethiopia. *Description:* Tuberous plant, resembling gladiolus but with less dense flower spikes; flowers white with reddish-brown patch in the centre. Very fragrant. *Requirements:* A sheltered situation, loose and well-drained soil. *Cultivation:* Plant out 6 to 8 cm deep, but not until beginning of May. After the first autumn frosts lift the corms, clean, and store at a temperature of 15 to 18 °C. *Propagation:* By cormlets. *Uses:* In groups in annual or perennial beds. Cut flowers will open in water down to the last bud. *Varieties:* The var. *murielae* PERRY, with large funnel-shaped flowers is generally grown.

Ornamental Onion   *Allium giganteum* REGEL

Liliaceae   100—150 cm   VI—VIII   ○ ◐ □ ◨

Origin: Himalayas. *Description:* Purplish-pink flowers in umbels up to 20 cm across. *Requirements:* Likes lime, light, well-drained soil and a fairly warm situation. At higher altitudes needs a good winter cover. *Cultivation:* Plant bulbs 10 to 15 cm deep in September or October. They may be left in the same place for several years. If it is necessary to lift them, do so in late summer after the leaves have turned completely yellow. *Propagation:* By bulblets. Plants grown trom seed take 3 years before they start flowering. *Uses:* In perennial beds; also attractive as cut and dried flowers. *Varieties:* Only the type species; no varieties known.

Ornamental Onion   *Allium karataviense* REGEL

Liliaceae   20—25 cm   IV—V   ○ ◐ □ ◨

Origin: Turkestan. *Description:* Usually only 2 to 3 broad, blue-green leaves edged with narrow band of red. The umbel of greyish-pink flowers is decorative even after they have faded. *Requirements:* Fairly light, well-drained soil, in a warm situation. Likes lime. *Cultivation:* Plant bulbs 8 to 10 cm deep in September to November. In harsher climates cover with evergreen branches as protection against dry frost. May be left in the same spot 2 to 4 years. *Propagation:* as for *A. giganteum. Uses:* Best in rock gardens or between low-growing perennials. *Varieties:* Only the type species to date.

Windflower, Poppy Anemone   *Anemone coronaria* L.

Ranunculaceae   15—35 cm   IV—VI   ◐ ◨

Origin: Mediterranean. *Description:* Tuberous anemones have greatly divided leaves, and flowers with a larger number of stamens and pistils. *Requirements:* Rather moist, humus-rich but well-drained soil. *Cultivation:* Plant tubers 5 to 8 cm deep in early November. Before planting soak them in tepid water for 24 hours. After the plants have died back lift the tubers and store in a dry place. They may be stored for several years before being replanted. *Propagation:* Best by seed, which will produce flower-bearing tubers after two years. *Uses:* Mostly for cutting. *Varieties:* Most widely sold in a mixture of colours, with single flowers—"De Caen" varieties; or double flowers—"St. Brigid" varieties.

Top left: *Acidanthera bicolor* var. *murielae.* Top right: *Allium giganteum.* Bottom left: *Allium karataviense.* Bottom right: *Anemone coronaria.*

Bulbs

Begonia tuberhybrida voss.

Begoniaceae   25—40 cm   VI—X   ◕ ● ▨

Origin: This hybrid is derived from South American species. *Description:* Flattened tubers from which rise soft stems with large, showy flowers. *Requirements:* Slightly acid, humus-rich soil with plenty of nutrients. *Cultivation:* Put grown-on plants outdoors in late May, not before, because they are intolerant of even the slightest frost. Apply liquid feed once a week, ideally a 0.1% solution of compound fertilizer. Lift plants after the first autumn frost, clean tubers and store till spring in a dry place at a temperature of 7 to 8°C. *Propagation:* By cutting large tubers into pieces with at least one eye each. Nurserymen propagate them from seed sown in February in boxes in the greenhouse. *Uses:* In ornamental beds in parks and gardens, on graves, in window-boxes or urns, particularly on the eastern and northern side of the house. *Varieties:* The many varieties available are divided into several groups, such as "Gigantea"—large single flowers; "Gigantea flore plena"—large double flowers; "Gigantea fimbriata"—double flowers with fringed petals; "Multiflora"—smaller single flowers; "Pendula flore plena"—pendent double flowers. Each group contains the following varieties, named according to colour: 'White', 'Yellow', 'Orange', 'Pink', 'Carmine-red', 'Scarlet-red', and 'Dark Red'.

Indian Shot   *Canna indica* hybrids

Cannaceae   60—200 cm   VI—IX   ○ ▨

Origin: Central America. *Description:* Fleshy roots, longish ovate leaves and spectacular flowers coloured red, orange, pink or yellow. *Requirements:* Deep, rich soil containing humus, a warm and sheltered situation. *Cultivation:* Put outdoors in late May or early June after all danger of frost is past, having grown on for about 10 weeks before that in boxes at a temperature of 15° to 18° C. Plant in beds 8 to 12 cm deep and 40 to 70 cm apart. After the first autumn frost cut back stems to about 10 cm above the ground, and store rootstock with its ball of soil in a dry place at a temperature of 5 to 10° C for the winter. *Propagation:* By cutting larger roots into pieces with at least one large eye each. *Uses:* As solitary specimens or small groups of several plants in the lawn. Also popular plants for decoration in parks and public areas, as well as in large urns and other containers on terrace or patio. *Varieties:* Many attractive varieties are currently available, e.g. 'Feuerzauber'—deep red with red foliage; 'Gartenschönheit'—carmine-pink with green foliage; 'Gruss aus Rom'—blood red with green foliage; 'Hamburg'—salmon-pink with red foliage; 'J. B. van der Schoot'—lemon-yellow spotted with red, green foliage; 'Reine Charlotte'—scarlet with broad yellow margin; 'The President'—bright scarlet with green foliage; and many more.

Top left: *Begonia tuberhybrida* 'Dark Red'. Top right: *Begonia tuberhybrida* 'Yellow'. Bottom left: *Canna indica* hybrid 'Reine Charlotte'. Bottom right: *Canna indica* hybrid 'The President'.

Bulbs

Glory-of-the-Snow   *Chionodoxa luciliae* BOISS.

Liliaceae   10 – 15 cm   III—IV   ○◐▨

Origin: Asia Minor. *Description:* Very small bulbs, strap-shaped leaves, one-sided racemes of star-like flowers. *Requirements:* Rather moist, humus-rich, deep soil. *Cultivation:* Plant bulbs 6 to 8 cm deep from September to mid-November. If they are to be moved to another site do so in mid-July. *Propagation:* By bulblets or seed. In congenial conditions they seed themselves. *Uses:* In rock gardens or under deciduous shrubs or trees. *Varieties:* The type species has blue flowers with white centre. Var. *alba* AYE is white, var. *rosea* WITTE pink.

Autumn Crocus   *Colchicum* hybrids

Liliaceae   10 — 25 cm   VIII—X   ○◐□▨

Origin: Asia Minor. *Description:* Crocus-like flowers appear before the broad leaves, which grow in during spring. *Requirements:* Deep, nourishing soil; sufficient moisture in spring; dry conditions in summer. *Cultivation:* Must be planted out in mid-August, 10 to 20 cm deep. May be moved in July. *Propagation:* By offsets of the tuber, produced in considerable numbers. *Uses:* Together with low-growing perennials and ornamental grasses or in rock gardens. *Varieties:* Most widely grown are 'Autumn Queen'—pinkish-violet with white throat; 'Lilac Wonder'—lilac-pink; 'Water Lily'—lavender-pink, double; 'The Giant'—amethyst-violet.

Montbretia   *Crocosmia masonorum* N. E. BR.

Iridaceae   80 — 100 cm   VII—VIII   ○▨

Origin: South Africa. *Description:* Corms, sword-shaped leaves, funnel-shaped flowers arranged in two rows. *Requirements:* Good garden soil. *Cultivation:* Plant as gladiolus. In an open site it requires a support so that it is not uprooted by the wind. *Propagation:* By cormlets, which usually take two years to develop and bear flowers. Overwinter in a ventilated room at a temperature of 5 to 8 °C. *Uses:* In groups together with low-growing perennials or annuals. Also good for cutting. *Varieties:* The type species has vivid orange flowers.

Crocus chrysanthus HERB.

Iridaceae   5 — 8 cm   III—IV   ○◐▨

Origin: Eastern regions bordering the Mediterranean. *Description:* Small round corms, long narrow leaves, globular flowers on short stalks. *Requirements:* Well-drained soil with plenty of nutrients. Dry conditions in summer. *Cultivation:* Plant 6 to 8 cm deep in September or October. Leave in the same site 3 to 4 years. *Propagation:* By cormlets. *Uses:* Best together with low-growing perennials or in rock gardens; also attractive under deciduous shrubs or trees. *Varieties:* Type species has yellow flowers with golden-yellow throat; there are many pretty varieties and forms, ranging from creamy-white to bronze-brown and lilac-blue.

Top left: *Chionodoxa luciliae.* Top right: *Colchicum* hybrid 'Lilac Wonder'. Bottom left: *Crocosmia masonorum.* Bottom right: *Crocus chrysanthus.*

Bulbs

Crocus neapolitanus HORT. ex MORDANT *(C. vernus* WULF.*)*

Iridaceae   8—15 cm   III—IV   ○ ◑ ◪

Origin: Garden crocuses are derived from species native to the Mediterranean. *Description:* Usually flattened, round corms of various sizes and long, narrow leaves, often with a prominent white stripe. They appear at the same time as the flowers, or later. The flowers are borne on short stems so that they appear to be growing directly from the ground; before they open they are encased in a membranous sheath. *Requirements:* Well-drained soil with plenty of nutrients. Moisture in spring and autumn, dry conditions in summer. *Cultivation:* Plant 6 to 8 cm deep in second half of September or October. May be left undisturbed for several years. If they must be moved, lift them in late June or July. Clean the corms and store in a dry, cool place until time to plant out. *Propagation:* Garden varieties by cormlets. *Uses:* In beds together with low-growing perennials, under ornamental shrubs, in rock gardens; also in turf, although they need to be replaced after a time as early cutting of the lawn will hinder growth. Large-flowered varieties in windowboxes and troughs on the balcony; may also be forced in flower pots or bowls. *Varieties:* Intensive breeding and selection has produced numerous attractive large-flowered varieties. Most widely grown are 'Dutch Yellow'—smaller, golden-yellow flowers; 'Enchantress'—porcelain-blue tinged with silver; 'Jeanne d'Arc'—white with violet-tinged tube; 'Kathleen Parlow'—snow white; 'Little Dorrit'—pale lilac-silver; 'Pickwick'—white with dark blue stripes; 'Remembrance'—purplish-blue; 'Sky Blue'—violet-blue with silvery-white stripes; 'Striped Beauty'—silvery-grey with purplish-violet stripes and dark blue tube; 'Violet Vanguard'—lilac-violet, and others.

Cyclamen purpurascens MILL. *(C. europaeum* L. emend. AIT.*)*

Primulaceae   8—15 cm   VIII—IX   ◑ ● ◪

Origin: Central and southern Europe. *Description:* Flattened, globose tubers producing roots only in an upward direction and to the sides. The leaves, growing directly from the tuber, are heart-shaped, evergreen, with silvery markings on the upper side and red on the underside. Flowers up to 15 mm across, pleasantly scented. Fruit a globose capsule filled with small, dark-skinned seeds. As it ripens the flower-stalk winds around the capsule like a spiral. *Requirements:* A warm, sheltered situation, best of all semi-shade or shade. Well-drained, humus-rich, alkaline soil. *Cultivation:* Plant in spring so that top of tuber is covered by only about 3 cm of soil. The longer it is left undisturbed in the same site the greater its beauty. *Propagation:* By seed sown in dishes in a cold greenhouse or frame. *Uses:* In rock gardens or under deciduous shrubs or trees. *Varieties:* Only the type species, with purplish-pink flowers, is cultivated.

Top left: *Crocus neapolitanus* 'Sky Blue'. Top right: *Crocus neapolitanus* 'Striped Beauty'. Bottom left: *Crocus neapolitanus* 'Violet Vanguard'. Bottom right: *Cyclamen purpurascens.*

Bulbs

Dahlia hybrids (derived from *D.* × *cultorum* THORSR. et REIS., *D. variabilis* HORT and other species)

Compositae   30—180 cm   VII—X   ○ ◪

Origin: Mexico. *Description:* Rising from the tuber are hollow stems with opposite, usually tripartite leaves; flowers composed of tongue-shaped and tubular petals on long stems grow from the leaf axils. *Requirements:* Any soil that is not too heavy and soggy. Add well-rotted compost or manure-enriched peat to the soil and dig over in the autumn. A sheltered situation. *Propagation:* As dahlias do not tolerate frost, plant tubers in late April or early May. Tall, vigorous varieties should be spaced 60 to 80 cm apart, low-growing and less robust varieties 30 to 50 cm apart. The soil layer above the tubers should be 8 to 10 cm thick. Plants grown from cuttings should not be put out before 20 May. Put stakes in when planting for later support. Remove all but the three strongest shoots to promote flowering and encourage larger blooms. Hoe the soil occasionally, and water in dry weather. Proprietary feeds may be applied until the end of July. Remove faded flowers promptly. As soon as the top parts are burned by the first autumn frosts cut back the stems to about 10 cm above the ground and lift the tubers. Turn upside down to drain water from the hollow stems and spread on the ground to dry. Then clean and overwinter in a cool, frost-free place at a temperature of 4 to 6°C. Smaller tubers and precious novelties should be stored in sand, sawdust or dry peat so they do not dry out. Make frequent checks during the winter and remove all diseased tubers promptly, or at least cut off decaying parts and sprinkle the cut surface with powdered charcoal. *Propagation:* By division of tubers—each portion must contain a piece of collar with a bud. Also by cuttings of plants that have started growth. For this purpose put parent plants in a box containing sand and peat in February and spray lightly; at a temperature of 15 to 20°C the tubers will begin to produce shoots. As soon as the shoots have 3 to 4 pairs of leaves cut them off and insert in a box with sand and peat, where they will take root after about 1 or 2 weeks at a temperature of 15 to 20°C. Single dahlias may also be multiplied from seed sown under glass in March. *Uses:* Dahlias are popular flowers for cutting, even though they are not very long-lived. They are planted in larger or smaller groups in beds. Tall varieties are good as solitary specimens or to conceal unattractive spots in the garden. Low varieties may be used also for edging and in boxes or urns on the balcony. *Varieties:* The wide range is subject to frequent changes; the following includes only the principal groups and examples.
"Cactus Dahlias"—double, narrow petals, rolled and sharply pointed, e.g. 'Alice'—light carmine-red; 'Apple Blossom'—lilac-pink with paler centre; 'Baby Fontenau'—pale pink; 'Bacchus'—blood red; 'Choral'—white; 'Doris Day'—bright red; 'Firebird'—fiery red; 'Fortune'—dark pink; 'Golden Autumn'—golden yellow; 'Golden Heart'—orange-red with golden-yellow centre; 'Madame Elizabeth Sawyer'—carmine-pink; 'Orfeo'—wine-red; 'Piquant'—vermilion red with white tips; 'Sternchen'—creamy-yellow; and many others.

Top left: *Dahlia* hybrid 'Mignon'. Top right: *Dahlia* hybrid 'Baby Fontenau'. Bottom left: *Dahlia* hybrid 'Alice'. Bottom right: *Dahlia* hybrid 'Choral'.

Bulbs

Dahlia hybrids *(D.* × *cultorum* THORSR. et REIS., *D. variabilis* HORT.*)*

Compositae (continued)   30—180 cm   VII—X   ○ ◪

"Decorative Dahlias"—large, double flowers with broad, smooth ray petals, e.g. 'Arabian Night'—blackish-red; 'Brandaris'—scarlet-orange with golden-yellow centre; 'Broeder Justinus'—dark orange-yellow with golden centre; 'Chinese Lantern'—orange-red with yellow centre; 'Class'—yellow; 'Gerrie Hoek'—pure pink; 'Glory van Heemstede'—pure sulphur-yellow; 'House of Orange'—orange; 'Lavender Perfection'—pale lilac; 'Majuba'—dark carmine-red; 'Nálada'—pale reddish-orange with white tips; 'Red and White'—red with white patch; 'Requiem'—purple with darker centre; 'Scarlet Beauty'—scarlet; 'Severin's Triumph'—salmon-pink with darker centre; 'Schweizerland'—red with white tips; 'Snowstorm'—pure white; 'Tartan'—dark purplish-violet with white tips.

"Pompon Dahlias"—double, almost ball-like flowers composed of funnel-shaped petals. Most widely cultivated varieties are 'Albino'—pure white; 'Barbara Purvis'—white; 'Bell Boy'—vivid red; 'Capulet'—dark purplish-violet with brown shading; 'Diblík'—red; 'Glow'—orange; 'Heloise'—dark chestnut brown; 'Kochelsee'—vivid red; 'Kašpárek'—orange-red; 'Lipoma'—lilac-pink; 'Magnificat'—orange-red on yellow ground; 'New Baby'—orange with yellow centre; 'Odin'—pure yellow; 'Oranjefest'—orange; 'Punch'—violet; 'Stolze von Berlin'—lilac-pink; 'Zonnegoud'—canary-yellow with bronze tinge.

"Collerette Dahlias"—between the tubular petals in the centre and the outer row of ray petals there is a kind of 'collar'—a single row of small petals of a different colour, e.g. 'Accuracy'—dark orange with lemon-yellow collar; 'Bride's Bouquet'—pure white; 'Can Can'—light purple with cream collar; 'Clair de Lune'—yellow-green with white collar; 'Geerling's Elite'—orange-red with yellow collar; 'Grand Duc'—dark red with yellow tips and yellow-white collar; 'Kaiserwalzer'—light red with yellow collar; 'La Cierva'—wine-purple with white collar; 'La Gioconda'—light scarlet-red with white collar; 'Libretto'—dark velvety-red with white collar; 'Music'—pink with pure white collar.

"Mignon Dahlias"—single flowers with outer row of ray petals and central disc of short, tubular, yellow petals, e.g. 'Golden River'—vivid yellow; 'Jet'—apricot-yellow; 'Mies'—lilac-pink; 'Murillo'—lilac-pink with blackish-red band; 'Nelly Geerlings'—vivid scarlet; 'Rote Funken'—scarlet-red with dark foliage; 'Sneezy'—pure white; 'Soleil'—canary-yellow; 'Tapis Rouge'—vivid red; 'Zons'—dark velvety-red.

"Anemone-flowered Dahlias"—raised centre of yellow tubular petals and one or more rows of ray petals. Most widely grown are 'Bridal Gown'—creamy-white; 'Bridesmaid'—white with creamy centre; 'Brio'—orange-red; 'Comet'—dark carmine-red; 'Branato'—orange-red; 'Guinea'—dark yellow with pale centre; 'Honey'—bronze-pink with yellow centre; 'Magic Favourite'—dark red; 'Roulette'—purplish-pink.

Top left: *Dahlia* hybrid 'Nálada'. Top right: *Dahlia* hybrid 'La Cierva'. Bottom left: *Dahlia* hybrid 'Kašpárek'. Bottom right: *Dahlia* hybrid 'Diblík'.

Bulbs

Winter Aconite *Eranthis hyemalis* SALISB.

Ranunculaceae   7 — 15 cm   II — IV   ◑ ◪

Origin: Southern Europe and Asia Minor. *Description:* Irregularly formed tuber, flowers 2 to 3 cm across, open only in sun. Palmate leaves do not appear until after flowering. *Requirements:* Ordinary garden soil. *Cultivation:* Plant tubers 5 to 7 cm deep in September or October. May be left undisturbed in the same place for many years. May be moved soon after leaves have died back. *Propagation:* By seed sown in boxes; plants will bear flowers after 2 to 3 years. *Uses:* Under deciduous trees and shrubs, for spring bedding, in rock gardens. *Varieties:* Besides the type species, the varieties 'Glory' — with larger flowers, green leaves; and 'Guinea Gold' — large-flowered with bronze leaves, are also grown.

Foxtail Lily *Eremurus robustus* REGEL

Liliaceae   200 — 300 cm   VI — VII   ○ □ ◪

Origin: Turkestan. *Description:* Tuberous, octopus-like root. Long, broad leaves which eventually arch downwards. Long spike of star-like flowers on a tall, stout stem. *Requirements:* Rather light, well-drained soil, a warm and sheltered situation. *Cultivation:* Plant 8 to 15 cm deep in well-drained soil in September or October. Move after 4 to 6 years, preferably in August. *Propagation:* May be increased from seed; plants bear flowers after 4 to 6 years. *Uses:* As a solitary specimen in turf or among low-growing perennials. Also as cut flowers for large vases. *Varieties:* Only the type species is cultivated with its flowers pinkish at first, later white with brownish vein down the centre of each petal; pleasantly scented.

Foxtail Lily *Eremurus stenophyllus* BAK.

Liliaceae   70 — 120 cm   VI — VII   ○ □ ◪

Origin: Central Asia. *Description:* Long, narrow leaves, stem terminated by shorter spike of yellow flowers. *Requirements, cultivation, propagation* and *uses:* As for *E. robustus*. *Varieties:* The type species has dark yellow flowers with orange stripes on the outside of the petals. It has yielded many attractive varieties, such as the 'Shelford Hybrids', 'Ruiter Hybrids' and the like, available in a mixture of colours or in separate varieties.

Pineapple Flower *Eucomis natalensis* HORT.

Liliaceae   30 — 70 cm   VI — VIII   ○ ◪

Origin: South Africa. *Description:* Large bulb, from which grow strap-shaped leaves and stem, with spike of yellow-green flowers ending in a tuft of leaves. *Requirements:* Well-drained soil, full sun, a sheltered situation. *Cultivation:* Plant out during second half of April; store in a cool, frost-free place for the winter. *Propagation:* By offsets from the bulb, also by seed sown in a semi-warm greenhouse. *Uses:* In beds among exotic plants. *Varieties:* Only the type species and sometimes the white variety 'Alba' are grown.

Top left: *Eranthis hyemalis.* Top right: *Eremurus robustus.* Bottom left: *Eremurus stenophyllus* var. *bungei.* Bottom right: *Eucomis natalensis.*

Bulbs

Freesia hybrids

Iridaceae   60 – 100 cm   VII – IX

Origin: South Africa. *Description:* Longish corms from which grow narrow, sword-shaped leaves and a one-sided spike of 8 to 10 funnel-shaped flowers. *Requirements:* Rather light, humus-rich, fresh and nourishing soil. A warm, sheltered situation. *Cultivation:* Plant out 3 to 5 cm deep, but not until May. May be grown-on in pots from March. *Propagation:* By offsets of the corm, or by seed sown under glass in March or April. *Uses:* In smaller groups in beds, in bowls and for cutting. *Varieties:* Available in a mixture of colours as well as separate varieties, such as 'Apollo' – white; 'Aurora' – yellow; 'Blauer Wimpel' – azure blue; 'Carnival' – orange-scarlet; 'Margaret' – rosy-purple.

Crown Imperial   *Fritillaria imperialis* L.

Liliaceae   60 – 100 cm   IV – V

Origin: Asia Minor. *Description:* Bulbous plant with hanging, bell-like flowers and lanceolate leaves. *Requirements:* Deep, rich, well-drained soil. *Cultivation:* Plant bulbs 15 to 25 cm deep in September or October, and leave undisturbed for 3 to 4 years. If necessary lift in late June. *Propagation:* By offsets of the bulb, growth of which may be promoted by making incisions in the basal plate. Plants grown from seed bear flowers after 3 to 5 years. *Uses:* Singly or in smaller groups in beds. *Varieties:* The type species has orange-red flowers. Varieties also come in yellow and dark red.

Snake's Head Fritillary, Guinea Flower   *Fritillaria meleagris* L.

Liliaceae   20 – 40 cm   IV – V

Origin: Europe. *Description:* Small bulb from which grow narrow leaves; hanging, bell-like flowers. *Requirements:* Well-drained soil, a sheltered situation. *Cultivation:* Plant bulbs 6 to 10 cm deep in October, and leave undisturbed for 5 to 10 years. *Propagation:* By offsets of the bulb and by seed. *Uses:* In groups for spring bedding, in rock gardens, under deciduous shrubs or trees. *Varieties:* The type species has purplish flowers with chequered pattern; varieties also come in white, pink and other colours.

Snowdrop   *Galanthus elwesii* HOOK.

Amaryllidaceae   15 – 25 cm   II – III

Origin: Mediterranean region. *Description:* Leaves grey-green, strap-shaped, up to 3 cm wide; very early flowers up to 4 cm across. *Requirements:* Ordinary, loose soil that is reasonably moist. *Cultivation:* Plant bulbs 5 to 8 cm deep in late August, and leave undisturbed for about 4 years. May be moved even during the flowering period with a ball of soil round the roots. *Propagation:* By offsets of the bulb, division of large clumps when flowers are fading, and also by seed sown in boxes. *Uses:* In perennial beds, rock gardens and under deciduous shrubs or trees. *Varieties:* The type species is most widely cultivated, though there are also a number of varieties.

Top left: *Freesia* hybrids. Top right: *Fritillaria imperialis.* Bottom left: *Fritillaria meleagris.* Bottom right: *Galanthus elwesii.*

Bulbs

Gladiolus hybrids

Iridaceae   30—150 cm   VI—IX   ○ ◪

Origin: The species from which the garden forms are derived come from central and south Africa, the Mediterranean region and Europe. *Description:* Sword-shaped leaves growing in pairs from corms that make new corms every year. Spike of cornucopia-shaped flowers with petals joined at the base to form a tube. *Requirements:* Almost any garden soil that is sufficiently moist and nourishing. *Cultivation:* Plant out between mid-April and mid-June, 8 to 12 cm deep and about 15 cm apart. Cut spikes off below the lowest flower before they have faded completely to prevent the formation of seed and consequent weakening of the plant. Lift corms in late September or early October. Cut off the stem just above the corm, clean it, and dry at a temperature of 25 to 30°C for 3 to 5 days. Store in a dry and well-ventilated place at a temperature of 5 to 10°C for the winter. *Propagation:* As a rule gladioli are increased by means of cormlets, which may be sown outdoors as early as April. Before doing so soak them in water for 1 to 2 days so they will germinate more readily. With proper care some plants flower the year they are sown. Varieties that make few new corms and cormlets may be increased by cutting the corms into portions, making sure that each has at least one well-developed bud and a piece of basal plate. Allow the cut surface to dry, and then plant out in the same way as whole corms. Plants grown from seed show marked variation in the shape and colour of the flower, height, and other characteristics. *Uses:* Best of all in groups of 5 to 20 specimens of a single variety in beds among annuals or perennials, but chiefly grown for cutting. May also be forced. *Varieties:* A very wide range, with new ones constantly being added. They are divided into three main groups: early-flowering, mid-season and late-flowering.

Early-flowering: 'Acca Laurentia' — scarlet-orange with yellow markings; 'American Express' — yellow with darker throat; 'Abu Hassan' — dark violet-blue; 'Firmament' — lobelia-blue; 'Flowersong' — yellow with carmine patch; 'Friendship' — pink with creamy-yellow throat; 'Gold Dust' — butter-yellow; 'Johann Strauss' — orange-red; 'Leuwenhorst' — pure pink; 'Lustige Witwe' — purplish-violet with white throat; 'Mansoer' — velvety red; 'Morning Kiss' — white with red throat; 'Pandion' — pale violet with darker flecks; 'Toulouse Lautrec' — orange with yellow patch and red markings; 'White Friendship' — cream-white, ruffled.

Mid-season: 'Alfred Nobel' — pink with white throat; 'Bloemfontein' — salmon-orange with yellow patch; 'Blue Conqueror' — dark violet-blue; 'Dr Fleming' — pale pink; 'Fidelio' — rosy-purple with darker patch; 'Mabel Violet' — wine-violet with white stripe; 'Pactolus' — yellow with red eye; 'Patriot' — orange-scarlet; 'Sans Souci' — scarlet-red; 'Silhouet' — lilac-grey with rose markings; 'Snow Princess' — white; 'Spotlight' — light yellow with scarlet-red eye.

Late-flowering: 'Albert Schweitzer' — bright red with darker eye; 'Aristocrat' — carmine-red with purplish tinge; 'Elan' — soft rose with white throat; 'Firebrand' — carmine-red with white stripes; 'New Europe' — vivid red; 'Picardi' — salmon; and many more.

Top left: *Gladiolus* hybrid 'Alfred Nobel'. Top right: *Gladiolus* hybrid 'Toulouse Lautrec'. Bottom left: *Gladiolus* hybrid 'White Friendship'. Bottom right: *Gladiolus* hybrid 'Albert Schweitzer'.

Common Hyacinth *Hyacinthus orientalis* L.

Liliaceae 20–30 cm IV–V ○◑◪

Origin: Middle East. *Description:* Large globular bulb, strap-shaped leaves and compact spike of very fragrant flowers. *Requirements:* Light, well-drained, nourishing soil. *Cultivation:* Plant bulbs, ideally 10 cm deep, in October; lift every year in late June, clean and store in a dry place until time to plant out again. *Propagation:* By offsets of the bulb, growth of which may be promoted by making incisions in the basal plate. *Uses:* In groups for bedding, also in troughs and bowls. The largest bulbs may be used for forcing. *Varieties:* The number of varieties used to run into thousands, but nowadays only several of the best forms are cultivated, mainly 'Anna Marie'—pale pink; 'Bismarck'—porcelain blue; 'Carnegie'—white; 'City of Haarlem'—yellow; 'Delft's Blue'—blue; 'Jan Bos'—carmine-red; 'Lady Derby—pink; 'L'Innocence'—pure white; 'Ostara'—dark blue; 'Perle Brilante'—pearly-blue; 'Pink Pearl'—dark pink; and several more.

Dwarf Bulbous Iris *Iris danfordiae* BOISS.

Iridaceae 10–12 cm III–IV ○◑□◪

Origin: Asia Minor. *Description:* Dwarf bulbous irises have long pointed bulbs with greatly reticulated tunic; leaves erect, linear, stiff, appearing at the same time as flowers which are very early. Shortened stem topped by a single flower. *Requirements:* Sandy-loamy, well-drained, slightly alkaline soil. A warm situation that is dry in summer so the bulbs can ripen properly. *Cultivation:* Plant 5 to 8 cm deep in October. May be left undisturbed for 2 to 3 years, but it is best to lift the bulbs in mid-June, clean them and store in a dry place until time to plant out again. *Propagation:* By growing on offsets of the bulb, or by seeds sown in pots. *Uses:* For early spring bedding, rock gardens, also for forcing in pots. *Varieties:* Only the type species is grown. The flowers are lemon-yellow with an orange stripe and green spots.

Spring Snowflake *Leucojum vernum* L.

Amaryllidaceae 15–25 cm III–IV ◑◪■

Origin: Central and southern Europe. *Description:* Small, globular bulbs with green-white skin, leaves strap-shaped, glossy dark green, one or two bell-shaped flowers to a stem. *Requirements:* Humus-rich, nourishing, preferably rather moist soil. Plants are fully hardy. *Cultivation:* Plant bulbs 8 to 10 cm deep in August. Move every 4 to 6 years about 6 weeks after flowering. *Propagation:* By offsets when the bulbs are being moved. Also by seeds sown in boxes; these will develop into flower-bearing plants in 2 to 3 years. *Uses:* For spring bedding, in the rock gardens and for cutting. *Varieties:* The type species has white flowers with striking yellow-green patch at the tip of each petal. Var. *carpaticum* has yellow-tipped flowers and var. *vagneri* green-tipped flowers.

Top left: *Hyacinthus orientalis* 'Carnegie'. Top right: *Hyacinthus orientalis* 'Pink Pearl'. Bottom left: *Iris danfordiae.* Bottom right: *Leucojum vernum.*

Bulbs

Lilies *Lilium* hybrids

Liliaceae   40—180 cm   VI—IX   ○ ◑ ◪

Origin: Type species come from Asia, North America and Europe. *Description:* Some species make annual stem roots just below the soil surface in addition to roots from the base of the bulb. Leaves are narrow, elongate; flowers may be trumpet-shaped, bell-shaped, cup-shaped, bowl-shaped, flat-faced or Turk's-cap. *Requirements:* Deep, humus-rich, moist but well-drained soil. The site where they are planted should be shaded by neighbouring perennials, low shrubs and ornamental grasses. *Cultivation:* Bulbs should be planted at a depth of two to three times the size of the bulb. Early-flowering species are planted at the beginning of the dormant period, i.e. in mid-September. Late-flowering species may also be planted in spring. Cover the soil where bulbs are put with a layer of manure-enriched peat or well-rotted compost to prevent the soil from caking and drying out, and to keep it cool; this also prevents the growth of weeds. Provide tall species with stakes to which they may later be tied. Remove faded flowers promptly to prevent formation of seed. Leave bulbs in the same place for a number of years, only moving them when they begin to bear few flowers and the bulbs constantly disintegrate. *Propagation:* Chiefly by small offsets of the bulb, by bulbils which form in the leaf axils and by bulb scales. Botanical species and certain varieties may be increased from seed: sow seed in boxes in a mixture of good, composted soil, coarse sand and fine peat; cover with glass and put in a warm place. Species in which the cotyledon grows up above the ground will germinate within 3 to 6 weeks at a temperature of 18 to 20°C; species in which the cotyledon remains below the ground require a temperature of 20 to 25°C and many of the seeds do not germinate until the following year. As soon as the seeds germinate, remove the glass and put the seedlings in a light place. The following spring move them to a frame or nursery bed. Water regularly during the growing period and protect against fungus disease by spraying every two weeks with copper fungicide. Once a month feed with organic or mineral compound fertilizer in liquid form. In autumn, before the frosts, cover the bed with a layer of composted soil or manure-enriched peat about 5 cm thick. *Uses:* In groups of several bulbs of the same species in perennial beds, lower species also in rock gardens. Excellent plants for cutting and forcing. *Varieties:* The range of botanical species and their varieties is very wide, and new ones are being added every year. To aid selection, therefore, they are divided according to external characteristics and origin into nine separate groups. The ones most widely cultivated are:
"Asiatic hybrids" — usually 75 to 110 cm high. Flower in June. Divided according to shape of flower into the following three subgroups:
a) lilies with upward-facing, bowl-shaped flowers, e.g. 'Cinnabar' — chestnut-red; 'Destiny' — yellow; 'Enchantment' — orange-red; 'Harmony' — orange-yellow; 'Red Bird' — red; etc.
b) lilies with outward-facing flowers, e.g. 'Brandywine' — pale yellow tinged with orange; 'Paprika' — dark red; 'White Gold' — white tinged with apricot; and others.
c) lilies with pendent Turk's-cap flowers, e.g. 'Burgundy' — dark wine-red; 'Citronella' — lemon-yellow; 'Sonata' — salmon-orange; etc.

Top left: *Lilium* hybrid 'Red Bird'. Top right: *Lilium* hybrid 'Black Butterfly'. Bottom left: *Lilium* hybrid 'White Gold'. Bottom right: *Lilium* hybrid 'Paprika'.

Bulbs

Lilies *Lilium* hybrids

Liliaceae (continued) 40—180 cm VI—IX   ○ ◐ ◨

"Trumpet-shaped hybrids"—usually 120 to 180 cm high. Petals long and neatly curved. Very good growers and very long-lived. In Europe they usually flower in July. Recommended varieties include 'African Queen'—apricot; 'Damson'—fuchsia-pink; 'Golden Splendour'—dark yellow; 'Green Magic'—greenish-white; 'Honeydew'—greenish-yellow; 'Limelight'—lemon-yellow; 'Pink Perfection'—pink; 'Royal Gold'—golden-yellow; 'Sentinel'—pure white, and others.

"Oriental hybrids"—grow to a height of 120 to 180 cm. Usually do not flower until August and September. They are divided according to the shape of the flower into several subgroups:

a) lilies with bowl-shaped flowers—e.g. 'Bonfire'—large flowers with broad carmine-red band down the centre of the petals and narrow white margin; 'Empress of China'—large, chalk-white flowers with reddish-brown dots; 'Empress of India'—dark carmine-red flowers with recurved white margins; 'Empress of Japan'—white flowers with broad golden-yellow stripes down the centre of each petal and chestnut dots; 'Magic Pink'—pale pink flowers spotted dark red, etc.

b) lilies with flat-faced flowers—e.g. 'Imperial Crimson'—carmine-red with white edge and silvery throat; 'Imperial Gold'—broad white petals with golden-yellow stripe and chestnut-red spots; 'Imperial Silver'—white heavily spotted with scarlet-red; 'Nobility'—ruby-red with white markings; 'Sunday Best'—white with purplish-red stripe down the centre of each petal, and others.

c) lilies with Turk's-cap flowers—e.g. 'Allegra'—pure white with green star in the centre; 'Jamboree'—carmine-red with white margin and dark red spots; 'Red Champion'—dark pink spotted red; 'White Champion'—white with greenish star in the centre; etc.

Lily *Lilium leucanthum* BAK.

Liliaceae 100—140 cm VII—VIII   ○ ◐ ◨

Origin: Central China. *Description:* Bulb pale yellow tinged with cinnamon, makes stems with numerous stem roots. Leaves long and narrow; large trumpet-shaped flowers, usually clusters of 3 to 5, pleasantly scented. *Requirements:* Good, humus-rich soil, and thick protective cover for the winter. *Cultivation:* Plant bulbs 15 to 25 cm deep in well-drained soil. Leave in the same place for several years. *Propagation:* Sow under glass in spring; seedlings usually do not start bearing flowers until the third year. *Uses:* In beds together with perennials or low woody plants. *Varieties:* The type species has creamy white flowers with yellow throat. Var. *centifolium* is a more vigorous form, with as many as 15 flowers coloured rosy pink outside, white inside with pale yellow throat.

Top left: *Lilium leucanthum*. Top right: *Lilium* hybrid 'Golden Splendour'. Bottom left: *Lilium* hybrid 'Black Beauty'. Bottom right: *Lilium* hybrid 'Jamboree'.

Bulbs

Grape Hyacinth *Muscari armeniacum* BAK.

Liliaceae   15—20 cm   IV—V   ○ ◑ ▣

Origin: Asia Minor. *Description:* Bulbous plant with ground rosette of narrow, strap-shaped leaves. Stems terminated by compact heads (racemes) of flask-like, short-stalked flowers. *Requirements:* Loose, nourishing soil that is not too moist. *Cultivation:* Plant bulbs 6 to 12 cm deep in September or October. May be lifted in July; generally left in the same spot for about 3 years. *Propagation:* By offsets of the bulb, produced in great numbers. *Uses:* In beds and in rock gardens; as underplanting for tall bulbs, or under deciduous trees or shrubs. Also good for forcing and cutting. *Varieties:* Besides the type species, with cobalt-blue flowers, the varieties 'Cantab'—light blue; and 'Heavenly Blue'—gentian blue, are also cultivated.

Daffodil *Narcissus* hybrids

Amaryllidaceae   7—45 cm   III—V   ○ ◑ ▣

Origin: Mediterranean region and Alps. *Description:* Tunicated bulbs from which grow strap-shaped leaves. Hollow stem ending in one or more flowers with stalks growing from a membranous sheath. Perianth segments are joined to form a trumpet, in the mouth of which is a petal-like central ring or corona which may be a trumpet, cup or eye. *Requirements:* Deep, loose, nourishing soil that is reasonably moist. *Cultivation:* Plant out in late August or September, as they require greater warmth for rooting than tulips; garden varieties at a depth of 12 to 18 cm. Lift bulbs in July every 3 or 4 years, grade, and put out again in autumn. *Propagation:* By offsets of the bulb which must not, however, be separated from the parent bulb by force. *Uses:* In smaller or larger groups of a single species in parks and gardens. When planted in turf, grass should be left uncut as long as possible to allow the foliage time to die down. Also popular for cutting and for forcing. *Varieties:* The large number of botanical species, varieties and several thousand garden forms are divided for purposes of selection into several groups:
"**Trumpet Narcissi**"—with long trumpet corona. The most widely cultivated varieties include 'Beersheba'—pure white; 'Covent Garden'—yellow; 'Dutch Master'—pure yellow; Explorer'—pale yellow; 'Golden Harvest'—golden-yellow; 'King Alfred'—lemon-yellow; 'Magnet'—white with lemon-yellow trumpet; 'Mount Hood'—cream-white; 'Queen of Bicolors'—cream with canary-yellow trumpet; 'Unsurpassable'—canary yellow; and many more.
"**Large-cupped Narcissi**"—with long cup- or saucer-shaped corona. The best-known varieties are: 'Birma'—dark yellow with orange-red corona; 'Carlton'—golden-yellow, 'Flower Record'—white with yellow corona and orange margin; 'Fortune'—yellow, corona with orange-red margins; 'Helios'—yellow with orange corona, 'La Argentina'—white with yellow-orange stripe on corona; 'Mercato'—white with yellow-orange corona with red margin; 'Rosy Sunrise'—cream-white with salmon-pink corona; 'Sempre Avanti'—white with pale orange corona; and many others.

Top left: *Muscari armeniacum*. Top right: *Narcissus* hybrid 'Golden Harvest'. Bottom left: *Narcissus* hybrid 'Birma'. Bottom right: *Narcissus* hybrid 'Rosy Sunrise'.

Daffodil   *Narcissus* hybrids

Amaryllidaceae (continued)   7—45 cm   III—V   ○ ◑ ◼

"**Small-cupped Narcissi**"—with smaller cup- or saucer-shaped corona. Attractive varieties include: 'Aflame'—white with red corona; 'Barrett Browning'—cream with orange-yellow corona; 'Edward Buxton'—primrose-yellow with orange corona; 'La Riante'—white with dark orange corona; 'Mary Housley'—white with yellow corona edged orange; 'Verger'—white with orange-red corona; etc.

"**Double Narcissi**"—always have six or more petals. Examples are 'Golden Ducat'—pale yellow; 'Indian Chief'—sulphur-yellow with several orange petals; 'Mary Copland'—cream with orange petals in the centre; 'Texas'—golden-yellow with fiery-red petals; 'Twink'—white with several orange petals in the centre; 'Van Sion'—deep yellow, etc.

"**Triandrus Narcissi**"—generally have 2 to 6 flowers to a stem with cup- or trumpet-shaped corona. Most widely cultivated are 'Shot Silk'—white with yellow corona; 'Silver Chimes'—white with small yellow corona; 'Thalia'—pure white; and 'Tresamble'—white with cream-yellow corona.

"**Cyclamineus Narcissi**"—narrow trumpet corona and recurved perianth, e.g. 'February Gold'—pale yellow with yellow-orange corona; 'Peeping Tom'—golden-yellow.

"**Jonquilla Narcissi**"—very tender, fragrant with scent of orange, e.g. 'Golden Perfection'—pure yellow; 'Suzy'—yellow with orange corona; 'Trevithian'—lemon-yellow.

"**Tazetta Narcissi**"—3 to 12 flowers on a stem. Most widely cultivated varieties include 'Cheerfulness'—cream with double centre; 'Cragford'—white with small orange corona; 'Geranium'—white with dark orange corona; 'Laurens Koster'—cream with lemon-yellow corona; 'Yellow Cheerfulness'—primrose-yellow with double centre; and others.

"**Poeticus Narcissi**"—collar-like corona, pleasantly scented, very late-flowering. Chiefly the variety 'Actaea'—white with yellow corona edged red. Many dainty miniature species are also available for the rock garden.

Star of Bethlehem   *Ornithogalum umbellatum* L.

Liliaceae   15—30 cm   V—VI   ○ ◑ □ ◼

Origin: Europe, Asia Minor, North Africa. *Description:* Ground rosette of linear leaves with white median stripe. Flowers starlike, about 3 cm across, open in sunny weather between 11 a.m. and 3 p.m. *Requirements:* Light, loose, nourishing soil. *Cultivation:* Plant bulbs 8 to 10 cm deep in October. Leave undisturbed in the ground for several years; otherwise lift in July or August. *Propagation:* By offsets of the bulb, produced in great numbers. Also by seeds sown under glass; flower-bearing plants will develop in 2 to 3 years. *Uses:* In rock gardens, as edging for beds, and under deciduous shrubs or trees. *Varieties:* Only the type species, with white flowers striped green on the outside, is grown.

Top left: *Narcissus* hybrid 'Mary Housley'. Top right: *Narcissus* hybrid 'Fortune'. Bottom left: *Narcissus* hybrid 'Indian Chief'. Bottom right: *Ornithogalum umbellatum*.

Bulbs

Pleione bulbocodioides ROLFE *(P. limprichttii* SCHLECHTER*)*

Orchidaceae   10 — 15 cm   IV — V   ◐ ☑

Origin: Tibet. *Description:* Green, conical pseudo-bulbs, from which grow stems with flowers about 7 cm across and, later, lanceolate leaves. *Requirements:* This ground orchid does not tolerate lime, and needs good drainage. *Cultivation:* Plant in spring with the top of the pseudo-bulb protruding from the soil. Mist frequently with soft water. In autumn and winter it needs dry conditions. Provide a good protective cover for the winter. *Propagation:* By offsets of the pseudo-bulb in spring. *Uses:* In rock gardens in a position facing north-east or in a flower bowl. *Varieties:* The only species that can be grown outdoors.

Striped Squill   *Puschkinia scilloides* ADAMS *(P. libanotica* ZUCC.*)*

Liliaceae   7 — 20 cm   III — IV   ○ ◐ ☑ ■

Origin: Asia Minor. *Description:* Bulb small, globose; strap-shaped leaves emerge at the same time as the flower stems, with one-sided racemes of small, bell-shaped flowers. *Requirements:* Ordinary garden soil. *Cultivation:* Plant 6 to 10 cm deep in September or October. Move in August, but may be left undisturbed for a number of years. *Propagation:* By seed sown in boxes; these will develop into flower-bearing plants in 2 years. Also by offsets of the bulb, which are not produced in great numbers. *Uses:* In rock gardens and under deciduous shrubs or trees. *Varieties:* Besides the type species, with flowers striped pale blue, also the white form 'Libanotica Alba'.

Spanish Bluebell   *Scilla hispanica* MILL. *(S. campanulata* AIT.*)*

Liliaceae   25 — 35 cm   V — VI   ○ ◐ ☑

Origin: Spain and Portugal. *Description:* Large bulb, ground rosette of strap-shaped leaves, loose racemes of bell-shaped flowers. *Requirements:* Rich, well-drained soil. *Cultivation:* Plant 6 to 10 cm deep in September or October. Move after several years, preferably in August. *Propagation:* By offsets of the bulb; also by seeds sown in boxes, which will develop into flower-bearing plants in 2 or 3 years. *Uses:* For spring bedding, and for cutting. *Varieties:* The type species is blue-violet, varieties also blue, pink or white.

Tiger Flower   *Tigridia pavonia* KER-GAWL.

Iridaceae   30 — 60 cm   VII — IX   ○ ☑

Origin: Mexico, Peru. *Description:* Corm firm, ovoid, leaves iris-like. Flowers, up to 15 cm across and borne in loose panicles, open in succession, each lasting only one day. *Requirements:* Rich, well-drained soil and a warm situation. *Cultivation:* Plant 5 to 10 cm deep during second half of April. Lift in October and store for the winter in a box filled with sand in a frost-free place. *Propagation:* By offsets of the bulb or by seeds sown under glass in early spring. *Uses:* In mixed beds. *Varieties:* Most widely cultivated in a mixture of colours including white, yellow, pink, scarlet and carmine.

Top left: *Pleione bulbocodioides.* Top right: *Puschkinia scilloides.* Bottom left: *Scilla hispanica.* Bottom right: *Tigridia pavonia.*

Bulbs

Tulipa violacea BOISS. et BUHSE.

Liliaceae   7—10 cm   III—IV   ○ ◐ ◪

Origin: Iran. *Description:* Leaves fairly narrow, usually 3 to 5 in a ground rosette. Flowers cup-shaped, opening wide in the sun, purplish-violet with yellow basal patch. *Requirements:* A sheltered situation. *Cultivation* and *propagation:* As for *Tulipa fosteriana* hybrids. *Uses:* Mainly in rock gardens. *Varieties:* Besides the type species, also the variety 'Yellow Centre' — vivid violet with deep yellow basal patch.

Water-lily Tulip   *Tulipa kaufmanniana* hybrids

Liliaceae   15—30 cm   III—IV   ○ ◐ ◪

Origin: Turkestan. *Description:* Flowers cup-shaped, opening wide in the sun, petals bluntly tipped, with carmine-red stripe on the outside. *Requirements, cultivation, propagation* and *uses:* As for *Tulipa fosteriana* hybrids. *Varieties:* The type species in cream-white with carmine stripe and yellow basal patch. The variety 'Shakespeare' is salmon-pink, tinged orange; 'The First' — cream with carmine stripe; 'Vivaldi' — yellow-white, striped red on the outside; and many more.

Tulip   *Tulipa fosteriana* hybrids

Liliaceae   15—40 cm   IV   ○ ◐ ◪

Origin: Central Asia. *Description:* Broad, grey-green leaves, stem terminating in a large flower, coloured scarlet-red with black basal patch margined yellow. *Requirements:* Good garden soil that is not acidic; plenty of moisture in spring, dry conditions in summer so that the bulbs will ripen. *Cultivation:* Best time for planting is from mid-September to mid-October. Prepare the soil in time by forking over deeply and then raking level. Plant bulbs 8 to 12 cm deep. Remove faded flowers in time so that the bulbs do not expend unnecessary energy on the formation of seed. Tulips may be left in the same place for several years, but it is better to lift them carefully after the top parts have died, about 6 to 8 weeks after flowering (early-flowering species at the end of June, others in July). Several days after lifting, remove old skins and store bulbs in a dry, well-aired place until time to put outdoors. *Propagation:* Tulips produce seeds quite readily, but these would not yield flower-bearing plants until 3 to 6 years after sowing; a much quicker method is by offsets of the bulb. *Uses:* Best in rock gardens, also in turf. *Varieties:* The type species is no longer cultivated, only the varieties, chiefly 'Red Emperor' — with large, glossy, scarlet-red flowers; and 'Purissima' — pure white.

Top left: *Tulipa violacea.* Top right: *Tulipa kaufmanniana* hybrid 'Vivaldi'. Bottom left: *Tulipa kaufmanniana* hybrid 'Shakespeare'. Bottom right: *Tulipa fosteriana hybrid 'Purissima'.*

Bulbs

Tulip   *Tulipa* L.

Liliaceae   15 — 80 cm   IV — V   ○◑▨

Origin: Asia and Europe. *Description:* Bulb usually composed of four fleshy tunics. Erect stem with 3 to 4 broadly lanceolate leaves. Flower six-petalled. *Requirements:* Early-flowering varieties need full sun; late-flowering varieties tolerate partial shade. *Cultivation* and *propagation:* As for preceding species. *Uses:* Garden tulips are planted in smaller or larger groups of a single variety in spring in bedding schemes among perennials, biennials, etc. Small, early-flowering tulips are used also for forcing in pots, and the taller varieties for cutting. *Varieties:* The number of varieties runs into thousands; for purposes of selection they are therefore divided according to characteristics into the following groups:

"**Single Early Tulips**" — about 15 to 25 cm high. Flower outdoors during first half of April. Used chiefly for forcing in pots, but also for planting outdoors, e.g. 'Brilliant Star' — scarlet-red with black basal patch edged with yellow; 'Ibis' — dark pink with white markings; 'Prince of Austria' — orange-red; etc.

"**Double Early Tulips**" — 25 to 30 cm high. Flower in mid-April. Double flowers on stout stems. Used for forcing in pots and for planting outdoors, e.g. 'Boule de Neige' — pure white; 'Orange Nassau' — orange-red; 'Peach Blossom' — dark pink; etc.

"**Mendel Tulips**" — 40 to 50 cm high. Flower in late April. Used chiefly for forcing for cutting, e.g. 'Krelages Triumph' — dark red.

"**Triumph Tulips**" — 30 to 60 cm high. Flower in late April and early May. Used for bedding and for forcing for cutting, e.g. 'Hindenburg' — garnet-red with paler margin; 'Paris' — dark red with yellow margin, etc.

"**Lily-flowered Tulips**" — 30 to 60 cm high. Flowers slender with reflexed petals. Do not flower until late May. 'Aladdin' — scarlet with reddish-yellow edge; 'China Pink' — pale pink; 'Mariette' — dark pink; 'Queen of Sheba' — chestnut red with yellow edge; 'Red Shine' — dark red; 'West Point' — primrose yellow; 'White Triumphator' — pure white; etc.

"**Darwin Tulips**" — 50 to 60 cm high. Flower during first half of May. Suitable chiefly for cutting. Varieties: 'Allard Pierson' — reddish-brown; 'All Bright' — blood red; 'Aristocrat' — pure red; 'Bartigon' — scarlet red; 'Campfire' — blood red; 'Clara Butt' — salmon pink; 'Coplands Rival' — purplish-pink; 'Demeter' — violet-blue; 'Golden Age' — yellow, shaded orange; 'Insurpassable' — pale violet; 'Magier' — white with violet edge; 'Mamasa' — yellow; 'Most Miles' — blood red; 'Niphetos' — cream-yellow; 'Paul Richter' — bright red; 'Philip Snowden' — pinkish-red; 'Pink Attraction' — silvery violet-pink; 'Pride of Haarlem' — carmine-pink; 'Queen of Night' — blackish-red; 'Rose Copland' — lilac-pink; 'Sweet Harmony' — lemon-yellow with white edge; 'Utopia' — carmine-red; 'William Copland' — lilac-red; 'Zwanenburg' — pure white; etc.

Top left: *Tulipa* 'Prince of Austria'. Top right: *Tulipa* 'White Triumphator'. Bottom left: *Tulipa* 'Queen of Sheba'. Bottom right: *Tulipa* 'Aristocrat'.

Bulbs

Tulip   *Tulipa* L.

Liliaceae (continued)   15—80 cm   IV—V   ○ ◐ ■

"Darwin Hybrids"—50 to 60 cm high. Large flowers on stout stems. Flower during second half of April. Used for planting outdoors and for forcing. Varieties: 'Apeldoorn'—orange-scarlet; 'Beauty of Apeldoorn'—yellow with red veining; 'Dardanelles'—cherry-scarlet; 'Deutschland'—red; 'Diplomate'—bright red; 'Dover'—scarlet-red; 'Golden Apeldoorn'—yellow; 'Gudoshnik'—yellow with red veining; 'Holland's Glory'—orange-scarlet; 'Jewel of Spring'—yellow with narrow red edge; 'Lefeber's Favourite'—vivid red; 'Oxford'—purplish-scarlet; 'Parade'—scarlet-red; 'Spring Song'—scarlet, etc.

"Parrot Tulips"—35 to 65 cm high. Flowers fringed or laciniate, fantastic shapes. Usually flower in mid-May. Varieties: 'Apricot Parrot'—orange-red; 'Black Parrot'—chestnut blackish-purple; 'Blue Parrot'—violet-blue; 'Erna Lindgreen'—bright red; 'Fantasy'—flesh pink; 'Fire Bird'—dark red, 'Karel Doorman'—carmine with narrow yellow edge; 'Miss Kay'—brownish-red; 'Orange Favourite'—orange; 'Orange Parrot'—orange-brown; 'Red Champion'—red; 'Red Parrot'—bright red; 'Sunshine'—golden-yellow; 'Texas Gold'—pale yellow; 'White Parrot'—white; etc.

"Breeder Tulips"—55 to 70 cm high. Flowers in soft pastel hues. Flower during second half of May. Varieties: 'Bacchus'—dark violet-blue; 'Cherbourg'—golden-yellow with bronze shading; 'Dillenburg'—orange-red with bronze-yellow edge; 'Georges Grappe'— lavender-blue; 'Jago'—brownish-red with yellowish-brown edge; 'Louis XIV.'—purple with broad golden-yellow edge; 'Orange Delight'—bronze-orange; 'Panorama'—mahogany-red; 'President Hoover'—reddish-orange; 'Tantalus'—pale yellow with violet shading; etc.

"Single Late Tulips" (syn. "Cottage Tulips")—40 to 60 cm high. Do not flower until second half of May. Varieties: 'Advance'—salmon-pink with violet-tinged median ridge; 'Artist'—violet-pink with green markings; 'Groenland'—pink with green markings; 'Golden Harvest'—lemon-yellow; 'Halcro'—red with carmine median ridge; 'Inglescombe Yellow'—yellow; 'Lincolnshire'—deep red; 'Princess Margaret Rose'—yellow shading to red; 'Renown'—carmine-red; 'Rosy Wings'—salmon-pink; etc.

"Rembrandt Tulips"—45 to 65 cm high. Flowers smaller, with variegated markings. Flower during second half of May, e.g. 'Cordell Hull'—red with white marbling.

"Double Late Tulips"—40 to 60 cm high. Flowers large, compact, on stout stems. Flower during second half of May. Varieties: 'Bonanza'—yellow with red veins; 'Clara Garder'—purplish-pink; 'Coxa'—orange-red with yellow edge; 'Eros'—large, dusky rose, 'Gerbrand Kieft'—carmine-red with white edge; 'Gold Medal'—yellow; 'Livingstone'—scarlet-red; 'Mount Tacoma'—white with green veins; 'Nizza'—yellow, striped red; 'Porthos'—bright red; 'Symphonia'—carmine-red; 'Uncle Tom'—dark chestnut-red; 'Yosemite'—violet-pink with white edge, etc.

Top left: *Tulipa* 'Holland's Glory'. Top right: *Tulipa* 'Apricot Parrot'. Bottom left: *Tulipa* 'Coxa'. Bottom right: *Tulipa* 'Porthos'.

Broad-leaved Trees and Shrubs

Indian Mallow *Abutilon × milleri* HORT.

Malvaceae   150—200 cm   VI—X   ○ ◪

Origin: Hybrid of South American parentage. *Description:* Evergreen shrub with palmate, long-stalked leaves. Flowers bell-like, with variously coloured calyx. *Requirements:* Does well in a cool greenhouse. *Cultivation:* May be put in a sheltered spot in the garden after mid-May. *Propagation:* By cuttings or seed. *Uses:* Good for larger containers on terrace or balcony. Overwinters in a light and cool greenhouse. *Varieties:* The type species has yellow flowers with red calyx; the form 'Variegata' has yellow-spotted foliage.

Dutchman's Pipe *Aristolochia macrophylla* LAM.
(A. durior auct. non HILL*)*

Aristolochiaceae   600—1000 cm   V—VII   ○ ◉ ◪

Origin: North America. *Description:* Deciduous twining climber with large, heart-shaped leaves. Flowers greenish-yellow, purplish-brown inside, resembling pipe-bowls. *Requirements:* Nourishing soil, regular watering. *Cultivation:* Appreciates an occasional application of feed. *Propagation:* By layering or seed sown in a greenhouse. *Uses:* To make green, practically solid walls on a framework, and to cover north- and west-facing walls. Can also climb up a chain suspended from the branch of a tall tree, or up a pillar. *Varieties:* Normally only the type species is cultivated.

Barberry *Berberis thunbergii* DC.

Berberidaceae   100—150 cm   V   ○ ● ◪

Origin: Japan. *Description:* Deciduous shrub, usually with attractively coloured foliage. *Requirements:* Ordinary garden soil. *Cultivation:* May be thinned in spring. *Propagation:* The type species may be multiplied by seed, forms and varieties chiefly by cuttings. *Uses:* As a solitary specimen, in groups and to make low hedges. *Varieties:* The type species has small leaves that turn red in autumn; flowers yellow, fruits cylindrical, vivid red. The variety 'Atropurpurea' has purplish-red leaves that turn carmine-red in autumn; 'Atropurpurea Nana' is usually only 30 to 60 cm high; 'Rose Glow'—mottled pink leaves.

Bougainvillea glabra CHOISY

Nyctaginaceae   300—600 cm   VI—IX   ○ ◪

Origin: Brazil. *Description:* Evergreen climbing plant with ovate leaves. Flowers bland yellowish-white with brightly coloured bracts. *Requirements:* Overwinters in a greenhouse at a temperature of 5 to 8°C, with occasional watering. *Cultivation:* In congenial climates may be put outdoors in a sheltered spot, best of all against a south-facing wall, from April onwards. *Propagation:* By cuttings, preferably in June. *Uses:* To cover pergolas, garden gateways and other constructions. *Varieties:* Besides the type species, with vivid lilac-pink bracts, most widely cultivated is the variety 'Sanderiana', with dark violet bracts.

Top left: *Abutilon × milleri.* Top right: *Aristolochia macrophylla.* Bottom left: *Berberis thunbergii* 'Atropurpurea Nana'. Bottom right: *Bougainvillea glabra.*

Broad-leaved Trees and Shrubs

Heather   *Calluna vulgaris* HULL

Ericaceae   20—50 cm   VII—X   ○ ◑ ◪

Origin: Birch and pine stands of Europe and Asia Minor. *Description:* Broom-like branching evergreen shrubs with small, evergreen, linear leaves and bell-like flowers. *Requirements:* Poor, acid, sandy soil. *Cultivation:* Clip occasionally before growth starts, to keep tufts low and compact. *Propagation:* The lower parts of shoots root readily in hilled soil, and may later be separated from the parent plant. In larger numbers by seed or cuttings in summer. *Uses:* In larger groups in heath gardens. *Varieties:* Very many attractive varieties of various heights with white, pink or lilac-red flowers and variously coloured foliage, e.g. 'Cuprea'—pink; 'Golden Feather'—golden orange foliage; 'Peter Sparkes'—double pink flowers.

Allspice   *Calycanthus occidentalis* HOOK. et ARN.

Calycanthaceae   200—400 cm   VI—VIII   ○ ◑ ◪

Origin: California: *Description:* Erect deciduous shrub with oval leaves up to 15 cm long. Flowers reddish-brown, up to 5 cm across. Bark very aromatic. *Requirements:* Good, well-drained garden soil. *Cultivation:* Remove old shoots from time to time, preferably at end of winter. *Propagation:* By division of stronger shrubs; also by layering and seeds. *Uses:* As a solitary specimen or in mixed plantings. *Varieties:* Normally only the type species is cultivated.

Cassia didymobotrya L.

Leguminosae   150—300 cm   VII—X   ○ ◪

Origin: Tropical Africa. *Description:* Deciduous shrub with odd-pinnate leaves and five-petalled flowers in racemes up to 30 cm long. *Requirements:* Nourishing, humus-rich soil. Grown in a cool greenhouse, but may be put outdoors in summer. *Cultivation:* Liberal and regular watering, limited from November to March. *Propagation:* By imported seeds which usually develop into flower-bearing plants the following year. Also by cuttings. *Uses:* In larger containers on terrace or resting place or other sheltered spots in the garden in summer. *Varieties:* Only the type species with yellow flowers is cultivated as a cool glasshouse shrub.

Japanese Quince   *Chaenomeles* hybrids

Rosaceae   60—200 cm   IV—V   ○ ◑ ◪

Origin: Hybrids of East Asiatic parentage. *Description:* Deciduous shrubs with striking flowers up to 4 cm across, followed in autumn by aromatic, quince-like fruits which may be used to make cider. *Requirements:* Any garden soil. Fully hardy. *Cultivation:* Tolerates hard pruning. *Propagation:* By layering or root cuttings. Varieties are grafted on species rootstock. *Uses:* Singly, in groups and free-growing hedges. *Varieties:* Recommended varieties include 'Nivea'—pure white with large fruits, 'Crimson and Gold'—flowers dark red with golden-yellow stamens; 'Knap Hill Scarlet'—large-flowered, salmon-orange; 'Boule de Feu'—carmine-red; etc.

Top left: *Calluna vulgaris* 'Cuprea'. Top right: *Calycanthus occidentalis.* Bottom left: *Cassia didymobotrya.* Bottom right: *Chaenomeles* hybrid.

Broad-leaved Trees and Shrubs

Clematis hybrids

Ranunculaceae	200—400 cm	VI—IX	○ ◑ ▨

Origin: South-eastern Europe and Asia. *Description:* Deciduous, climbing plants with four- to eight-petalled flowers. *Requirements:* Fresh, well-drained, nourishing soil, lightly shaded at the base of the plant. *Cultivation:* Plant outdoors in spring with root neck about 10 cm above the soil surface. *Propagation:* By layering, softwood cuttings and grafting. *Uses:* To cover walls, fences, pergolas, gateways, etc. *Varieties:* Recommended large-flowered varieties include 'Lasurstern'—deep blue; 'Nelly Moser'—pale pink with red median stripe; 'The President'—dark violet; and 'Ville de Lyon'—carmine-red.

Cornelian Cherry   *Cornus mas* L.

Cornaceae	200—500 cm	II—IV	○ ◑ □ ▨

Origin: Central Europe and Asia. *Description:* Small deciduous tree with small red fruits (drupes). *Requirements:* No special needs. *Cultivation:* Does not need regular pruning. *Propagation:* By seed which must be stratified. *Uses:* Singly, in smaller groups and under taller trees. *Varieties:* Only the type species, with small golden-yellow flowers is cultivated; the form 'Variegata' has white-edged leaves.

Cotoneaster horizontalis DECNE.

Rosaceae	50—100 cm	V—VI	○ ◑ ▨

Origin: China. *Description:* Spreading deciduous shrub with herring-bone twigs and small oval leaves about 16 mm long, coloured dark green but changing to red in autumn. Fruits are coral-red and remain on the shrub until late in winter. *Requirements:* Fairly easy to grow, fully hardy; in a sunny situation it bears more flowers and berries. *Cultivation:* May be pruned in March or April. *Propagation:* Fairly easy from seed, also by stooling and cuttings. *Uses:* Best of all in rock gardens, dry walls, on a slope and as a substitute for turf. *Varieties:* The type species has pink flowers; the form 'Variegata' white-spotted leaves, and 'Saxatilis' is of less robust, more prostrate habit.

Cotoneaster microphyllus WALL. ex LINDL.

Rosaceae	20—60 cm	V—VI	○ ◑ ▨

Origin: Himalayas. *Description:* Evergreen, prostrate shrub with small leaves, glossy dark green above and grey-felted below. Fruits small red berries produced in August, which remain on the shrub until winter. *Requirements:* A somewhat sheltered situation, otherwise fairly easy to grow. *Cultivation, propagation* and *uses:* As for the preceding species. *Varieties:* Besides the type species, also certain forms and varieties, e.g. var. *melanotrichus,* only 15 cm high; var. *thymifolius* with narrow leaves curling at the edges; the form 'Cochleatus'—particularly good for rock gardens.

Top left: *Clematis* hybrid 'Ville de Lyon'. Top right: *Cornus mas.* Bottom left: *Cotoneaster horizontalis.* Bottom right: *Cotoneaster microphyllus* 'Cochleatus'.

Broad-leaved Trees and Shrubs

Common Broom *Cytisus scoparius* LINK
(Sarothamnus scoparius WIMM. ex W.D.J. KOCH*)*

Leguminosae   50 — 100 cm   V — VI   ○ □

Origin: Europe. *Description:* Deciduous, broom-like shrub with small leaves. *Requirements:*
Light, well-drained soil and a sheltered situation. Intolerant of lime. *Cultivation:* Plant with
ball of soil, preferably in spring. Varieties require a protective cover of evergreen branches in
winter. *Propagation:* The type species may be increased from seed, varieties only by cuttings,
layering or grafting. *Uses:* As a solitary specimen in rock and heath gardens. *Varieties:* Besides
the type species many attractive varieties exist — yellow, orange, pink, carmine, purple, scarlet
and bicoloured, e.g. 'Zeelandia' — purplish-pink; 'Golden Sunlight' — bright yellow.

Mezereon *Daphne mezereum* L.

Thymelaeaceae   100 — 150 cm   III — IV   ○ ◑ ■

Origin: Europe. *Description:* Erect, deciduous, loosely branched shrub of slow growth. Flowers very early, before leaves appear. The red berries are poisonous. *Requirements:* Humus-rich,
well-drained soil. *Cultivation:* Does not tolerate transplanting; must be planted out with ball
of soil round the roots. *Propagation:* Fairly easy from seed, which must be stratified; also by
cuttings. *Uses:* In rock gardens or perennial beds. *Varieties:* The type species has pinkish-red
flowers, but plants grown from seed show marked variation in colour and may be salmon-
pink, reddish-purple or white. Pleasantly scented.

Angel's Trumpet *Datura suaveolens* H.B.K.

Solanaceae   200 — 300 cm   VII — X   ○ ◑ ■

Origin: Mexico. *Description:* Shrubby deciduous plant with glabrous, longish ovate leaves up
to 30 cm long. Flowers large, trumpet-shaped, five-petalled, pleasantly scented. *Requirements:*
Flowers profusely if watered liberally and given regular applications of feed. Fairly heavy,
nourishing soil. *Cultivation:* Glasshouse shrub. Optimum temperature for overwintering is
10 to 15°C. Cut back in spring and let plant make new shoots at a temperature of about
18°C. *Propagation:* By softwood cuttings in early summer, or by seed. *Uses:* In larger containers put outdoors in summer on the terrace or other suitable place in the garden. *Varieties:*
Besides the type species, the variety *flore pleno* HORT. — white, double, is also cultivated.

Deutzia × *rosea* REHD.

Saxifragaceae   70 — 300 cm   V — VII   ○ ◑ ■

Origin: The parents of these hybrids come from East Asia and America. *Description:* Richly
branching, deciduous shrub with bell-like flowers, about 2 cm across, arranged in short
panicles. *Requirements:* Does well in any garden soil. *Cultivation:* Removal of oldest branches
promotes the growth of new shoots. *Propagation:* By softwood cuttings in summer and
hardwood cuttings in autumn. *Uses:* As a solitary specimen or in groups; also for hedges.
Varieties: The type species has white flowers coloured reddish on the outside;
'Campanulata' — white; 'Carminea' — deep pink.

Top left: *Cytisus scoparius.* 'Zeelandia'. Top right: *Daphne mezereum.* Bottom left: *Datura
suaveolens.* Bottom right: *Deutzia* × *rosea.*

Broad-leaved Trees and Shrubs

European Spindle Tree *Euonymus europaeus* L.

Celastraceae   200—500 cm   V   ○ ◑ ☑

Origin: Europe. *Description:* Deciduous shrub with square twigs and elliptic-ovate leaves about 7 cm long, turning purplish-red in autumn. *Requirements:* Fairly easy to grow. *Cultivation:* Remove old and non-fruiting branches regularly. *Propagation:* By seed sown as soon as ripe, or in spring after stratification. Also by cuttings at end of winter or in August. *Uses:* In groups to cover unattractive features, or as underplanting. *Varieties:* Only the type species, which bears a great profusion of pink to light reddish fruits, is normally cultivated.

Japanese Spindle *Euonymus japonicus* L. f.

Celastraceae   150—200 cm   V—VI   ○ ◑ ☑

Origin: Asia. *Description:* Erect, evergreen shrub with dense foliage. Leaves up to 7 cm long, elliptic, glossy dark green. *Requirements:* Hardy in warm, coastal regions, very useful as a seaside hedge. *Cultivation:* Plant out with root ball. *Propagation:* By cuttings. *Uses:* Chiefly for decoration in a cool greenhouse, and for garden hedges and decoration, especially by the sea. *Varieties:* Many varieties with variegated or variously shaped leaves, e.g. 'Albomarginatus'—leaves edged silvery-white; 'Aureovariegatus'—dark green with golden-yellow spots.

Golden Bell *Forsythia × intermedia* ZAB.

Oleaceae   200—500 cm   IV—V   ○ ◑ ☑

Origin: Hybrid of Chinese parentage. *Description:* Deciduous shrub flowering before leaves on the previous year's shoots. *Requirements:* Any ordinary soil. *Cultivation:* Cut out old wood after flowering to promote the growth of new shoots. *Propagation:* By softwood cuttings in summer and hardwood cuttings in autumn. *Uses:* As a solitary specimen, in groups and in free-growing hedges. In winter branches with buds may be put in a vase, they will flower. *Varieties:* Tried and tested varieties include 'Primulina'—pale yellow; 'Spectabilis'—golden-yellow, and 'Beatrix Farrand'—chrome-yellow.

Chinese Witch Hazel *Hamamelis mollis* OLIV.

Hamamelidaceae   200—300 cm   II—IV   ○ ◑ ☑

Origin: China. *Description:* Spreading deciduous shrub, with young shoots and underside of leaves covered in light down. Flowers four-petalled, borne in clusters before the leaves. *Requirements:* Rich soil. Intolerant of lime. *Cultivation:* Plant with root ball. During flowering period protect with polythene sheet against damage by frost. *Propagation:* By layering or grafting on *H. virginiana* rootstock. *Uses:* As a solitary specimen in a striking position in the garden. *Varieties:* The type species is deep yellow; 'Pallida'—pale yellow, 'Brevipetala'—dark yellow with shorter petals.

Top left: *Euonymus europaeus*. Top right: *Euonymus japonicus* 'Aureovariegatus'. Bottom left: *Forsythia × intermedia*. Bottom right: *Hamamelis mollis*.

Broad-leaved Trees and Shrubs

Hebe andersonii hybrids *(H. × andersonii* COCK.*)*

Scrophulariaceae   50—200 cm   VIII—X   ○◐◨■

Origin: Derived from species native to New Zealand and Australia. *Description:* Evergreen, richly branched shrubs with oval or elongate leaves. Flowers borne in dense racemes. *Requirements:* A warm and sheltered situation, rich soil. *Cultivation:* May be plunged in a bed in summer, in winter preferably in a cool greenhouse at a temperature of 3 to 5°C. *Propagation:* By cuttings in spring or late summer. *Uses:* In the garden only in congenial climates, otherwise in the greenhouse. *Varieties:* Recommended varieties include 'Alicia Amherst'—violet; 'Great Orme'—pink; 'La Seduisante'—carmine; 'Pink Wand'—bright pink, etc.

Ivy   *Hedera helix* L.

Araliaceae   30—2000 cm   IX—X   ○●◨

Origin: Europe and Asia. *Description:* Evergreen, climbing plants with leathery, mostly lobed leaves. Yellow-green flowers in umbels. *Requirements:* Practically any garden soil. *Cultivation:* Tolerates even hard pruning. *Propagation:* By cuttings. *Uses:* To climb up walls, wire netting, or tall trees. Also as a substitute for turf in shade. *Varieties:* 'Conglomerata'—a dwarf form with wavy leaves; 'Sagittifolia'—small leaves with long pointed lobes; 'Gold Heart'—bright yellow variegation.

Hortensis   *Hydrangea macrophylla* SER.

Saxifragaceae   100—200 cm   VI—VIII   ○◐◨■

Origin: Japan. *Description:* Deciduous shrubs. Most have flower-heads with fertile flowers in the centre, sterile flowers on the edge, and a brightly coloured calyx. *Requirements:* A sheltered situation and slightly acid soil. *Cultivation:* In alkaline soil the flowers are red, in acid soil, blue. Usually damaged by severe dry frosts but will put out new shoots from the base again in spring. *Propagation:* By softwood cuttings, which root readily. *Uses:* Singly or in small groups in turf or among perennials. *Varieties:* H. macrophylla is a well-known house plant which can also be grown outdoors. There are many varieties with flat or almost globular flower heads in colours including white, pink, carmine-red and blue.

Hortensis   *Hydrangea paniculata* SIEB.

Saxifragaceae   100—200 cm   VII—VIII   ○◐◨■

Origin: China and Japan. *Description:* Sparsely-branched deciduous shrub with stout shoots. Leaves longish ovate, up to 25 cm long. Dome-shaped flower heads 15 to 30 cm long. *Requirements, cultivation, propagation* and *uses:* As for the preceding species. *Varieties:* The type species has white flowers that gradually change to pink; 'Grandiflora' has large flower heads composed only of sterile flowers; 'Praecox' flowers as early as July.

Top left: *Hebe andersonii* hybrid 'Pink Wand'. Top right: *Hedera helix* 'Sagittifolia'. Bottom left: *Hydrangea macrophylla*. Bottom right: *Hydrangea paniculata* 'Praecox'.

Broad-leaved Trees and Shrubs

Holly *Ilex aquifolium* L.

Aquifoliaceae 200—400 cm V—VI   ○ ● ▨ ■

Origin: Western Europe and Mediterranean. *Description:* Dense, evergreen shrub with spiny, leathery, glossy green leaves, toothed and wavy on the margin. Flowers small, white, followed by red berries. *Requirements:* Preferably rather heavy soil. *Cultivation:* Very hardy and useful for shaded or exposed sites. *Propagation:* By cuttings, and by seed that has been stratified. *Uses:* As a solitary specimen or in small groups or hedges. *Varieties:* The type species has leaves about 6 cm long. A number of attractive varieties exist: 'Golden Queen'—yellow margined leaves; 'Bacciflava'—yellow fruits; and many others.

Beauty Bush *Kolkwitzia amabilis* GRAEBN.

Caprifoliaceae 200—300 cm V—VI   ○ □ ▨

Origin: China. *Description:* Small deciduous shrub of loose habit with slightly drooping shoots. Clusters of bell-like flowers on short stalks. *Requirements:* Nourishing, well-drained soil. Intolerant of permanently soggy soil. *Cultivation:* Plant out in spring. Removal of oldest branches promotes growth of new shoots. If damaged by severe dry frosts will again put out new shoots from the base. *Propagation:* By ripe cuttings in late summer. *Uses:* As a solitary specimen in turf. *Varieties:* The type species has flowers coloured soft pink with yellow patch inside; variety 'Rosea'—a deeper pink.

Golden Rain *Laburnum × watereri* DIPP.

Leguminosae 250—350 cm V—VI   ○ ◕ □ ▨

Origin: Hybrid of species native to southern Europe and Asia Minor. *Description:* Sparsely branched deciduous shrub or tree with trifoliate leaves. Yellow, pea-shaped flowers hanging in long chains. *Requirements:* Easy to grow; tolerates even a smoke-laden atmosphere, and likes lime. *Cultivation:* Damaged by frost in severe winters but puts out new shoots again from the base. *Propagation:* By seed sown in spring. Varieties are budded on *L. anagyroides* stock. *Uses:* As a solitary specimen or in mixed groups in the garden. *Varieties:* The flower trusses are 30 to 40 cm long in the species; in var. 'Vossii' they are up to 50 cm long, coloured golden-yellow.

Common Privet *Ligustrum vulgare* L.

Oleaceae 50—300 cm VI—VII   ○ ◕ □ ▨

Origin: Europe. *Description:* Evergreen or semi-evergreen shrub of dense, upright habit with ovate-lanceolate leaves about 6 cm long. Flowers white, grouped in terminal, many-flowered panicles. Fruits round, black berries. *Requirements:* No special needs. Vigorously growing shrub that tolerates even the smoke-laden atmosphere of industrial areas. *Cultivation:* Tolerates frequent trimming. *Propagation:* By softwood and hardwood cuttings. *Uses:* Good for clipped hedges. *Varieties:* Besides the type species several other forms, e.g. 'Lodense'—only 50 cm high with semi-persistent leaves, particularly well suited for low hedges.

Top left: *Ilex aquifolium.* Top right: *Kolkwitzia amabilis.* Bottom left: *Laburnum × watereri.* Bottom right: *Ligustrum vulgare.*

Broad-leaved Trees and Shrubs

Honeysuckle *Lonicera tatarica* L.

Caprifoliaceae 200—300 cm V—VI   ○ ● □ ☑

Origin: Central Asia. *Description:* Deciduous shrub of broad, dense habit. Flowers short-stalked, labiate. Fruits red berries. *Requirements:* Does best in soil that is not too heavy but fresh. *Cultivation:* Tolerates hard pruning, best done in spring. *Propagation:* By seed and cuttings in summer. *Uses:* In groups; also to cover unattractive features. *Varieties:* The type species has pink flowers and bright red berries; var. 'Grandiflora'—large white flowers; 'Rosea'—pale pink; and 'Zabelii'—vivid red flowers.

Magnolia × *soulangeana* SOUL. BOD.

Magnoliaceae 300—500 cm IV—V   ○ ☑

Origin: Hybrid of East Asian parentage. *Description:* Tall, deciduous shrub or tree. Flowers borne on naked wood. *Requirements:* A light and fully sheltered situation. Deep, humus-rich, slightly acid soil. *Cultivation:* The first few years after planting out, cover the soil round the roots with a layer of dry leaves and pine needles before the frosts. If there is danger of light night-time frosts cover shrubs with polythene sheets. *Propagation:* Usually by layering or by seed that has been stratified. Varieties also by softwood cuttings or by grafting onto species stock. *Uses:* As a solitary specimen or in smaller groups. *Varieties:* The original hybrid has large, obovate leaves, whitish-pink cup-shaped flowers tinged red on the outside. Unscented. Var. 'Alba Superba'—white; 'Lennei'—purplish-pink; 'Rustica Rubra'—purplish-red.

Magnolia stellata MAXIM.

Magnoliaceae 250—300 cm III—IV   ○ ☑

Origin: Japan. *Description:* Deciduous, leaves longish ovate, up to 8 cm long. Flowers star-like, white, pleasantly scented, petals narrower than in other species, produced before leaves appear. *Requirements, cultivation, propagation* and *uses:* As for preceding species. *Varieties:* Besides the type species also cultivated is var. 'Rosea' with rose-tinted flowers, but it is of weaker habit.

Oregon Grape *Mahonia aquifolium* NUTT.

Berberidaceae 80—180 cm IV—V   ◑ ● ☑

Origin: North America. *Description:* Evergreen, sparsely branching shrub. Leaves glossy, alternate, pinnate, toothed. Fruits blue berries. *Requirements:* Easy to grow; likes lighter, nourishing soil. *Cultivation:* Does not need regular pruning. *Propagation:* By offshoots or by seed sown outdoors. *Uses:* As underplanting to trees and shrubs or in low, freely growing hedges. *Varieties:* Besides the type species with large leaves and dense clusters of small, vivid yellow flowers, there are several varieties, e.g. 'Undulata' with wavy leaves.

Top left: *Lonicera tatarica.* Top right: *Magnolia* × *soulangeana.* Bottom left: *Magnolia stellata.* Bottom right: *Mahonia aquifolium.*

Broad-leaved Trees and Shrubs

Crab Apple *Malus* hybrids

Rosaceae 200—300 cm IV—V ○ ▣

Origin: Hybrids of many species native to Europe, Asia and North America. *Description:* Deciduous trees or shrubs, often with attractively coloured leaves and decorative fruits. *Requirements:* Fresh, nourishing soil. Tolerates atmosphere of industrial areas. *Cultivation:* Do not prune, merely thin. *Propagation:* Varieties are budded on apple wildlings. *Uses:* Chiefly as solitary specimens or in tree avenues. *Varieties:* E.g. 'Aldenhamensis'—red, semi-double flowers; 'Eleyi'—wine-red flowers, dark purple leaves and deep red fruits; 'Lemoinei'—single, dark red flowers; 'John Downie' —large red and yellow fruits.

Oleander *Nerium oleander* L.

Apocynaceae 200—400 cm VI—IX ○ ▣

Origin: Mediterranean region. *Description:* Branching, evergreen shrub with lanceolate, grey-green leaves up to 15 cm long. Flowers single or double in many-flowered cymes, pleasantly scented. *Requirements:* Regular watering, nourishing soil, a sheltered situation. *Cultivation:* Glasshouse shrub. Overwinter in a light place at a temperature of 2 to 8 °C. *Propagation:* Fairly easy by terminal cuttings, as they root even in water. *Uses:* Very good for terrace, balcony or resting place in summer. *Varieties:* Many varieties in colours including pink, red, white, cream-yellow, orange as well as bicoloured forms.

Osmanthus heterophyllus P.S. GREEN *(Olea aquifolium* SIEB. et ZUCC.*)*

Oleaceae 200—400 cm IX—X ○ ▣

Origin: Japan. *Description:* Evergreen shrub with leathery, toothed leaves resembling those of holly. Flowers small, white, sweetly scented. *Requirements:* A sheltered situation. *Cultivation:* Will grow in any soil and shaded site. *Propagation:* By seed sown as soon as it is ripe or by cuttings in August. *Uses:* Outdoors as hedges or background, otherwise in large containers placed out on terrace, balcony, etc. in summer. *Varieties:* Many attractive varieties, e.g. 'Gulftide' with differently shaped leaves.

Mountain or Tree Paeony *Paeonia suffruticosa* ANDR.
(P. arborea DONN*)*

Paeoniaceae 100—200 cm V—VI ○ ◑ ▣

Origin: China and Japan. *Description:* Deciduous, large, divided leaves with greyish down on the underside. Flowers large, single, semi-double or double. *Requirements:* Deep, fresh, well-drained soil. *Cultivation:* Plant in September, with union of scion and rootstock about 8 cm below the surface of the soil; a light cover for the winter is recommended. *Propagation:* Woody paeonies are grafted on *P. lactiflora* rootstock in late summer. *Uses:* As a solitary specimen or in groups. *Varieties:* The type species is seldom cultivated; available in its stead are many attractive varieties in colours including white, pink, red, salmon, orange and yellow.

Top left: *Malus* hybrid. Top right: *Nerium oleander.* Bottom left: *Osmanthus heterophyllus* 'Gulftide'. Bottom right: *Paeonia suffruticosa.*

Broad-leaved Trees and Shrubs

Virginia Creeper *Parthenocissus quinquefolia* PLANCH. emend. REHD.

Vitaceae   800—1000 cm   VII—VIII   ○ ◑ ▧

Origin: North America. *Description:* Deciduous climbing plant with five-lobed leaves and insignificant yellow-green flowers. Fruits black berries. *Requirements:* Ordinary garden soil; leaves colour better in full sun. *Cultivation:* Tie to a support at first. *Propagation:* By cuttings. *Uses:* Invaluable for covering the wall of a house, high walls, or the trunk of a tall tree, from the top of which it hangs in an attractive display. *Varieties:* The type species is hardy but does not always possess organs of attachment, and young plants must therefore be tied in at first.

Mock Orange *Philadelphus virginalis* hybrids
(P. × virginalis REHD.*)*

Saxifragaceae   150—400 cm   VI—VII   ○ ◑ □ ▧

Origin: Southern Europe, Asia and North America. *Description:* Deciduous, rather thickly branched shrub of upright habit. *Requirements:* Will grow even in poor soils; tolerates atmosphere of industrial areas. In a situation that is too shaded it bears few flowers. *Cultivation:* Cut out old shoots from time to time to promote the growth of new ones. *Propagation:* By softwood and hardwood cuttings. *Uses:* In freely growing hedges and to conceal unattractive places. *Varieties:* Crossing of the type species has yielded many attractive varieties with single, semi-double and double flowers, e.g. 'Virginal' with pure white, double flowers up to 5 cm across and pleasantly scented.

Russian Vine *Polygonum baldschuanicum* REGEL
(Bilderdykia baldschuanica D.A. WEBB*)*

Polygonaceae   800—1000 cm   VII—X   ○ ● □ ▧

Origin: Central Asia. *Description:* Deciduous twining plant with lace-like sprays of small flowers. *Requirements:* Ordinary garden soil with sufficient nutrients; tolerates atmospheric pollution. *Cultivation:* Is not damaged by hard pruning. To climb to the required height it needs a framework of wooden trellis or wire. *Propagation:* By softwood and hardwood cuttings. *Uses:* To cover an unsightly feature or for quick screening. *Varieties:* The type species has white flowers tinged a delicate pink, coloured a darker shade on the reverse.

Shrubby Cinquefoil *Potentilla fruticosa* L.

Rosaceae   30—150 cm   V—IX   ○ ▧

Origin: South-east Asia and North America. *Description:* Low, richly branched deciduous shrub with small leaves and five-petalled flowers borne practically the whole summer long. *Requirements:* Deep but not unduly heavy soil. *Cultivation:* Should be thinned every year by removal of older shoots. *Propagation:* By softwood cuttings. *Uses:* In the rock garden, perennial bed and in front of taller shrubs. *Varieties:* The type species is about 120 cm high, with yellowish-white flowers; many attractive varieties with white, yellow and almost orange blooms are also cultivated, e.g. 'Hurstbourne'—a dwarf shrub with bright yellow flowers; 'Katherine Dykes'—primrose yellow; Vilmoriniana—silvery leaves, white flowers.

Top left: *Parthenocissus quinquefolia.* Top right: *Philadelphus virginalis* hybrid 'Virginal'. Bottom left: *Polygonum baldschuanicum.* Bottom right: *Potentilla fruticosa* 'Hurstbourne'.

Broad-leaved Trees and Shrubs

Prunus laurocerasus L. (*Laurocerasus officinalis* M.J. ROEN.)

Rosaceae	100—200 cm	IV—V	○●□■

Origin: South-eastern Europe and Asia Minor. *Description:* Evergreen shrub of spreading habit with leathery, longish ovate leaves and small white flowers in narrow, upright racemes. Fruits blackish-red drupes. *Requirements:* Good nourishing soil and preferably a sheltered situation. Likes lime. *Cultivation:* Regular pruning is not necessary. *Propagation:* The type species may be increased by seed sown in spring, varieties by cuttings. *Uses:* As underplanting for taller trees. *Varieties:* Besides the type species also cultivated are attractive varieties such as 'Caucasica'—large, broad leaves; 'Otto Luyken'—narrow, pointed leaves; 'Reynvaanii'—of upright habit, narrow, pale green leaves; 'Rotundifolia'—of compact habit, small round leaves; 'Schipkaensis'—of vigorous habit, large, dark green leaves; and 'Zabeliana'—of low, spreading habit with narrow leaves.

Bird Cherry *Prunus padus* L.

Rosaceae	800—1000 cm	IV—V	○●◪■

Origin: Europe and Asia. *Description:* Shrubby deciduous tree with drooping branches, elliptic, pointed leaves and fragrant white flowers in pendent racemes. *Requirements:* Easy to grow, hardy, likes lime. *Cultivation:* Does not need pruning. *Propagation:* By seed that has been stratified. *Uses:* To cover unsightly features or as underplanting. *Varieties:* Besides the type species, also cultivated is the variety 'Watereri' with long white racemes.

Almond *Prunus triloba* LINDL.

Rosaceae	150—250 cm	IV—V	○◪

Origin: China. *Description:* Spreading, richly branched, deciduous shrub with obovate to three-lobed leaves. *Requirements:* Good garden soil and a sheltered situation. *Cultivation:* Does not need regular pruning. *Propagation:* By grafting on *Prunus domestica* rootstock. *Uses:* As a solitary specimen or in smaller groups. *Varieties:* The type species has pale pink flowers, but most widely cultivated is var. 'Multiplex', with double pink flowers.

Firethorn *Pyracantha coccinea* M.J.ROEM.

Rosaceae	200—400 cm	V—VI	○◖□◪

Origin: South-eastern Europe and Asia. *Description:* Evergreen shrub with dense cymes of white flowers followed by lovely red fruits. *Requirements:* Thrives in any garden soil, preferably on the dry rather than moist side. *Cultivation:* Plant with ball of soil, preferably in spring. Stands up well to hard pruning. *Propagation:* By cuttings in summer; also by seed sown in open ground after it has been stratified. *Uses:* As a solitary specimen, wall shrub, in small groups and to make an impenetrable hedge. *Varieties:* Several varieties with attractive fruits are cultivated, e.g. 'Golden Charmer'—golden-yellow fruits; 'Kasan'—scarlet-red fruits; 'Orange Charmer'—orange fruits; 'Lalandei'—orange-red fruits.

Top left: *Prunus laurocerasus.* Top right: *Prunus padus.* Bottom left: *Prunus triloba* 'Multiplex'. Bottom right: *Pyracantha coccinea.*

Broad-leaved Trees and Shrubs

Rhododendron hybrids

Ericaceae 150—300 cm V—VI ○●◪■

Origin: Hybrids derived from various species native mostly to Asia and North America. *Description:* Evergreen shrubs with leathery, entire leaves and clusters of large, funnel-shaped flowers. *Requirements:* Humus-rich acid soil, improved with addition of leaf-mould and peat. High atmospheric moisture and some shade is also favourable to growth. Water used for watering must not contain lime. *Cultivation:* The best time for planting is in April or May. Place the root ball in water for several hours until it is well soaked. Hybrid varieties are usually more resistant to frost. The plants may require watering also in winter. Remove faded flowers with care. To promote flowering apply diluted liquid manure. *Propagation:* By layering, cuttings and grafting, usually on *R. caucasica* 'Cunningham's White' stock. *Uses:* As solitary specimens or in groups in the partial shade of deciduous trees or taller shrubs. *Varieties:* Many attractive varieties coloured white, pink, red, violet and other colour combinations are cultivated nowadays. Tried and tested varieties include, for example, 'Antonín Dvořák'—carmine-violet; 'Aurora'—dark pink, late-flowering; 'Cunningham's White'—white, early-flowering; 'Don Juan'—vivid red, early-flowering; 'Duke of York'—pink with an eye, mid-season; 'Omega'—carmine-pink, late-flowering; and many more.

Rhododendron ledikamense HORT.

Ericaceae 40—100 cm V ◕◪■

Origin: Himalayas. *Description:* Small, rather sparsely branched, semi-deciduous shrub. *Requirements, cultivation,* and *propagation:* As for preceding species. *Uses:* In rock or heath gardens. *Varieties:* Normally only the type species is cultivated.

Rhododendron molle G.DON *(Azalea mollis* BL.*)*

Ericaceae 100—150 cm IV—V ◕●◪■

Origin: Asia. *Description:* Pale green, deciduous foliage. Flowers yellow, dotted green. *Requirements, cultivation, propagation* and *uses:* As for preceding species. *Varieties:* Vast numbers of garden varieties in yellow, orange, red and pink, e.g. 'Dagmar'.

Japanese Azalea *Rhododendron obtusum* PLANCH.

Ericaceae 30—70 cm IV—V ◕●◪■

Origin: Japan. *Description:* Small, evergreen shrub of broadly spreading habit with pink flowers. *Requirements, cultivation, propagation* and *uses:* As for preceding species. *Varieties:* The type species is no longer cultivated; it has been replaced by many attractive varieties such as 'Misík' with pink blooms; 'Amoenum'—brilliant magenta; and others.

Top left: *Rhododendron* hybrid 'Antonín Dvořák'. Top right: *Rhododendron ledikamense.* Bottom left: *Rhododendron molle* 'Dagmar'. Bottom right: *Rhododendron obtusum* 'Misík'.

Broad-leaved Trees and Shrubs

Rhododendron schlippenbachii MAXIM.

Ericaceae	150 — 200 cm	IV — V	◐ ◪ ■

Origin: Korea and Manchuria. *Description:* Funnel-shaped flowers coloured whitish-pink with brownish-red dots inside. Deciduous shrub. *Requirements, cultivation, propagation* and *uses:* As for other rhododendrons. *Varieties:* Normally only the type species, with flowers about 7 cm across, is cultivated.

Rhodotypos scandens MAK.   *(R. kerrioides* SIEB. et ZUCC.*)*

Rosaceae	100 — 200 cm	V — VI	○ ◐ ☐ ◪

Origin: Japan and China. *Description:* Dense deciduous shrub with leaves about 10 cm long; it is thorny, the bark brownish. Flowers pure white, about 4 cm across. Fruits, small black nutlets, rest in the centre of the large sepals. *Requirements:* Fairly undemanding. *Cultivation:* Damaged by frost in severe winters but puts out new shoots again in spring. *Propagation:* By softwood cuttings, or by seed sown as soon as it is ripe. *Uses:* In smaller groups in mixed plantings. *Varieties:* Only the type species is cultivated; no known varieties to date.

Flowering Currant   *Ribes sanguineum* PURSH

Saxifragaceae	150 — 250 cm	IV — V	○ ◐ ☐ ◪

Origin: California. *Description:* Upright deciduous shrub with palmate leaves. Twigs covered with racemes of five-petalled flowers which appear before the leaves. Fruits blue-black berries. *Requirements:* Nourishing soil. *Cultivation:* Regular pruning after flowering keeps the shrubs low. *Propagation:* Chiefly by cuttings. *Uses:* Good for planting in mixed groups or in groups of one kind. *Varieties:* The type species has pink flowers and dark green leaves with prominent veins, felted on the underside. There are also varieties with more vividly coloured flowers, e.g. 'Atrorubens' — small, dark red flowers; 'Carneum' — large, light red flowers; 'King Edward VII' — of smaller habit, dark red; 'Pulborough Scarlet' — of more vigorous habit, with striking carmine-scarlet flowers.

Rose Acacia   *Robinia hispida* L.

Leguminosae	150 — 200 cm	V — VI	○ ☐

Origin: Mexico and USA. *Description:* Sparsely branched, deciduous thornless shrub with twisted branches and odd-pinnate leaves. Flowers in short, drooping racemes, unscented. *Requirements:* Does better in poor soil than one that is too rich; tolerates a smoke-laden atmosphere. Needs a sheltered situation, as the fragile twigs are easily broken by the wind. *Cultivation:* Remove root suckers regularly. *Propagation:* By grafting on *R. pseudoacacia,* either just above the ground or in the crown. *Uses:* As a solitary specimen or in smaller groups. *Varieties:* The type species has pink flowers and is only 150 cm high, so the tree form is more widely cultivated. The variety 'Macrophylla' is of more vigorous habit and flowers about two weeks earlier.

Top left: *Rhododendron schlippenbachii.* Top right: *Rhodotypos scandens.* Bottom left: *Ribes sanguineum.* Bottom right: *Robinia hispida.*

Broad-leaved Trees and Shrubs

Ramanus Rose   *Rosa rugosa* THUNB.

Rosaceae   150—200 cm   VI—IX   ○ ◑ ▣

Origin: China, Japan, Korea. *Description:* Fairly dense, deciduous, stout shoots with dark green, crinkled leaves, carmine-red flowers and large hips. *Requirements:* Will grow even in poor sandy soil, very hardy. *Cultivation:* See next species. *Propagation:* By seed or by root suckers. *Uses:* As a solitary specimen or in groups; also very good for making an impenetrable hedge. *Varieties:* Besides the type species, several varieties are cultivated, such as 'Blanc Double de Coubert'—white, double; 'Frau Dagmar Hastrop'—pale pink; 'Roseraie de l'Hay'—purplish-red, fragrant; 'Pink Grootendorst'—smaller, salmon-pink flowers; etc.

Roses   *Rosa* hybrids

Rosaceae   15—300 cm   V—X   ○ ▣

Origin: Asia. *Description:* Thorny, upright or climbing, deciduous shrubs. Flowers borne singly or in cymes. *Requirements:* Deep, fresh, humus-rich soil that is well-drained and nourishing, with a pH of 6 to 7. *Cultivation:* Before planting in autumn dig over the ground to a depth of at least 40 cm and add farmyard manure or dung-enriched peat. The best time for planting is from mid-October to the end of November. Before doing so, shorten the roots by about one-third to half their length. Top parts are pruned in spring — hybrid tea, floribunda and standard roses to the third or fourth bud as a rule, climbing and shrub roses to the fifth or seventh bud. The union of the bud and rootstock should be covered with about 5 cm of soil. Hybrid tea and floribunda roses should be spaced 25 to 35 cm apart, miniature roses 20 to 25 cm apart, standards 120 to 150 cm apart, and shrub roses 100 to 300 cm apart, depending on their size. During the first half of March each year cut back hybrid teas and floribundas to three to five buds. In the case of climbing and shrub roses pruning is limited to removing old wood and non-flowering shoots. Newly planted roses should not be given feed until after they have become established. Older roses may always be given an application of compound fertilizer in March, distributed at the rate of 100 grams per square metre, and then again every 2 weeks until the end of July, distributed at the rate of 30 grams per square metre. In the autumn, bend standard roses to the ground, insert tops in shallow holes and cover with soil, and wrap bracken round the stem. In the case of shrub roses heap soil about 20 cm high round the base. *Propagation:* By budding on *R. canina* rootstock. *Uses:* Hybrid tea, floribunda and miniature roses always in groups of at least three to five specimens of a single variety. Dwarf roses are also used in rock gardens, in bowls and boxes. Climbing roses beside a wall, pergola, pillar, gateway, on slopes and so on. Shrub roses are best planted singly because they need plenty of space. *Varieties:* The range is very wide, and varieties are therefore divided into several groups:
"Hybrid Tea Roses"—The stem usually terminates in a single large flower. Good for cutting. Recommended varieties include 'Bettina'—peachy orange-yellow; 'Dr. A. J. Verhage'—golden-yellow;

Top left: *Rosa rugosa.* Top right: *Rosa rugosa*—hips. Bottom left: *Rosa* hybrid 'Bettina'. Bottom right: *Rosa* hybrid 'Dr A. J. Verhage'.

Broad-leaved Trees and Shrubs

Roses *Rosa* hybrids

Rosaceae (continued)   15 – 300 cm   V – X   ○ ◪

'Ena Harkness' — carmine-red; 'Geheimsrat Duisberg' — pure yellow; 'Gloria Dei' — yellow edged with pink; 'Grace de Monaco' — pink; 'Intermezzo' — silvery-blue; 'Josephine Bruce' — dark red; 'Königin der Rosen' — yellow edged with orange; 'Konrad Adenauer' — blood-red; 'Kordes Perfecta' — cream edged with pink; 'Message' — greenish-white; 'Maria Callas' — dark pink; 'Michele Meilland' — silvery-pink; 'Montezuma' — salmon-red; 'Neue Revue' — yellowish-white edged with red; 'New Yorker' — pure red; 'Pascali' — white; 'Piccadilly' — red with golden-yellow reverse; 'Poinsettia' — scarlet-red; 'President Herbert Hoover' — orange; 'Queen of Bermuda' — orange-red; 'Rendez-vous' — vivid pink; 'Spek's Yellow' — golden-yellow; 'Sterling Silver' — silvery-blue; 'Super Star' — fiery orange; 'Sutter's Gold' — vivid yellow and orange; 'Tahiti' — yellow and pink; 'Texas Centennial' — orange-red; 'Tzigane' — scarlet-red with yellow reverse; 'Uncle Walter' — scarlet-red; 'Westminster' — red with yellow reverse; 'Wiener Charme' — orange-brown; 'Virgo' — white, and many more.

"Floribunda Roses" — Stems terminate in a cluster of smaller or larger flowers. Of moderately low height, they are good mainly in groups in beds. Popular varieties include 'Alain' — dark red; 'Allgold' — golden-yellow; 'Circus' — yellow and red; 'Concerto' — orange-red; 'Dagmar Späth' — pure white; 'Fanal' — vivid red; 'Farandole' — brick-red; 'Fashion' — salmon-pink; 'Gelbe Holstein' — golden-yellow; 'Kordes Sondermeldung' — scarlet-red; 'Lilli Marleen' — fiery red; 'Masquerade' — golden-yellow to red; 'Orange Triumph' — scarlet-red and orange; 'Pinocchio' — salmon-pink on yellow; 'Polka' — soft rose; 'Rimosa' — yellow; 'Rumba' — yellow and red; 'Salmon Perfection' — salmon-red; 'Sarabande' — orange-red; 'Schweizer Gruss' — velvety red; 'Spartan' — orange-red; 'Titian' — salmon-pink; 'Europeana' — dark red; and others.

"Climbing Roses" — Make long shoots that divide in ensuing years. The blossoms are upright or slightly drooping clusters. Varieties that are usually rewarding include 'Blaze' — carmine-red; 'Climbing Goldilocks' — pure yellow; 'Cocktail' — red with cream centre; 'Coral Dawn' — coral-pink; 'Danse des Sylphes' — bright red; 'Dorothy Perkins' — pink; 'Dortmund' — fiery red; 'Excelsa' — carmine-red; 'Fugue' — garnet-red; 'Golden Climber' — golden-yellow; 'Golden Showers' — lemon-yellow; 'Guinée' — dark velvety red; 'New Dawn' — pale pink; 'Paul's Scarlet Climber' — scarlet-red; etc.

"Miniature Roses" — Tiny bushes with small leaves and small flowers, e.g. 'Baby Darling' — orange; 'Baby Masquerade' — yellow and pinkish-red; 'Bit o'Sunshine' — canary-yellow; 'Colibri' — orange-yellow; 'Cri-Cri' — pink; 'Little Buckaroo' — scarlet-red with white centre; 'Little Flirt' — yellow-red; 'Perla de Alcanada' — dark carmine-red; 'Perla Rosa' — pink; 'Scarlet Gem' — orange-scarlet; 'Trinket' — pink; 'Yametsu Hime' — white and pink; etc.

Top left: *Rosa* hybrid 'Maria Callas'. Top right: *Rosa* hybrid 'Neue Revue'. Bottom left: *Rosa* hybrid 'Queen of Bermuda'. Bottom right: *Rosa* hybrid 'Europeana'.

Willow *Salix × erythroflexuosa*

Salicaceae   300—400 cm   IV—V   ○ □ ☑

Origin: South America. *Description:* Deciduous tree with slender, drooping branches. *Requirements:* No special soil requirements. *Cultivation:* Stands up well to pruning. *Propagation:* By softwood cuttings. *Uses:* As a solitary specimen. *Varieties:* Besides the type species, there is also var. 'Flexuosa', of markedly drooping habit.

Bridal Wreath *Spiraea × arguta* ZAB.

Rosaceae   150—200 cm   IV—V   ○ ◐ □ ☑

Origin: Hybrid derived from species native to South-East Asia. *Description:* Deciduous shrubs with slender, dark brown, arching twigs covered with a profusion of dainty, snow-white flowers borne in clusters. *Requirements:* Any garden soil; tolerates a smoke-laden atmosphere, but in a shaded situation it bears few flowers. *Cultivation:* Remove older shoots regularly after flowering. *Propagation:* By softwood or hardwood cuttings. *Uses:* As a solitary specimen in smaller gardens, otherwise in groups or as freely-growing hedges. *Varieties:* Normally only the type species is cultivated.

Spiraea bumalda hybrids *(S. × bumalda* BURVENICH*)*

Rosaceae   50—80 cm   VI—IX   ○ ◐ □ ☑

Origin: Varieties descended from species native to South-east Asia. *Description:* Dense deciduous shrubs with angular stems and lanceolate leaves. *Requirements:* Fairly easy to grow, tolerate a smoke-laden atmosphere. *Cultivation:* Prune in winter or early spring. Regular applications of feed are appreciated. *Propagation:* By cuttings and also by root suckers. *Uses:* As hedges. *Varieties:* The type species has whitish-pink flowers; most widely cultivated varieties include 'Anthony Waterer'—carmine-pink; 'Froebelii'—dark purple; 'Pruhoniciana'—pure pink.

Lilac *Syringa vulgaris* hybrids

Oleaceae   200—500 cm   V—VI   ○ ◐ ☑

Origin: South-eastern Europe. *Description:* Deciduous shrubs or trees, with heart-shaped leaves and panicles of pleasantly scented flowers. *Requirements:* Flower profusely only in deep, nourishing soil. *Cultivation:* Remove suckers growing from the rootstock. *Propagation:* By budding on *S. vulgaris* rootstock. *Uses:* Singly or in groups. *Varieties:* Numerous attractive varieties differing in height, shape of flower clusters, colour and form of the flower, e.g. 'Ambassadeur'—blue, single; 'Andenken an Ludwig Späth'—dark purplish-red, single; 'Decaisne'—light blue, single; 'Marechal Foch'—lilac pink, single; 'Marie Legraye'—white, single; 'Primrose'—pale yellow, single; 'Charles Joly'—purplish-red, double; 'Katherine Havemeyer'—lilac-pink, double; 'Madame Lemoine'—white, double; etc.

Top left: *Salix × erythroflexuosa*. Top right: *Spiraea × arguta*. Bottom left: *Spiraea bumalda* hybrid 'Anthony Waterer'. Bottom right: *Syringa vulgaris* hybrid 'Ambassadeur'.

Broad-leaved Trees and Shrubs

Tamarisk   *Tamarix pentandra* PALL.

Tamaricaceae   300—600 cm   VII—IX   ○ □ ▨

Origin: Southern Europe and Asia. *Description:* Broom-like shrubs, green only in summer, with small, deciduous scale-like leaves. Multi-divided panicles with large number of minute pink flowers. *Requirements:* Rather light, well-drained soil. Intolerant of lime. *Cultivation:* Plant in spring with root ball; older plants do not tolerate transplanting. *Propagation:* By softwood and hardwood cuttings. *Uses:* Best as a solitary specimen; by the seaside also to make a hedge. *Varieties:* The type species is pink, the variety 'Rubra' pinkish-red.

Viburnum carlesii HEMSL.

Caprifoliaceae   120—180 cm   IV—V   ○ ◑ □ ▨

Origin: Korea. *Description:* Broadly-spreading deciduous shrub with felted shoots and five-petalled flowers in cymes. Fruit is a blackish-blue drupe. *Requirements:* Fresh, nourishing garden soil. *Cultivation:* Plant out with root ball. Does not need regular pruning. *Propagation:* By softwood cuttings and grafting on *V. lantana* stock. *Uses:* As a solitary specimen or in small groups. *Varieties:* The type species has very sweet-scented flowers, coloured white tinged with red. There are a number of attractive varieties of deeper hues, e.g. 'Aurora' — red at first, later pink; 'Diana' is similar.

Weigela hybrids

Caprifoliaceae   150—300 cm   V—VII   ○ ◑ ▨ ■

Origin: Hybrids derived from species native to South-east Asia. *Description:* Upright, deciduous shrubs with slightly arching branches and clusters of tubular flowers. *Requirements:* Flower profusely only in sufficiently nourishing soil. *Cultivation:* Apply well-rotted farmyard manure regularly in autumn. Remove old, faded shoots to promote growth of new ones. *Propagation:* By softwood cuttings. *Uses:* Rewarding shrubs for group planting at lower altitudes. *Varieties:* Favourite varieties include 'Bristol Ruby'—dark carmine flowers with lighter throat; 'Eva Rathke'—carmine-red, shorter; 'Newport Red'—violet-red, tall.

Wisteria sinensis SWEET

Leguminosae   800—1000 cm   IV—VI   ○ ▨

Origin: South-east Asia. *Description:* Twining deciduous climber of vigorous growth with odd-pinnate leaves composed of 7 to 13 leaflets and long pendulous sprays of sweet pea-type flowers. *Requirements:* Flowers much better in nourishing soil. Likes a warm and sheltered situation. *Cultivation:* Cut back strong shoots to about 20 cm from the ground at beginning of August to promote more profuse flowering. *Propagation:* By layering. *Uses:* To cover pergolas or house walls—it needs a support. *Varieties:* The type species is lilac-blue, but there are also varieties coloured greyish-blue and white; most highly prized are varieties with pure blue flowers.

Top left: *Tamarix pentandra.* Top right: *Viburnum carlesii.* Bottom left: *Weigela* hybrid 'Bristol Ruby'. Bottom right: *Wisteria sinensis.*

Coniferous Trees and Shrubs

Cedar *Cedrus atlantica* MANETTI ex CARR.

Pinaceae   500—3000 cm   ○ □ ◩

Origin: Algeria and Morocco. *Description:* Evergreen tree with asymmetrical crown. Needles stiff, sharp, in clusters; cones erect, disintegrate when ripe. *Requirements:* Well-drained soil, a warm and sheltered situation. *Cultivation:* Requires a protective cover for the winter the first few years after planting out. *Propagation:* By seed and cuttings. Garden forms are grafted on *C. atlantica* stock. *Uses:* Striking as a solitary specimen in a large expanse of turf. *Varieties:* Besides the type species, several garden forms are also cultivated, such as 'Glauca', with steel-blue needles; and 'Pendula'—a pendulous form with drooping branch tips.

Lawson Cypress *Chamaecyparis lawsoniana* PARL.

Cupressaceae   200—2000 cm   III—IV   ○ ◕ □ ◩

Origin: California and Oregon. *Description:* Richly branched, narrowly conical evergreen tree with grey-green, scale-like needles. *Requirements:* Good garden soil and a sheltered situation. *Cultivation:* Plant with root ball, preferably in September or April. *Propagation:* The type species may be multiplied from seed, varieties by cuttings or by grafting on species stock. *Uses:* As a solitary specimen or in free groupings; also for hedges. Dwarf forms in rock gardens and large urns. *Varieties:* Besides the type species several interesting varieties are also cultivated, such as 'Allumii'—metallic-blue, 5 to 10 m high; 'Ellwoodii'—blue-green, 2 to 3 m high; 'Filiformis'—green, filamentous, pendulous twigs, only 2 m high; 'Minima Glauca'—shell-like twigs with blue-green needles, 1 m high; 'Lutea'—golden-yellow foliage.

Hinoki Cypress *Chamaecyparis obtusa* SIEB. et ZUCC. ex ENDL.

Cupressaceae   100—2000 cm   III—IV   ○ ◕ □ ◩

Origin: Japan. *Description:* Evergreen shrub or tree of broad conical habit; twigs spread fan-like, leaves are scale-like, dark green. *Requirements:* A sheltered situation, atmospheric moisture and good soil. *Cultivation:* Plant with root ball, preferably in spring or early autumn. *Propagation:* The type species may be multiplied by seed, varieties usually by cuttings. *Uses:* Lower forms in rock gardens or combined with perennials; others in groups or as solitary specimens. *Varieties:* Besides the type species, other attractive varieties are 'Crippsii'—pendulous twigs with golden-yellow needles, up to 5 m high; 'Nana'—only 60 cm high, very dense, of flattened, globose habit; 'Nana Gracilis'—100 to 150 cm high, very slow growing, twigs in fan-like arrangement covered with green, scale-like needles; 'Pygmaea'—no taller than 2 m, twigs spread fan-like, covered with brownish-green needles; 'Tetragona Aurea'—conical, dwarf form with golden-yellow twigs.

Top left: *Cedrus atlantica.* Top right: *Chamaecyparis lawsoniana* 'Minima Glauca'. Bottom left: *Chamaecyparis obtusa* 'Tetragona Aurea'. Bottom right: *Chamaecyparis obtusa* 'Nana Gracilis'.

Coniferous Trees and Shrubs

Common Juniper *Juniperus communis* L.

Cupressaceae   30 — 1000 cm   IV — V   ○ ◑ □ ▨

Origin: Europe, Asia and North America. *Description:* Evergreen shrub or tree with slender cylindrical crown. Leaves needle-pointed, grey-green with white stripe on the upper side. *Requirements:* No special needs but does best in well-drained soil. Intolerant of atmospheric pollution. *Cultivation:* The comparatively shallow and dense root system makes it possible to transplant even older plants. *Propagation:* The type species may be multiplied by seed, which must be stratified when ripe; varieties by cuttings or by grafting on species rootstock. *Uses:* Columnar forms as solitary specimens in natural settings, in heath gardens or in turf; dwarf forms also in the rock garden. *Varieties:* The type species grows to a height of 10 m in the wild. Var. 'Compressa' is only 1 m high, slow growing, columnar, with pale green foliage on dense, upright twigs; 'Hibernica' (syn. 'Stricta') is columnar, up to 4 m high, with blue-green needles; 'Hornibrookii' is prostrate, only 50 cm high and up to 2 m across, with dense, pale-green needles; 'Oblonga Pendula' is columnar, about 3 m high, with drooping branches and soft green needles; 'Repanda' is only 30 cm high and 150 cm across, with dark green needles.

Shore Juniper *Juniperus conferta* PARL.

Cupressaceae   30 — 100 cm   ○ ◑ □ ▨

Origin: Japan and Sakhalin. *Description:* Prostrate evergreen shrub with scale-like needles. *Requirements:* Good garden soil, reasonably well-drained. *Cultivation:* Transplant with root ball, preferably in spring. *Propagation:* By cuttings. *Uses:* As ground cover, also in rock gardens. *Varieties:* Normally only the type species is cultivated; no varieties or forms are known to date.

Juniper *Juniperus squamata* BUCH.-HAM. ex LAMB.

Cupressaceae   50 — 300 cm   ○ ◑ □ ▨

Origin: Afghanistan and China. *Description:* Spreading, irregularly branched evergreen shrub with needles in whorls of three. *Requirements:* Easy to grow. Likes well-drained soil; tolerates dry conditions. *Cultivation:* Plant in spring or early autumn. *Propagation:* Quite easy, best by cuttings. *Uses:* As a solitary specimen in turf, in perennial beds, smaller forms in rock gardens. *Varieties:* The type species is not much grown; more popular are the varieties, e.g. 'Blue Star' — a new form of attractive habit with silvery-blue needles; 'Meyeri' — a slow-growing form, of upright habit, about 2 m high with deep blue needles; 'Wilsonii' — a dwarf form of rather upright habit, suitable for larger rock gardens.

Top left: *Juniperus communis* 'Compressa'. Top right: *Juniperus communis* 'Hibernica'. Bottom left: *Juniperus conferta*. Bottom right: *Juniperus squamata*.

Coniferous Trees and Shrubs

Colorado Spruce   *Picea pungens* ENGELM.

Pinaceae   100—2000 cm   ○ ◐ ◩ ■

Origin: North America. *Description:* Conical evergreen tree with branches in regular whorls. Shallow root system. Square needles cover twigs entirely; cones drooping, do not disintegrate. *Requirements:* Atmospheric moisture, clean air and good garden soil. *Cultivation:* Grafted spruces should be tied to a stake at first. *Propagation:* The type species by seed sown in open ground in spring; varieties by grafting on species stock in the greenhouse. Dwarf forms by cuttings. *Uses:* As a solitary specimen, also in smaller groups, and in hedges; dwarf forms also in the rock garden. *Varieties:* 'Glauca'—the name given to forms with blue-green needles; 'Glauca Globosa'—a dwarf blue-green form about 1 m high.

Bosnian Pine   *Pinus heldreichii* CHRIST. *(P. leucodermis* ANT.*)*

Pinaceae   50—800 cm   ○ ☐ ◩

Origin: Balkans. *Description:* Slow-growing evergreen tree of broad pyramidal habit. Soft green needles and upright twigs. *Requirements:* Fairly undemanding; will grow even in poor, stony soil. *Cultivation:* Older plants do not transplant well. *Propagation:* By grafting on native pine species stock in the greenhouse. *Uses:* As a solitary specimen, the dwarf form mainly in rock gardens. *Varieties:* 'Schmidtii' (*leucodermis* 'Pygmy')—a fairly rare, dwarf, thickly-branched form, only 50 cm high.

Common or English Yew   *Taxus baccata* L.

Taxaceae   60—1500 cm   III—IV   ○ ● ◩

Origin: Europe. *Description:* Slow-growing, evergreen thickly branched shrub or tree. Needles flat, dark green, lighter on the underside. Fruit a red aril. *Requirements:* Any garden soil. *Cultivation:* Does not tolerate dry frost and must therefore be provided with a protective cover of evergreen branches. *Propagation:* By stratified seed, also by cuttings in summer and autumn. *Uses:* As a solitary specimen or in groups. Stands up well to pruning and is therefore used for clipped hedges. *Varieties:* Besides the type species, several varieties are also cultivated, such as 'Elegantissima'—a shrub of irregular habit, 3 to 5 m high, with golden yellow needles; 'Erecta' (syn. 'Stricta')—of broader pyramidal habit; 'Fastigiata' (syn. 'Hibernica')—narrow, columnar, up to 3 m high; 'Repandens'—60 cm high and up to 3 m wide, dark green needles.

Arbor-vitae   *Thuja orientalis* L.

Cupressaceae   100—800 cm   IV—V   ○ ◩ ■

Origin: China. *Description:* Crown ovate-conical. Evergreen branches arranged in fan-shape; leaves scale-like, light green, brownish in winter. *Requirements:* A fairly warm situation. *Cultivation:* Add a large quantity of peat when planting. *Propagation:* The type species by seed, varieties by cuttings. *Uses:* As a solitary specimen or in groups, also in hedges. *Varieties:* Of the varieties most widely grown are 'Aurea', with golden-yellow needles; and 'Nana', a dwarf form with green foliage.

Top left: *Picea pungens* 'Glauca Globosa'. Top right: *Pinus heldreichii* 'Schmidtii'. Bottom left: *Taxus baccata*. Bottom right: *Thuja orientalis* 'Aurea'.

254

INDEX OF SCIENTIFIC NAMES

263

265